SOCIAL HISTORY
OF
AMERICAN EDUCATION

SOCIAL HISTORY OF

VOLUME I:

AMERICAN EDUCATION

COLONIAL TIMES TO 1860

Edited with commentary by

RENA L. VASSAR

San Fernando Valley State College

RAND MCNALLY & COMPANY • CHICAGO

Rand McNally Education Series
B. Othanel Smith, Advisory Editor

Copyright © 1965 by Rand McNally & Company
All rights reserved
Printed in U.S.A. by Rand McNally & Company
Library of Congress Catalogue Number 65:18594

CONTENTS

VOLUME I

v

III. THE FREE SCHOOL MOVEMENT

THE SOUTH: "NOT YET PREPARED TO EDUCATE ALL."

Preface

The public school system is so much a part of the American ideal of democracy and equality that little attention has been given to the wide differences in educational opportunities that existed in this country for approximately 250 years. Free universal education has become the accepted principle—but only gradually and often over staunch opposition—as during the nineteenth century state after state accepted the responsibility of education for all: first on the elementary level, then secondary; and finally with the state universities and the land grant colleges the keystone was set in the public education arch. By the closing decades of the last century, publicly supported free schooling had become a natural right in theory and in practice, although equal opportunity remains in many areas an unfulfilled ideal.

The purpose of this collection of historical writings is to highlight the divergencies that have long existed in educational opportunities among social and racial groups, and to explain in part how the idea of free universal education came to triumph—in principle by the mid-nineteenth century, and in practice during the present century. In such an approach the complexities of America's educational past become apparent, and, by contrast, the present uniformity and extensiveness of public education seems a startling accomplishment, considering the degree of individual responsibility and the extreme diversity in methods that dominated the colonial and early national eras.

Today, school and education are virtually synonymous, although formal institutions of learning played only a small role in the early years of the American experiment when the family and church were the principal instruments for training and disciplining and for perpetuating the cultural heritage. Individualism in the educational realm explains to a large extent the tremendous variations in educational opportunities and practices during colonial years; the assumption by the separate states of responsibility for schooling is the key to the standardization and uniformity of education in modern America, despite the highly decentralized system. It should not be forgotten that the first Americans were transplanted Englishmen who accepted the idea of education as an individual matter. The transformation of this concept over a period of two centuries into that of public responsibility is one of the major themes of American educational history.

The democratic impulse to provide equality of educational opportunity contributed to unifying the nation and to creating a uniform educational system throughout the nation. This so-called Jacksonian tradition has dominated educational development in both the nineteenth and twentieth centuries. In 1954, the United States Supreme Court reiterated this principle in the famous Brown case. In the last two decades, however, another theme — the Jeffersonian concept of excellence in education — has become a significant issue. In a sense, the present concern with excellence in education has its origin in the overwhelming success of the American nation in achieving equality of educational opportunity.

The extensive bibliography of the history of education attests to the fact that this is not a neglected field of research; but until recent years the traditional approach was a narrow one, concentrating on the institutional developments or the history of a particular school or college rather than on the social and intellectual implications of educational practices, theories, and developments. Thus, the long accepted interpretation was in progressive terms: the emergence of the American public school and the constant movement toward improved and diversified mass education. This is an oversimplified picture of America's educational past: it overlooks the complex interrelationships between education and the forces of change.

The deeper one goes into the rich sources, the more complicated the subject of educational developments becomes; and these

selections will undoubtedly raise as many questions as they answer. This would certainly be a measure of the success of such a
compilation. The principal problem in organizing a volume of this
nature is the matter of selecting from the vast resources those items
that are most pertinent and representative. In general, this presen-
tation emphasizes four major themes: education as a reflection of
the social and economic order; the evolution of the American idea
of free universal education; the role of the school in social change;
and the problem of mass education in a complex modern society.

An attempt has been made to reveal the developments of education through a wide sampling of contemporary writings gathered
from many different books, newspapers, and periodicals not always
readily available to the student of American educational and social
history. Necessity—of time and space—determined the exclusion of
material pertaining to the important developments of popular and
adult education. In putting the final editorial touches on the manuscript, the desire to start anew in reading, selecting, and discarding
came over the editor. If patience and perseverance grow with age,
then perhaps these other fascinating aspects of America's educational past will be drawn together in a similar collection in the
future.

The history is organized into six sections, presenting educational trends and problems from colonial times to the present. The
introductory essay for each part offers the continuity; contemporary
writings exemplify and reflect the significant developments and
ideas of the period. In the essays the numbers in parentheses refer
to the selections. The dates in the table of contents and in the head-
ings of each selection indicate when the items first appeared. Ed-
iting has been kept to a minimum in an effort to give the reader the
full flavor of the age itself.

Rena L. Vassar

Bloomington, Indiana
July, 1964

PART I:

EDUCATIONAL BEGINNINGS
IN AMERICA

THE USUAL approach to education in the colonial era was in terms of Massachusetts' "Old Deluder Satan Law" of 1647, the well-known endowed schools, the perennial school dame, *The New England Primer*, and Latin grammar education as preparation for college training. Yet even in the relatively simple society that was carving a place for itself in western civilization, education was a far more complex matter than the rude little school house or the dedicated school master or dame. One of the striking features of colonial education is the variety of ways and means the colonists found to educate their youth and prevent complete social and cultural disorganization.

The school was the formal institution for preserving and perpetuating the cultural heritage; and though it steadily grew in importance and popularity during colonial years, in the first century of settlement the school was a secondary agency compared to the educational role of the family and the church. The family looked after the physical and spiritual needs of its offspring and was the principal means by which the child acquired his religious, moral, and vocational training—and literary knowledge if there was time available. The church was an all-pervasive influence in the daily lives of the colonists, adults, and children. It set the standards of behavior, established moral and universal values, perpetuated doctrinal concepts, and supervised the lives of its communicants. Through sermons and visitations and through promises and threats, the church was a significant instrument of education.

This traditional role played by the social and religious institutions in education was English and European in origin. The colonists brought these customs and applied them to the wilderness conditions. Thus the early history of American education is basically the story of Old World practices undergoing inevitable changes and modifications as a result of the transfer to the New World. Pioneer life, the constant struggle to survive, and the social disorganization of frontier existence all contributed toward undermining social stability and cultural vitality and influenced the availability and effectiveness of education.

The colonists showed ingenuity and practicality in adapting old methods to the new environment and in evolving innovations in the never-ending struggle against the erosive forces of frontier life. When the family was failing to carry out its duties and responsibilities as the principal educator and supervisor of morals and character, the provincial governments of Puritan New England, for example, took steps to require parents and masters to train children in letters, vocational arts, religious doctrine, and the laws of the land. Massachusetts Bay Colony, the seat of orthodoxy, was the first to act, and the famous law of 1642 became in historical perspective the supreme example of the Puritans' interest in education and of early state action to promote education. Yet the law did not pertain to schools but placed the requirement of training squarely on parents and masters, who had long held that role in England; it provided a system of fines and punishment for neglect. America's first educational legislation reflected the established and traditional pattern of relying on the family rather than the school.

Connecticut and New Haven soon followed the Massachusetts precedent, but other colonists sought other means for preserving and perpetuating the social and cultural heritage. Since the apprenticeship system was a tried and proven way to educate youth in a trade, the colonists expanded the English practice to include in the contractual relationship the requirement of training the apprentice in the rudiments of learning. By provincial legislation or by custom, this scheme based on indentures became the means of training, educating and caring for the orphaned and pauper classes in the colonies. This system should not be confused with the regular custom of apprenticeship, which also placed children with other families for the express purpose of providing vocational education plus careful and strenuous supervision of the child's personal and religious conduct, which a loving and indulgent parent feared he might not acquire properly amid family surroundings. In theory the objectives were similar to the system used for the dependent classes: vocational, religious, and character training as well as in the letters and physical care in return for obedience and service; but the classes of children involved were vastly different. Apprenticeship contracts in all the colonies followed a similar pattern requiring the master to teach his apprentices — male or female — reading, and usually writing and cyphering for the boys. When eighteenth-century economic developments demanded more vocational services from the apprentice, there was a modification in the custom, which required the master to send the youth to a night school to receive his training in the letters (and thus not interfere with the full assistance the young apprentice gave to his master during the day).

As the colonial period progressed, the tutor, the indentured servant serving as teacher, the minister or lay reader, the school dame, and the school master assumed more and more of the educational responsibilities, formerly held by the family, for the academic and religious training of children. By the closing years of the colonial era, the school as a formal instrument of education had achieved great importance in the learning process. Although these institutions—the common schools of New England, the church schools among the Dutch, Quakers, and Anglicans, the endowed schools, and the provincial institutions of the southern colonies—ranged widely in organization and quality, their purposes, objectives and methods of education were remarkably similar. Their purpose was to provide training in the letters and in religion, to develop moral character, and to prepare the children for citizenship and for their position in life. They were institutions of practical training, matching the needs of the society. That small class of young men who were to enter ministerial, professional, or political realms received additional education in the classics in order to prepare them for college entrance. This training was also highly standardized: Latin and Greek language, grammar, and classical authors.

Despite the apparent similarity of their intellectual outlook and educational methods and viewpoints, some variations did exist from the beginning among the colonies, religious denominations, and social classes. In theory, if not in practice, only the Puritan colonies provided regular publicly-supported and supervised education for all economic and social groups. There was no religious test for entrance into one of the town schools. Fees and public funds supported the schools, and those unable to make these payments were exempted, a common practice throughout the English colonies. Class differentiation was much more pronounced in the southern colonies. Colonial legislation usually pertained only to the pauper and orphaned classes. The few provincial schools that came into existence in these colonies could care for a very small proportion of the population. The result was that families who could pay for their children's training by hiring a tutor or sending their children abroad were assured of regular education of a high

5

quality, but the vast portion of the colonists had to rely on any available teacher (who was frequently an overburdened indentured servant, an itinerant missionary, a poorly trained minister, or the parent himself). There came to exist a wide difference in the availability and kind of education of the children of the substantial tidewater planter and those of the backcountry settler. In the middle colonies, the religious sects—Quaker, Lutheran, Catholic, Dutch Reformed, and Anglican—looked out for the education of their offspring. Here again there were variations, depending on the compactness of settlement, the vitality of the religious community, and the existence of educated leadership.

In considering educational differences among the colonies and classes, one must not forget two groups in American society who posed special educational as well as social and economic problems. The Indian and Negro are usually overlooked or treated apart from the dominant white society. At first there was widespread interest among the colonists—as missionary or church groups, as political units, or as individuals with deep humanitarian interests—in the welfare, education, and training of these subjected people. As the social order grew more complex, the interest steadily declined. Not until the late nineteenth century was there as much systematic effort made to educate and assimilate these minority groups as there had been in the seventeenth and early eighteenth centuries.

This is merely a cursory view of educational developments in colonial America, and the contemporary items selected highlight variations as well as similarities in methods and objectives among religious and social groups. Rather than including such famous public documents as the Massachusetts Laws of 1642 and 1647 or the charters of well-known institutions, the emphasis here is on the viewpoints of the educational leaders and on the personal experiences of the school men or students of that era.

To represent fully the Puritan outlook on education it would be necessary to include examples of provincial legislation which set the requirements, records of town meetings which reveal how the laws were implemented, and court cases which show the system of enforcement. In addition, sermons and religious tracts which set forth the Puritan concept of learning, excerpts from the child rearing books which provided rules and advice for parents and masters on the care and discipline of children, and school books themselves would all be important evidence. The two selections by Cotton Mather and John Barnard do not fit into these categories, but they are excellent and representative examples of the Puritan idea of education (1) (2). Mather, the archetype of the strenuous and orthodox Puritan, presents the model Puritan family with its ideal relationship of parent and child engaged in the never-ending pro cess of education. *Bonifacius*, published in 1710, reflects a transitional period of Puritan development: On the one hand is the concept of a controlled society and of disciplined individuals and the subordination of the individual to the supreme being; but also apparent is the humanitarian strain of Puritanism with its emphasis on love, the general welfare of society, and human relationships. Although Mather's critics belittled and ridiculed his concern for man and society as "do goodism," his attitude, shown in the subtitle, "With Humble Proposals of Unexceptional Methods to Do Good in the World," was sincere and well-founded and in keeping with the eighteenth-century humanitarian outlook.

The passages pertaining to education and training excerpted from this lengthy essay reveal both the narrow and broad approaches of the Puritan to education. Mather neatly sums up the traditional Puritan view. Though his emphasis is on the family's role in preparing the child for his ultimate place in the universe, Mather also points out that the family has a holy obligation to train the child in the letters and in a vocational art. To fall short would be failure on the part of the parent to carry out the Lord's will. Who is to receive such training? Everyone—boys and girls, orphans and paupers, slaves and servants, too—is to get special attention in order to develop his religious senses and moral character; and if possible all are to learn to read, so that they might study the Bible.

John Barnard's brief autobiographical excerpt is a personal revelation of the educational process. While Mather concentrates on the model family and the ideal relationship, Barnard presents the intimate details of child life and school life in colonial New England. He reveals the various means by which a child might be educated: the school dame, the school master, or self-instruction. The account also presents the popular educational methods used in the seventeenth and eighteenth centuries. One may be struck by the precosity of the child who learned Latin and Greek at eight and entered Harvard College at fifteen, but this was common in that era.

In turning from Puritan education with its emphasis on preparation for life and for God to that of the Quakers, one immediately becomes aware of the striking similarity in ideas and views. The Quaker, like the Puritan and every other religious group in early America, looked upon the school and the family, along with the religious meeting, as the principal instruments for perpetuating the doctrinal views of the sect. Religious training was an integral part of all forms of education, and it is difficult to define the exact relationship between the school and the church or to separate the body of believers from the church organization. The Puritans were not unique; all schools in colonial America provided religious education. In the case of the Quakers, the local meeting played a significant role in establishing schools and supervising the training process. Anthony Benezet and Isaac Zane, two leading Quaker figures of the late eighteenth century, express in their report exactly what educational role the meetings were expected to play.

It is interesting to compare Thomas Budd's ideas about public responsibility and state supervision of education with Puritan New England's accomplishments (3). Despite William Penn's early efforts to use the state as a promoter and supervisor of education, Pennsylvania did not follow the early Puritan pattern but fell back on the old system of making education a family and church matter (4). As Benezet and Zane's report indicates, the members of the meeting often were lax in fulfilling their obligations (5).

Perhaps the humanitarian note is stronger in the Quaker writings than in the Puritan ones, but the most important difference between these two religious sects lies in the kind of education advocated. Here the Quaker stands out in contrast to the traditional concepts and practices of education. William Penn was one of a small group in England and America who criticized classical education. He expressed emphatically and specifically the idea of practical, useful, and vocational education as the primary role of the school. He did not completely reject classical education, which was considered highly utilitarian in terms of preparation for college entrance and professional and political responsibilities, but Penn's emphasis was on the kind of training that would prepare one

8

for a vocation and for the business world. With no ministry, the Quakers had less need for higher education than other sects. Furthermore, Penn seriously questioned the usefulness of learning "a strange Tongue or Two," a criticism also voiced by a small minority of English educational reformers. Penn argued that English, not Latin or Greek, was the language of the daily world and of the business world. This same theme runs throughout Quaker writings on education. Though not a member of the Society of Friends, Benjamin Franklin, a devoted citizen of Quaker Pennsylvania, expressed these same thoughts more elaborately in his "Idea of the English School" (1751) and sought to put them into practice by founding such a school in Philadelphia.

Another noteworthy aspect of the Quaker viewpoint on education is the new approach in regard to the methods of training and disciplining children. Here the idea of learning through meaningful activity and through using nature is similar to the views of education reformers of the nineteenth century. Penn was sharply critical of the standard techniques of learning through memorizing, parsing, drilling, and repeating.

The next section is a collection of documents from court records which reveal the role the state assumed in caring for and educating the indigent and orphaned children (6). The intense concern over the extent of legislative action and court surveillance attests to the keen desire of society as a whole to see that the children of the dependent class would be able to assume responsibility for their own welfare upon reaching maturity and not become public charges. The indentures and contracts tell in simple (and often awkward) language how the system operated, but they do not answer the question of how successful it was as an educational device. The master could easily subordinate education in an effort to obtain maximum service from his charge, whom he fed, clothed, and housed. Though brief and impersonal, the records nonetheless tell a great deal about the kind of education, the length of service, the type of payment, and the means for supervising such training. The ultimate purpose is clear: to produce capable and responsible members of society, well-grounded in Christian principles.

Following the indenture contracts is a group of selections dealing with the attempts of individuals and missionary societies to Christianize and educate the Negroes and Indians (7). In theory, the colonists, regardless of region or religion, showed a keen interest in the spiritual welfare of the "inferior sort" and sought to civilize and convert these heathens to western ways and the Christian religion. In practice, the efforts of the transplanted Englishmen were sporadic and varied considerably from colony to colony and family to family. There was no single central organization that had the mother country's blessings and assistance and the colonists' cooperation to undertake the formidable task of educating, in the broadest sense, the Indians and Negroes. It was largely left to individual families to carry on the task. As the slave was a part of the family unit, his education rested on the willingness and desire of his master to devote time and energy to his moral, religious, and even literary training such as it could be. Or the master could cooperate with the handful of dedicated missionaries who took the vast number of un-Christianized Indians and Negroes as their field.

There is an enormous difference between England and France and Spain in the New World in regard to missionary endeavors and accomplishments. Nowhere in English America was there the intensity, dedication, organization, and success of the Jesuits and Franciscans in their work in New France and New Spain. The most obvious reason for the difference is that the English colonies, albeit dominantly Protestant, were a mixture of denominations, each with a fairly well defined area of settlement. Missionary work under such conditions was purely local or provincial, and in this sense every denomination took an interest in the spiritual and moral training of the Negroes and Indians but with very little success.

Puritan writings frequently point out the importance of training and educating slaves and servants; John Eliot and a handful of ministers worked among the Indians of New England; and the Company of New England came into being as a missionary society in the seventeenth century. The Quakers of Pennsylvania followed the exemplary behavior of their founder in their relations with the Indians, in their demand that all children be educated, and in their concern for the welfare of the Negro. Yet, over-all, the accomplishments of these missionary groups or individuals were meager. The praying Indians of New England were few in number and frequently reverted to their old ways. Only the Quakers stand out in vivid contrast to the other colonists in their advanced humanitarian attitudes toward the slaves and Indians.

In 1701, the first well-organized missionary venture in the American colonies came into being in the form of the Society for the Propagation of the Gospel in Foreign Parts. The SPG, as it was known, was an outgrowth of the Society for the Promotion of Christian Knowledge, which now confined its efforts to revitalizing the spiritual, moral, and education life of Britain itself. Membership, composed of clerical and lay figures, was a veritable Who's Who of the Anglican Church and London Society who were bent on the reformation of manners and morals and the general uplift of the church and society in the colonies. This organization along with Dr. Bray's Associates (named for Thomas Bray who had served as Commissary in Maryland) provided men, funds, and books in a concerted effort to promote the Church of England and education in America. The Negroes, the Indians, and the backcountry—especially in the southern colonies—were their most fertile fields, but the dedicated servants worked everyplace. By 1704 New York City boasted a school for Negroes and Indians sponsored by the SPG and manned by Elias Neau, a transplanted French Huguenot.

The missionary organizations were far more successful in their endeavors among the Negroes than among the Indians. Such undertakings posed enormous problems, which letters of the members of Dr. Bray's Associates relate in detail. The cooperation of the master, the willingness of the Negro, and the patience and dedication of the minister-missionary were all key factors in the success or failure of this great crusade. That a handful of slaves learned to read and a few to write and that some were Christianized in the eighteenth century were due largely to the Anglican societies. The Bishop of London's decree in the early eighteenth century that baptism did not lead necessarily to manumission assisted the missionaries somewhat. In 1740, the colony of South Carolina reversed the trend when the assembly passed a law prohibiting the training of Negroes in reading and writing. (See p. 269).

The widespread concern for the moral and spiritual welfare of the Negroes was a combination of motives—religious, humanitarian, and utilitarian. Masters considered Christian training a means of comforting and reassuring these "lesser people" who accepted their servile status in this life that they could look forward to salvation along with the white race in afterlife, and that if they had undergone conversion they were equal before the supreme being. Also, the masters hoped that Christian doctrine would teach the servants to be obedient, trustworthy, responsible, and industrious — all the virtues desired of a servant class. As for training in the letters, to read was to read the Bible; thus such training also contributed to developing honest hardworking Christian slaves.

Many of these same motives applied to the attempts to educate and Christianize the Indians, but there was the added factor of a large population not enslaved but living side by side the white settlements — or more accurately speaking, in the pathway of white advance into the wilderness. Here, too, was a rich field for the missionary, and here was the practical matter of educating a people in order to live beside them peacefully. From the very beginning the missionary idea was to educate or recast the Indian into the dominant Western mold.

Eleazar Wheelock, the founder of Moor's Indian Charity School at Lebanon, Connecticut, which was to evolve into Dartmouth College at Hanover, New Hampshire, presents in his essay of 1770 the idealistic as well as practical reasons for Indian education (8). As a dedicated minister, the Reverend Mr. Wheelock joyfully accepted the call to work among the heathens and help uplift their race, but in stating his views, Wheelock realistically points out the importance of educating the Indian, so that he himself could undertake missionary work. Behind Wheelock's recognition that white missionaries were not successful in their work among the Indians lay more than a century of trying experiences on the part of individuals and servants of the New England missionary society.

Wheelock presented other practical arguments that were to become basic tenets of the national Indian policy in the nineteenth century: that to be educated, an Indian must be removed from his native environment, and that it was beneficial for Indians of different tribes to live together in order to learn the Englishman's ways and to adopt his religion. He also argued in favor of training Indians with English youth as a means of hastening Indian education and as a method of giving the whites the opportunity to learn the Indian tongue, a skill which would prove useful in negotiating with the natives as well as in teaching them.

Wheelock's dedication to the cause of Indian education and the Indian people helped create Dartmouth College, but such idealism was not adequate to overcome Indian as well as white prejudice and indifference. Dartmouth became another traditional college, and the course of Indian education was no more furthered by this institution than by the early efforts in Virginia to found an Indian College or by Harvard College's attempts to educate the natives. The belief in the efficacy of education as a solution to the problem of two cultures and two societies — one dominating and aggressive and the other struggling to survive — remained popular long after Wheelock's noble dream faded: first through the continued efforts of missionaries, and, after 1869, through the organized attempts of the federal government in its program based on boarding schools.

As the selections indicate, there was a widespread interest in education among the American colonists, who found many solutions to the problem of maintaining and perpetuating cultural life. In theory, by the eighteenth century, education was available to every social class and every segment of society, but a wide gulf existed between the ideal and the practice: regularity of education and quality of training varied considerably among social, economic, and geographic groups.

Schools were growing steadily in importance as a principal instrument of education, while parental and community responsibility was gradually declining. The common school of New England was limping along in the newly settled area; private institutions were beginning to flourish in the more populated centers of Boston, New York, Newport, Charles Town; the night school came into being to meet the needs of the apprenticed class. Various church groups continued to play a direct role in the establishment and maintenance of schools, and the Anglicans furthered education and religion through missionary undertakings. Society was in general committed to the principle of education for all, though, with the exception of New England, public responsibility remained limited largely to the dependent classes.

Differentiation in kinds, purposes, and objectives of education became apparent as society grew more complex and sophisticated and social stratification became more pronounced. The traditional education — the rudiments of learning for the masses, Latin and Greek for the young men who would seek college training — was not meeting the requirements of the commercial and business class who needed not Latin and Greek but more practical training in accounting, mathematics, geography, and the modern languages.

13

And the landed aristocracy wanted their children to receive the finishing touches of a gentleman's or lady's education. By mid-eighteenth century, the private institution or the tutor was meeting some of these needs, but such education was largely confined to the upper classes.

Benjamin Franklin was among the few who saw the need for a new kind of education, and he devoted his energies to creating in Philadelphia an institution that would cater to the demands of the emerging middle class. In his two essays, "Idea of the English School" and "Proposals Relating to the Education of Youth in Pennsylvania," Franklin sets forth the detailed rules and practical means by which the rising groups in America could imitate through formal education the pattern he himself followed through self-education (9) (10). Franklin's role in education goes far beyond his involvement in the founding of the Philadelphia Academy. In a real sense, he was the schoolmaster for the middle class of America; his autobiography set forth in literary form the rules by which the new American could learn. It was a handbook for the social order that was taking shape and form.

Many of the steps in this educational process are presented in his essay on the English School. He offers a detailed plan: literature to be studied (and imitated in style), English language, and practical and useful training. Any one of these schemes can be superimposed on the autobiography. Throughout, the theme is utilitarian. Franklin's hope was to found an institution that would fit a youth for any calling and any profession and to help him take his place in society where he would "serve Mankind, one's Country, Friends and Family." Thus Franklin provided the blueprints for an institution that would meet the needs of the individual, the family, the world of business, and the society in which he lived.

The final selection, excerpts from Philip Fithian's diary, represents another extreme in the spectrum of educational ideas and practices in the late colonial era (11). Fithian's account reveals the ideal education for the children of the southern aristocracy—boys and girls, children and adolescents. It is a warm, personal, and detailed revelation of the trials and tribulations and the joys and pleasures of a young Princeton graduate who took on the task of tutoring the children of the Robert Carter family in the classics and in religion. The diary presents a cross-section of plantation life and of the customs of the land, the kind of training the American gentry sought, and the educational techniques of the tutor. Beyond the factual information, the diary reveals the personality and ideas of its author and something about the intellectual and social milieu of Virginia on the eve of independence.

CHAPTER 1

THE PURITAN VIEW

The work of learning and of Grace too.

Cotton Mather, 1710

1. Bonifacius (1710)[1]

COTTON MATHER

Parents, Oh! How much ought you to be continually Devising, and even Travailing, for the Good of your Children. Often Devise; How to make them Wise Children; How to carry on a Desireable Education for them; an Education that shall render them Desireable; How to render them Lovely, and Polite Creatures, and Serviceable in their Generation. Often Devise, how to Enrich their Minds with valuable Knowledge; How to Instil Generous, and Gracious and Heavenly Principles into their Minds; How to Restrain and Rescue them from the Pathes of the Destroyer, and fortify them against their Special Temptations. There is a World of Good, that you have to Do for them. You are without Bowels, Oh! be not such Monsters! if you are not in a continual Agony to do for them all the Good that ever you can. . . .

I will Prosecute this Matter by Transcribing a Copy of PARENTAL RESOLUTIONS, which I have some-where met withal.

      ✿   ✿   ✿

'I would betimes entertain the Children with Delightful Stories out of the Bible. In the Talk, of the Table, I would go thro' the Bible, when the Olive Plants about my table are capable of being so Watered. But I would alwayes conclude the Stories with some Lessons of Piety, to be inferred from them.

'I would single out Some Scriptural Sentences, of the greatest Importance; and some also that have Special Antidotes in them against the Common Errors and Vices of Children. They shall

---

[1]Cotton Mather, *Bonifacius: An Essay upon the Good, that is to be Devised and Designed, by those Who Desire to Answer the Great End of Life and to Do Good While they Live* (Boston, 1710), pp. 52–70, 106–112, 147–48. Mather, whose name is virtually synonymous with Puritanism, was the son of Increase Mather and the grandson of two of the founders of Massachusetts Bay Colony, John Cotton and Richard Mather.

quickly get those Golden Sayings by heart, and be rewarded with Silver or Gold, or Some Good Thing, when they do it. . . .

'I would betimes cause my Children to Learn the Catechism. In Catechising of them, I would break the Answer into many Lesser and Proper Questions; and by their Answer to them Observe and Quicken their Understandings. I would bring every Truth, into some Duty and Practice, and Expect them to Confess it, and Consent unto it, and Resolve upon it. As we go on in our Catechising, they shall, when they are able, Turn to the Proofs, and Read them, and say to me, What they prove, and How. Then I will take my times to put nicer and harder Questions to them; and improve the Times of Conversation with my Family, which every man ordinarily has or may have, conferences on matters of Religion.

'Restless would I be, till I may be able to Say of my Children, Behold They Pray! I would therefore Teach them to Pray. But after they have Learnt a Form of Prayer, I will press them, to proceed unto Points which are not in their Form. I will show them the State of their own Souls; and on every Stroke Enquire of them, What they think ought now to be their Prayer. I will direct them, that every Morning they shall take one Text or Two out of the Sacred Scripture, and Shape it into a Desire, which they shall add unto their Usual Prayer. When they have heard a Sermon, I will mention to them over again the main Subject of it, and ask them thereupon, What they have now to Pray for. I will charge them, with all possible cogency, to Pray in Secret; And often call upon them, Child, I hope, you don't forget my charge to you, about Secret Prayer; Your crime is very great, if you do!

'I would betimes do what I can, to beget a Temper of Benignity in my Children, both towards one another and towards all other people. I will instruct them how Ready they should be to Communicate unto others, a part of what they have; and they shall see, my Encouragements, when they discover a Loving, a Courteous, an Helpful Disposition. I will give them now and then a piece of Money for them with their own Little Hands to dispense unto the Poor. Yea, if any one has hurt them, or vex'd them, I will not only forbid them all Revenge, but also oblige them to do a Kindness as soon as may be to the Vexatious Person. All Courseness of Language or Carriage in them, I will discountenance it.

'I would be Sollicitous to have my Children Expert, not only at

Reading handsomely, but also at Writing a fair Hand. I will then assign them such Books to Read, as I may judge most agreeable and profitable; obliging them to give me some Account of what they Read; but keep a Strict Eye upon them, that they don't Stumble on the Devils Library, and poison themselves with foolish Romances, or Novels, or Playes, or Songs, or Jests that are not convenient. I will set them also, to Write out such things as may be of the greatest Benefit unto them; and they shall have their Blank Books, neatly kept on purpose, to Enter such Passages as I advise them to. I will particularly require them now and then, to Write a Prayer of their own Composing, and bring it unto me; that so I may discern, what sense they have of their own Everlasting Interests.

'I Wish that my Children may as soon as may be, feel the Principles of Reason and Honor, working in them, and that I may carry on their Education, very much upon those Principles. Therefore, first, I will wholly avoid, that harsh, fierce, crabbed usage of the Children that would make them Tremble, and Abhor to come into my Presence. I will so use them, that they shall fear to offend me, and yet mightily Love to see me, and be glad of my coming home, if I have been abroad at any time. . . . I would raise in them, an High Opinion of their Fathers Love to them, and of his being better able to Judge What is Good for them, than they are for themselves. I would bring them to Believe, Tis best for them to be and do as I would have them. . . . I will never dispence a Blow, except it be for an atrocius Crime, or for a lesser Fault Obstinately persisted in; either for an Enormity, or for an Obstinancy. I would ever Proportion chastisements unto Miscarriages; not smite bitterly for a very small piece of Childishness, and only frown a little for some real Wickedness. Nor shall my Chastisements ever be dispensed in a Passion, and a Fury; but with them, I will first show them the Command of GOD, by Transgressing whereof they have displeased me. The Slavish Raving, Fighting Way of Education too Commonly used, I look upon it as a considerable Article in the Wrath and Curse of God, upon a miserable World.

'As soon as we can, weel get up to yet Higher Principles. I will often tell the Children, What cause they have to Love a Glorious Christ, who has Dy'd for them. And, How much He will be Well-pleased with their Well-Doing. And what a Noble Thing, tis to follow His Example; which Example I will describe unto them. I

19

will often tell them, That the Eye of God is upon them; the Great GOD knows all they do and Hears all they Speak. I will often tell them, That there will be a Time, when they must appear before the Judgment-Seat of the Holy LORD; and they must Now do nothing, that may Then be a Grief and Shame unto them. I will Set before them, the Delights of that Heaven that is prepar'd for Pious Children; and the Torments of that Hell that is prepared of old, for naughty ones. I will inform them of the Good Offices which the Good Angels do for Little Ones, that have the Fear of God and are afraid of Sin. . . .

'I would be very watchful and Cautious, about the Companions of my Children. I will be very Inquisitive, what Company they keep; If they are in hazard of being Ensnared by any Vicious Company, I will earnestly pull them out of it, as Brands out of the Burning. I will find out, and procure Laudable Companions for them. . . .

'I incline, that among all the Points of a Polite Education which I would endeavour for my Children, they may each of them, the Daughters as well as the Sons, have so much Insight into some Skill, which lies in the way of Gain, (the Limners, or the Scriveners, or the Apothecaries, or Some other Mystery, to which their own Inclination may most carry them,) that they may be able to Subsist themselves, and get something of a Livelihood, in case the Providence of God should bring them into Necessities. . . .

'As soon as ever I can, I would make my Children apprehensive of the main END, for which they are to Live; that so they may as soon as may be, begin to Live; and their Youth no be nothing but Vanity. I would show them, that their main END must be To Acknowledge the Great GOD, and His Glorious CHRIST; and bring Others to Acknowledge Him: And that they are never Wise nor Well, but when they are doing so. I would show them, what the Acknowledgments are, and how they are to be made. I would make them able to Answer the Grand Question, Why they Live; and what is the End of the Actions that they fill their Lives? Teach them, How their Creator and Redeemer is to be Obey'd in every thing; and how everything is to be done in Obedience to Him; Teach them, How even their Diversions, and their Ornaments, and the Tasks of their Education, must all be to fit them for the further Service of Him to whom I have devoted them. . . .'

✼   ✼   ✼

The School-Master has manifold Opportunities to Do Good. God made him sensible of his Obligations! We read, The Little Ones hath their Angels. It is an Hard work to keep a School. But it is a Good work; and it may be so done, as to be in some Sort like the Work of Angels. The Tutors of the Children may be like their Tutelar Angels. . . .

Tutors, will you not look upon the Children under your Wing as committed unto you, by the Glorious LORD, with a charge of this importance; Take them, and bring them up for me, and I will pay you your Wages! . . .

Sirs, Let it be a Great Intention with you, To instil Documents of Piety into the Children. Esteem it, Your and Their Great Interest, That they would So Know the Holy Scriptures as to be made Rise unto Salvation; and Know the Saviour, whom to know is Life Eternal, Oh! Take all occasions to Drop Some Honey out of the Rock upon them! Happy the Children, and as Happy the Master there they who made the Relation of their Conversion to Serious Piety, may say, There was a School-Master that brought us to CHRIST! You have been told; 'Certainly, Tis a Nobler work, to make the Little Ones Know their Saviour, than to know their Letters. The Lessons of Jesus are Nobler Things than the Lessons of Cato. A Sanctifying Transformation of their Souls, were a Nobler Thing, than meerly to construe Ovids Metamorphosis. He was a Good School-Master, of whom there was this Testimony given. . . .

CATECHISING; That should be a frequent and at least, a Weekly, Exercise of the School. And in the most Edifying, and Aplicatory, and Admonatory manner carried on . . . .

Dr. Reynolds, in a Funeral Sermon on an Eminent School-Master has a passage worthy to be written in Letters of Gold. 'If Grammar Schools have Holy and Learned men for over them, not only the Brains, but also the Souls of the Children might be there enriched, and the work of Learning and of Grace too, be Betimes wrought in them.' In order to this, tis to be proposed That you would not only Pray with your Scholars every day, but also take occasion from the Publick Sermons, and from Remarkable Occurences of Providence in your Neighbourhood, often to inculcate the Lessons of Piety upon the Children.

Tutors in the College, may do well Successively to treat each

21

of their Pupils alone, with all possible Solemnity and Affection, about their interior state; show them how to Repent of Sin, and Believe on Christ; and bring them to Express Resolutions of Serious Piety. Sirs, you may do a thousand Things, to render your Pupils Orthodox in their Principles, Regular in their Practices, Qualified for Services!

I have read this Experiment of One who had pupils under his charge; 'He made it his Custom, that in every Recitation, he would, from something or other occurring in it, make an occasion, to let fall some Sentence, which had a Tendency to promote the Fear of God in their Hearts; which thing Sometimes did indeed put him to more than a little Study; but the Good Effect Sufficiently Recompenced it!

If I should Press for certain Authors to be made Classical in the Grammar-Schools which are not commonly used there; Such as Castalio for the Latin Tongue, and Posselius for the Greek; or, if I should beg, with certain Modern Writers, That there may be a Northwest Passage found, for the Attaining of the Latin Tongue, that instead of, a Journey which may be dispatched in a Few Days, they may not wander, like the Children of Israel, many years in the Wilderness:' Or, if I should recite Austins complaints, of Little Boys Learning the filthy Actions of the Pagan Gods in the Schools, . . . and Luthers, 'That our Schools are more Pagan than Christian;' And the Reports and Wishes of a late Writer, who sayes; 'I knew an aged and famous School-Master, that after he had kept School about Fifty years, said with a Sad Countenance, That it was a great Trouble unto him that he spent so much Time in Reading Pagan authors to his Scholars, and wished it were customary to Read such a Book as Duports Verses upon Job, rather than Homer, and such Books. I pray God, put it in the Hearts of a Wise Parliament, to Purge our Schools; that instead of Learning Vain Fictions, and Filthy Stories they may be acquainted with Books containing Grave Sayings, and things that may make them truely Wise and Useful in the World:' I suppose, there will be little Notice taken of such Proposals: I had as good never mention them; Tis with Dispair that I make mention of them.

Among the Occasions to be taken for Instilling of Piety into the Scholars, there is One peculiarly at the Writing-Schools. An inveterate Sinner I have read of, Converted into Serious Piety, by

22

accidentally seeing that Sentence of Austin written in a Window; He that hath Promised Pardon to the Penitent Sinner, has not Promised Repentance to the Presumptious One. Who can tell what Good may be done to the Young Scholar, by a Sentence in a Copy-book? Let their Copies be of Sentences worthy to be had in Ever-lasting Remembrance; of Sentences, that shall have the brightest Maxims of Wisdom in them. . . .

At the Grammar School also, the Scholars may be ordered for their Exercises to turn such things into Latin, as may be likewise for their Instruction and Establishment, in the Principles of Chris-tianity. . . . Their Epistles, why may they not be on such Subjects as may most befriend Vertue in them!

I will add this; To carry on the Discipline of the School, with Rewards, as well as Punishments, is most certainly very Advise-able, very Preferrible. There may be Invented many ways of Rewarding, the Diligent and the Laudable; . . . a Child of any Ingenuity, under the Expectations and Encouragements of being Rewarded, will do to the uttermost. . . . If a Fault must be Pun-ished, Let Instruction, both unto the Delinquent and unto the Spectator, accompany the Correction. Let the Odious Nature of the Sin, that has Enforced the Correction, be declared; and let nothing be done in a Passion; all be done with all the Evidence of compas-sion that may be. . . .

2. Autobiography (1766)[1]

THE REVEREND JOHN BARNARD

I, John Barnard was born at Boston, 6th Nov. 1681; descended from reputable parents, viz. John and Esther Barnard, remarkable for their piety and benevolence, who devoted me to the service of God, in the work of the ministry, from my very conception and birth; and accordingly took special care to instruct me themselves in the principles of the Christian religion, and kept me close at school to furnish my young mind with the knowledge of letters. By that time I had a little passed my sixth year, I had left my reading school, in the latter part of which my mistress made me a sort of usher, appointing me to teach some children that were older than myself, as well as smaller ones; and in which time I had read my Bible through thrice. My parents thought me to be weakly, because of my thin habit and countenance, and therefore sent me into the country, where I spent my seventh summer, and by the change of air and diet and exercise I grew more fleshy and hardy; and that I might not lose my reading, was put to a school-mistress, and returned home in the fall.

In the spring of my eighth year I was sent to the grammar school, under the tuition of the aged, venerable, and justly famous Mr. Ezekiel Cheever. But after a few weeks, an odd accident drove me from the school. There was an older lad entered the school the same week with me; we strove who should outdo; and he beat me by the help of a brother in the upper class, who stood behind master with the accidence open for him to read out off; by which means he could recite his** three and four times in a forenoon, and the same

---

[1] "Autobiography of the Reverend John Barnard," *Massachusetts Historical Society Collections*, 3rd. ser. (1836), V, 178–87. Barnard took his degree from Harvard College in 1700 and became minister of a congregation in Marblehead. (** indicates illegible words in the original manuscript.)

in the afternoon; but I who had no such help, and was obliged to committ all to memory, could not keep pace with him; so that he would be always one lesson before me. My ambition could not bear to be outdone, and in such a fraudulent manner, and therefore I left the school. About this time arrived a dissenting minister from England, who opened a private school for reading, writing, and Latin. My good father put me under his tuition, with whom I spent a year and a half. The gentleman receiving but little encouragement, threw up his school, and returned me to my father, and again I was sent to my aged Mr. Cheever, who placed me in the lowest class; but finding I soon read through my ** in a few weeks he advanced me to the **, and the next year made me the head of it.

In the time of my absence from Mr. Cheever, it pleased God to take to himself my dear mother, who was not only a very virtuous, but a very intelligent woman. She was exceeding fond of my learning, and taught me to pray. My good father also instructed me, and made a little closet for me to retire to for my morning and evening devotion. But, alas! how childish and hypocritical were all my pretensions to piety, there being little or no serious thoughts of God and religion in me. . . .

Though my master advanced me, as above, yet I was a very naughty boy, much given to play, insomuch that he at length openly declared, "You Barnard, I know you can do well enough if you will; but you are so full of play that you hinder your classmates from getting their lessons; and therefore, if any of them cannot perform their duty, I shall correct you for it." One unlucky day, one of my classmates did not look into his book, and therefore could not say his lesson, though I called upon him once and again to mind his book; upon which our master beat me. I told master the reason why he could not say his lesson was, his declaring he would beat me if any of the class were wanting in their duty; since which this boy would not look into his book, though I called upon him to mind his book, as the class could witness. The boy was pleased with my being corrected, and persisted in his neglect, for which I was still corrected, and that for several days. I thought, in justice, I ought to correct the boy, and compel him to a better temper; and therefore, after school was done, I went up to him, and told him I had been beaten several times for his neglect; and since master would not correct him I would, and I should do so often as I was corrected

25

for him; and then drubbed him heartily. The boy never came to school any more, and so that unhappy affair ended.

Though I was often beaten for my play, and my little roguish tricks, yet I don't remember that I was ever beaten for my book more than once or twice. One of these was upon this occasion. Master put our class upon turning Aesop's Fables into Latin verse. Some dull fellows made a shift to perform this to acceptance; but I was so much duller at this exercise, that I could make nothing of it; for which master corrected me, and this he did two or three days going. I had honestly tried my possibles to perform the task; but having no poetical fancy, nor then a capacity opened of expressing the same idea by a variation of phrases, though I was perfectly acquainted with prosody, I found I could do nothing; and therefore plainly told my master, that I had diligently labored all I could to perform what he required, and perceiving I had not genius for it, I thought it was in vain to strive against nature any longer; and he never more required it of me. Nor had I any thing of a poetical genius till after I had been at College some time, when upon reading some of Mr. Cowley's works, I was highly pleased, and a new scene opened before me.

I remember once, in making a piece of Latin, my master found fault with the syntax of one word, which was not so used by me heedlessly, but designedly, and therefore I told him there was a plain grammar rule for it. He angrily replied, there was no such rule. I took the grammar and showed the rule to him. Then he smilingly said, "Thou art a brave boy; I had forgot it." And no wonder; for he was then above eighty years old. . . .

From the grammar school I was admitted into the college in Cambridge, in New England, in July, 1696, under the Presidentship of the very revered and excellent Dr. Increase Mather, (who gave me for a thesis, *Habenti dabitur*,) and the tutorage of those two great men, Mr. John Leverett, (afterwards President) and Mr. William Brattle (afterwards the worthy minister of Cambridge.) Mr. Leverett became my special tutor for about a year and a half, to whom succeeded Mr. Jabez Fitch, (afterwards the minister of Ipswich with Mr. John Rogers, who at the invitation of the church in Portsmouth, New Hampshire, removed to them.) Upon my entereing into college, I became chamber-mate, the first year, to a senior and junior sophister; which might have been greatly to my advantage, had they been of a studious disposition, and made any considerable progress in literature. But, alas! they were an idle pack, who knew but little, and took no pains to increase their knowledge. When therefore, according to my disposition, which was ambitious to excel, I applied myself close to books, and began to look forward into the next year's exercises, this unhappy pair greatly discouraged me, and beat me off from my studies, so that by their persuasions I foolishly threw by my books, and soon became as idle as they were. Oh! how baneful is it to be linked with bad company! and what a vile heart had I to hearken to their wretched persuasions! I never, after this, recovered a good studious disposition, while I was at college. Having a ready, quick memory, which rendered the common exercises of the college easy to me, and being an active youth, I was hurried almost continually into one diversion or another, and gave myself to no particular studies, and therefore made no great proficiency in any part of solid learning. . . .

In the last year of my being at college, it pleased God, in righteous judgment, so far to deliver me up to the corrupt workings of my own heart, that I fell into a scandalous sin, in which some of my classmates were concerned. This roused me more seriously to bethink myself of the wickedness of my heart and life; and though I had kept up some little show of religion, yet now I saw what a terrible punishment it was to be left of God, and exposed to his wrath and vengeance, and set myself upon seeking an interest in the favor of God, through the blessed Mediator; and resolved, through the grace of God assisting of me, to lead a sober, a righteous, and a godly life, and improve my time and talents in the service of my Maker and Redeemer, and applied myself more closely to my studies: but I found I could not recover what I had lost by my negligence.

In July, 1700, I took my first degree, Dr. Increase Mather being President; after which I returned to my honoured father's house, where I betook myself to close studying, and humbling myself before God with fasting and prayer, imploring the pardon of all my sins, through the mediation of Christ; begging the divine Spirit to sanctify me throughout, in spirit, soul, and body, and fit me for, and use me in the service of the sanctuary, and direct and bless all my studies to that end. I joined to the North Church in Boston, under the pastoral care of the two Mathers. . . .

While I continued at my good father's I prosecuted my studies; and looked something into the mathematics, though I gained but little; our advantages therefor being noways equal to what they have, who now have the great Sir Isaac Newton, and Dr. Halley, and some other mathematicians, for their guides. About this time I made a visit to the college, as I generally did once or twice a year, where I remember the conversation turning upon the mathematics, one of the company, who was a considerable proficient in them, observing my ignorance, said to me he would give me a question, which if I answered in a month's close application, he should account me an apt scholar. He gave me the question. I, who was ashamed of the reproach cast upon me, set myself hard to work, and in a fortnight's time returned him a solution to the question, both by trigonometry and geometry, with a canon by which to resolve all questions of the like nature. When I showed it to him, he was surprised, said it was right, and owned he knew no way of resolving it but by algebra, which I was an utter stranger to. I also gave myself to the study of the Biblical Hebrew, turned the Lord's prayer, the creed, and part of the Assembly's Catechism into Hebrew, (for which I had Dr. Cotton Mather for my corrector,) and entered on the task of finding the radix of every Hebrew word in the Bible, with design to form a Hebrew Concordance; but when I proceeded through a few chapters in Genesis, I found the work was done to my hand by one of the Buxtorfs. So I laid it by.

The pulpit being my great design, and divinity my chief study, I read all sorts of authors, and as I read, compared their sentiments with the sacred writings, and formed my judgment of the doctrines of Christianity by that only and infallible standard of truth; which led me insensibly into what is called the Calvinistical scheme, (though I never to this day have read Calvin's Works, and cannot call him master,) which sentiments, by the most plausible arguments to the contrary, that have fallen in my way, (and I have read the most of them,) I have never yet seen cause to depart from.

Through the importunity of my friends, I preached my first sermon, . . . to a society of young men, meeting on Lord's day evening for the exercises of religion, (to which I belonged) in the

August twelvemonth after I took my first degree; and some months after preached publicly at Gloucester. By August, 1702, I became almost a constant preacher, both on week days, and on the Lord's day. . . . This constant preaching took me off from all other studies. About two months before I took my second degree, the reverend and deservedly famous Mr. Samuel Willard, then Vice-President, called upon me, (though I lived in Boston), to give a common-place in the college hall; which I did, endeavoring to prove the divine inspiration and authority of the holy Scriptures. When I had concluded, the President was so good as to say openly in the hall, *"Bene fecisti, Barnarde, et gratias ago tibi."* Under him I took my second degree in July, 1703. . . .

CHAPTER 2

THE QUAKER OUTLOOK

The World . . . a great and stately Volume
of natural Things.

William Penn, 1693

3. Good Order Established in Pennsilvania and New-Jersey in America (1685)[1]

THOMAS BUDD

1. Now It might be well if a Law were made by the Governours and general Assemblies of Pennsilvania and New-Jersey, that all Persons inhabiting in the said Provinces, do put their Children seven years to the publick School, or longer, if the Parents please.

2. That Schools be provided in all Towns and Cities, and Persons of known honesty, skill and understanding be yearly chosen by the Governour and General Assembly, to teach and instruct Boys and Girls in all the most useful Arts and Sciences that they in their youthful capacities may be capable to understand, as the learning to Read and Write true English, Latine, and other useful Speeches and Languages, and fair Writing, Arithmatick and Book-keeping and the Boys to be taught and instructed in some Mystery or Trade, as the making of Mathematical Instruments, Joynery, Turnery, the making of Clocks and Watches, Weaving, Shoe making, or any other useful Trade or Mystery that the school is capable of teaching; and the Girls to be taught and instructed in Spinning of Flax and Wool, and Knitting of Gloves and Stockings, Sewing, and making of all sorts of useful Needle Work, and the Making of Straw Work, as Hats, Baskets, etc. or any other useful Art or Mystery that the School is capable of teaching.

3. That the Scholars be kept in the Morning two hours at Reading, Writing, Book-keeping etc. and other two hours at work in that Art, Mystery or Trade that he or she most delighteth in, and then let them have two hours to dine, and for Recreation; and in the

---

[1]Thomas Budd, *Good Order Established in Pennsilvania and New-Jersey in America, Being a true Account of the Country: With its Produce and Commodities there Made* (Philadelphia, 1685), pp. 14–15. Budd was an important figure in West Jersey politics, but eventually left the colony and the Society of Friends and returned to England where he joined the Baptist Church.

afternoon two hours at Reading, Writing, etc. and the other two hours at work at their several Imployments.

4. The seventh day of the Week the Scholars may come to school only in the fore-noon, and at a certain hour in the after-noon let a Meeting be kept by the School-Masters and their scholars, where after good instruction and admonishion is given by the Masters, to the Scholars, and thanks returned to the Lord for his Mercies and Blessings that are daily received from him, then let a strict examination be made by the Masters of the Conversation of the Scholars in the weekpast, and let reproof, admonition and correction be given to the Offendors, according to the quantity and quality of their faults.

5. Let the like Meetings be kept by the School-Mistresses, and the Girls apart from the Boys. By strictly observing this good Order, our Children will be hindred of running into that Excess of Riot and Wickedness that youth is incident to, and they will be a comfort to their tender Parents.

6. Let one thousand Acres of Land be given and laid out in a good place, to every publick School that shall be set up, and the Rent or income of it to go towards the defraying of the charge of the school.

7. And to the end that the children of poor People, and the Children of Indians may have the like good Learning with the Children of Rich People, let them be maintained free of charge to their Parents, out of the Profits of the school, arising by the Work of the Scholars, by which the Poor and the Indians, as well as the Rich, will have their Children taught, and the Remainder of the profits, if any be, to be disposed of in the building of School-houses and Improvements on the thousand Acres of Land, which belongs to the School.

4. SOME FRUITS OF SOLITUDE (1693)[1]

WILLIAM PENN

IGNORANCE

1. It is admirable to consider how many *Millions* of People come into, and go out of the World, *Ignorant of themselves,* and of the World they have lived in.

2. If one went to see *Windsor-Castle,* or *Hampton-Court,* it would be strange not to observe and remember the Situation, the Building, the Gardens, Fountains, &c. that make up the Beauty and Pleasure of such a Seat? And yet few People know *themselves;* No, not their *own Bodies,* the *Houses* of their Minds, the *most curious* Structure of the World; a *living walking* Tabernacle: Nor the *World* of which it was made, and out of which it is fed; which would be so much our Benefit, as well as our Pleasure, to know. We cannot doubt of this when we are told that the *Invisible Things of God are brought to light by the Things that are seen;* and consequently we read our Duty in them as often as we look upon them, to him that is the Great and Wise Author of them, if we look as we should do.

3. The *World* is certainly a great and stately *Volume* of natural Things; and may be not improperly styled the *Hieroglyphicks* of a better: But, alas! how very few Leaves of it do we seriously turn over! This ought to be the *Subject* of the Education of our *Youth,* who, at Twenty, when they should be fit for Business, know little or nothing of it.

EDUCATION

4. We are in Pain to make them Scholars, but not *Men*! To talk, rather than to know, which is true *Canting.*

---

[1]William Penn, *Some Fruits of Solitude in Reflections and Maxims* (Introduction by Edmund Gosse)(London, 1901), pp. 1–6.

5. The first Thing obvious to Children is what is *sensible;* and that we make no Part of their Rudiments.

6. We press their Memory too soon, and puzzle, strain and load them with Words and Rules; to know *Grammer* and *Rhetorick,* and a strange Tongue or two, that it is ten to one may never be useful to them; Leaving their natural *Genius* to *Mechanical* and *Physical,* or natural Knowledge uncultivated and neglected; which would be of exceeding Use and Pleasure to them through the whole Course of their Life.

7. To be sure, Languages are not to be despised or neglected. But Things are still to be preferred.

8. Children had rather be making of *Tools* and *Instruments* of Play; *Shaping, Drawing, Framing,* and *Building,* &c. than getting some Rules of Propriety of Speech by Heart: And those also would follow with more Judgment, and less Trouble and Time.

9. It were Happy if we studied Nature more in natural Things; and acted according to Nature; whose Rules are *few, plain and most reasonable.*

10. Let us begin where she begins, go her Pace, and close always where she ends, and we cannot miss of being good *Naturalists.*

11. The Creation would not be longer a Riddle to us: The *Heavens, Earth,* and *Waters,* with their respective, various and numerous Inhabitants: Their Productions, Natures, Seasons, Sympathies and Antipathies; their Use, Benefit and Pleasure, would be better understood by us: And an *eternal Wisdom, Power, Majesty* and *Goodness,* very *conspicuous* to us, thro' those sensible and passing Forms: The World wearing the *Mark* of its Maker, whose Stamp is everywhere *visible,* and the *Characters* very *legible* to the Children of Wisdom.

12. And it would go a great way to caution and direct People in their Use of the World, that they were better studied and known in the Creation of it.

13. For how could Man find the Confidence to abuse it, while they should see the Great Creator stare them in the Face, in all and every Part thereof?

14. Their Ignorance makes them insensible, and that Insensibility hardly in misusing this noble Creation, that has the Stamp and Voice of a Deity every where, and in every Thing to the Observing.

15. It is pity therefore that Books have not been composed for *Youth*, by some curious and careful *Naturalists*, and also *Mechanicks*, in the *Latin* Tongue, to be used in Schools, that they might learn Things with Words: Things obvious and *familiar* to them, and which would make the Tongue easier to be obtained by them.

16. Many able *Gardiners* and *Husbandmen* are yet Ignorant of the *Reason* of their Calling; as most *Artificers* are of the Reason of their own Rules that govern their excellent Workmanship. But a Naturalist and Mechanick of this sort, is *Master* of the Reason of both, and might be of the Practice too, if his Industry kept pace with his Speculation; which were very commendable; and without which he cannot be said to be a *complete* Naturalist or Mechanick.

17. Finally, if Man be the *Index* or *Epitomy* of the World, as *Philosophers* tell us, we have only to read our *selves* to be *learned* in it. But because there is nothing we less regard than the *Characters* of the Power that made us, which are so clearly written upon us and the World he has given us, and can best tell us what we are and should be, we are even Strangers to our own *Genius:* The *Glass* in which we should see that true instructing and agreeable Variety, which is to be observed in Nature, to the Admiration of that Wisdom and Adoration of that Power which made us all.

5. Some Observations Relating to the Establishment of Schools (1778)[1]

ANTHONY BENEZET AND ISAAC ZANE

It is the opinion of the Committee, that Friends having united with others, in employing such persons for Masters, who have not submitted to the operation of truth, hath had a tendency to strengthen a disposition in our youth to avoid the Cross, and unite with the spirit of the world; whereby many hurtful and Corrupt things have gained ground amongst us. On reviewing the Minutes of the Yearly Meeting, we find, that at several Meetings, particularly at and since the year 1750, the consideration of the importance of training up our Youth in useful Learning, under the tuition of religious, prudent persons, suitably qualified for that service, came weightily before the Meeting, when it was recommended, that Friends should exert themselves therein as fully as their circumstances would permit, and that the likeliest means to induce persons, properly qualified, to undertake the business, would be to have some certain income fixed, in consideration of which, the Master should be obliged to teach so many children, on behalf of each Monthly, or particular Meeting, as the said Meeting shall judge adequate to the Salary; and that no Master should be employed, but with the approbation of a Committee of the Monthly Meeting, appointed for that and other services, relating to such Schools: But we find, that notwithstanding those pressing recommendations, very little has been effectually done therein. We, therefore, think

---

[1]George S. Brookes, *Friend Anthony Benezet* (Philadelphia: University of Pennsylvania Press, 1937), pp. 492–95. The report was submitted to the Yearly Meeting in 1778. Benezet was a French Huguenot who joined the Society of Friends upon coming to Philadelphia. A successful businessman, he turned his attention to education and played an important role in its promotion in Philadelphia. He served as teacher of the Friends' school, established a girls' school in 1755, and helped establish a school for Negroes, where he taught.

it necessary, that it be recommended to the Quarterly and from thence to the Monthly and Preparative Meetings, that the former advice of collecting a fund, for the establishment and support of schools, under the care of a standing Committee appointed by the several Monthly or Particular Meetings, should generally take place, and that it be recommended by the Yearly Meeting, to Friends of each quarter, to send up the next year an account of what they have done therein. And we also think it necessary, that this weighty concern should in future become the continued care of the Yearly Meeting, by an annual Query; that so that matter may rest on a solid foundation, and every possible encouragement and assistance may be afforded to Friends in the Settlement of schools, procuring Master &c. thro' the whole extent of the Yearly Meeting. And notwithstanding some difficulties may appear in the raising of a sufficiency, fully to answer the end proposed, yet as improvements of this kind have often arisen from small beginnings, it is desired, that Friends be not discouraged, by their inability, but having faith in the Divine Blessing, being conferred on their benevolent intentions, would begin, by making some provision, agreeable to the circumstances of their respective Meetings. That within the compass of each Meeting, where the settlement of a school is necessary, a lot of ground be provided, sufficient for a garden, orchard, grass for a cow, &c. and that a suitable house, stable &c. be erected thereon. There are but few meetings but which may, in labour, in materials or money, raise so much as would answer this charge. Such a provision would be an encouragement for a staid person, with a family who will likely to remain a considerable time, perhaps his whole life, in the service, to engage therein. This will obviate the necessity Friends often think themselves under, of hiring no other but a single person, for a Master, on account of boarding him, from one house to another, amongst themselves; hence they are induced to bargain with transient persons, often of doubtful characters; some of whom have proved to be men of corrupt minds, and even their conduct immoral, yet they are seldom likely to remain in the service any longer than some employ more agreeable to support themselves offers: Whereby the Teachers miss the opportunity of improvement, which nothing will give, equal to that experience gained by long practice, in the education of the Youth. A service, which, however it may be slighted by many, if duly performed is as arduous to the teacher, as it is of advantage to the Youth: And which if it was sometimes undertaken by pious minded Persons, more from an inclination of benefiting the Youth, than from a desire of gain, would afford a satisfaction far exceeding that of spending their time either in supineness and ease, delighting themselves in the enjoyment of their wealth, or in the pleasure of amassing more. For indeed as the Apostle observes I Cor. 6, 20; 2 Cor. 5, 15, "Ye are not your own, for ye are bought with a price—that they which live should not henceforth live unto themselves but unto him which died for them." And here a sorrowful consideration occurs, which we desire to mention with caution & tenderness that is the backwardness so apparent amongst us to contribute that part of our substance, which the circumstance of things and the necessities of the people, have on different occasions made necessary; if this had not been the case, a matter of so great importance, as the virtuous education of our Youth, would not have lain neglected, for so long a course of years; after such pressing advices had been so expressly, handed down from the Yearly Meeting: Hence arises a Query, how far our neglect of applying to the necessary service of our fellowmen, such part of the goods many have laid up in store, is one of the causes of the deep affliction which now so feelingly attends, and how small a part of what has been forcibly taken from many, if it had been seasonably, and cheerfully contributed, would have answered the several good purposes, which have either been refused, or neglected by us.

The giving proper encouragement to such teachers as are capable by example and precept, to promote the growth of piety and virtue; as well as due instruction in our youth, and are likely to continue in the service, would be attended with farther advantages as well from the experience the teachers would necessarily gain, who in other respects may be incapable of supporting themselves by labour, to be educated and qualified to serve as School-Masters; a consideration well worth our particular care, as well from duty, as interest. The benefit of the youth and the means of a comfortable living for the Master, may be encreased by the conveniency which might be made, for boarding some children, under his care, whose distant situation might otherwise impede their instruction.

And if to what has been proposed, Friends were willing to add the promoting a subscription, towards a fund, the increase of which might be employed in paying the Master's Salary, if necessary, and promoting the Education of the poorer Friend's children; such a fund tho' it might be but small in the beginning being a fixed object, would draw the attention of Friends to contribute, whereas so long as there is no beginning made, this weighty service is neglected, by many who would be glad of giving encouragement to so necessary and good a work. And altho' many may not be able to give much, yet as they are willing to contribute, in proportion to their abilities, it will, like the widow's mite, entitle them to the blessing: People frequently appear to think it is at their option to do what they will with their substance, which they call their own, to give or to withhold, at their pleasure, forgetting that they are but as stewards; accountable to him who has entrusted them: Others think they are justifiable, tho' in the neglect of this plain duty, in order to heap up the more riches for their offspring, contrary to our blessed Saviour's express Command, "Lay not up for yourselves treasures on the earth," and notwithstanding the multiplied experience, daily before our eyes that riches, generally prove as wings to raise their children above truth; or as thick clay to bind them to the earth; but neither of these conclusions will stand the test of that Gospel Injunction, "Thou shalt love thy neighbour as thyself;" nor enable them to give a satisfactory account when that alarming proclamation will be made, "Steward give an account of thy stewardship, for thou mayest be no longer steward."

Signed on behalf of the Committee,
ANTHONY BENEZET
ISAAC ZANE

29th, 9th Month, 1778

CHAPTER 3

THE INDIGENT CLASS

To teach him his trade . . . , and to read and wright, etc.

Orphans' Court, Surry County, 1681

6. Indentures and Court Records (1646–1694)[1]

VIRGINIA

YORK COURT, 20 Oct., 1646. — It is ordered, with the consent of Mr. Edmund Chisman, father-in-law to John Lilly, orphant; William Barber, father-in-law to the orphans of John Dennett, viz.: Thomas Dennett, Margaret Dennett, and Sarah Dennett; and Daniel Foxe, father-in-law to the orphants of Clark & Munday, that the estates belonging to the said severall orphants, which this day they have filed on accot. of to this court shall henceforward with all there increase freely come and belong unto the said orphants with out any charges for the future subsistance or education of the said orphants or for their care, paines, or charge in preserving and looking to the said severall orphants estates, as long as they or any of them shall remaine under the tuition of the above said Edmund Chisman, William Barber, and Daniel Foxe, etc.

YORK COUNTY. — Orphants Court held August 24th, 1648.

Present: Capt. Nicholas Martin, Capt. John Chisman, Mr. Hugh Gwyn, Mr. Francis Willis, Mr. Francis Morgan.

Whereas John foster, orphant to John foster, late of Hampton p[ar]ish, deceased, whoe is left without any mentaynance or estate whatsoever, and Stephen Gill, godfather to the said foster, haveing made humble suite to this court that the said John foster, whoe hath by him beene already provided for and kept about a yeare, that he may have the tuition and bringing upp of the said John foster, and that he may be put with him for some certayne tyme by this court. It is therefore ordered that the said John foster shall live and remaine under tuition and bringing upp of the said Stephen Gill, for the space of nine yeares from the date hereof.

---

[1]Edgar W. Knight (Ed.), *Documentary History of Education in the South before 1860* (Chapel Hill: University of North Carolina Press, 1949), I, 53–55, 57–59. Some abbreviations have been spelled out to make the text more readable.

Dureing which tyme the said Gill is hereby injoined to p'vide sufficiently for the said foster, and take care that he bee brought upp in the feare of God and taught to Reade.

LANCASTER COUNTY, Jan'y 6, 1655. — The court hath ordered John, the base child of Thomas Mannan, borne of Eliza: Tomlin, shall, according to the will of the mother, bee kept by Roger Harris and his wife until he arrive at the Age of 18 years, he, the said Harris providing that the said child be taught to write and reade. And that the said Harris have all of the tobacco due from John Robinson paid him at the crop on the 10th of November next, the same being 600 and caske.

SURRY COUNTY, June 15, 1681. — Wm. Rogers bound apprentice to Thomas Bage to serve till 21 — his master to teach him his trade of blacksmith, and to read and wright, etc.

April 15, 1701. Sarah, the daughter of John Allen, dece'd., is bound to Thomas Bentley until she shall arrive at the age of eighteen years — the said Bentley obligeing himselfe to instruct her in the rudiments of the Christian Religion, to learne or cause her to be learnt to reade perfectly, and at the expiration of the said tearm to provide and give her a decent suit of Apparell, and ordered that Indentures be drawne accordingly.

May 4, 1697. Ordered that unless John Clements do put John High to school to learne to reade and write, he do appeare at the next court, and bring the said John with him, that the court may then do therein as shall be found fitt.

ELIZABETH CITY COUNTY, July 18, 1698. — Ann Chandler, orphan of Daniel Chandler, bound apprentice to Phyllemon Miller till 18 or day of marriage, to be taught to read a chapter in the Bible, the Lord's prayer, and ten commandments, and sempstress work.

ISLE OF WIGHT COUNTY. — At an Orphan's Court held on the 1st May, Anno 1694.

42

Present: Col. Arthur Smith, Capt. Henry Applewhait, Mr. Hen. Baker, Mr. Thos. Giles, Mr. Antho. Holladay, justices.

Charles Edwards having exhibited a peticon to this Court for Grace Griswood, an Orphan Girl, that she might live with him, the said Charles, till eighteen years old or marryed. It is thereupon ordered that the said Orphan doe live and abide with the said Edwards till age or marryage as aforesaid, and the said Charles doth hereby oblige himselfe to mainteyn her decently and see that she be taught to read, sew, spinn and knitt, and at the expiration of the tyme to have sufficient cloathing as shall be thought well by the court.

YORK COURT, May the 26th 1690. — Whereas Thomas Thorpe and Ellinor his wife sued Robt. Green to this court, and in their peticon declare that they did binde Richard Gilbert there son An Apprentice to the Defent. for the space of nine yeares by one Indenture under hand and seale to bee Instructed and taught in the Arts and Mistery of a taylor and to teach or cause him to be taught to read and to write a Leagable hand, and not to Imploye him to Labour in the Grownd, Excepting in helping to make corne for the Defendts. famely, but the Defendt. without regard to the said Indenture Dayley keeps the said Apprentice to Labour in the Ground from year to year and omitts giveing him Learning or teach him his trade which is to the said Apprentice utter Rewing and undoing. Therefore itt is ordered that the said Robt. Green doe at the next court Enter into a Bond of 4000 lb tobacco and cash, with good and sufficient security for the true pformance of the said Indenture and to fulfill every clause and Artickle therein expressed, according to the true Interest and meaning the same.

SOUTH CAROLINA

Order'd that Charles Purdy be bound to Mrs. Levis Planter until he is of the age of 21 years and that the Parish pay her ten pounds in Consideration of her giving him a years Schooling. (1733).

You may judge of my Hurry, when I tell you I am, (and have been these 4 Months) the sole Inhabitant of my Printing office, (excepting a Negro boy, whom I'm teaching to serve me at the Press). I discharged my villainous Apprentice; gave him two years time, quitted all Claims on him for Monies received and gamed away, for loss of Time, and Charges for taking up etc. etc. etc. A Lad very capable of the Business, and might have been of vast Service to me but for 3 years has always pulled the contrary way; owing to an unhappy affection for Drink, Play, and Scandalous Company. — [Letter by Peter Timothy, June 14, 1754.]

This Indenture Witnesseth that John Alston the sonne of William Alston of Hamersmith in the County of Midlesex gent doth put himselfe apprentice to James Jones of the County of Carolina merchant to Learne and follow his Art with him after the manner of an apprentice and to serve him his said master the full end and terme of Seaven yeares from the day of the date hereof dureing which said Terme he the aforesaid James Jones doth hereby covenant to finde unto his said Apprentice meate, drinke, apparell Lodgeing and all other necessaryes which shall be needfull and convenient for him provided neverthelesse and it is hereby further Agreed by and between the said James Jones and the aforesaid William Alston-father of the said John that if the said William Alston shall at any tyme or tymes hereafter cause to require or call home to him his said sone within the aforesaid Terme or seaven yeares and before that time be compleated he the said James Jones doth hereby covenant and Oblige himself to returne him Carefully (if alive) The said William defraying the money due for his passage into England and returne In Wittness whereof the p[ar]ties above named to these present Indentures have put their hands and seales Interchangeably this sixteenth day of May Anno Dni 1682.

CHAPTER 4

NEGROES AND INDIANS

The good and spiritual advantage of those poor unhappy creatures.

Eleazar Wheelock, 1762

7. LETTERS FROM MISSIONARIES (1761–1763)[1]

Associates Office Jany 6th 1763

Read a Letter from the Revd. Mr. Alexander Stewart dated Bath North Carolina Aug. 12. 1762 wherein he says "he made known the Associates Intention of supporting a Negroe School, and found the People at Bath and in his Several Chapelries approved of it and many of them promised to be encouragers of so good a Design But He says there are Difficulties almost peculiar to that Province. The Towns are Small, Bath particularly has the fewest Inhabitants of any, so that the Number of Negroes Sufficient for a School cou'd not be had in any one Town, that the Towns which abound with Negroes are situated on Rivers which are generally impassable, however, he Saith, he hath advertised for a Mistress, and will make an Essay on the Associates Plan.

The most probable Method of making the Associates Scheme take footing in that Province till it is better peopled he thinks wou'd be to divide their Salary among three or four Schoolmasters in different Towns, and that He will take upon him to visit the Several Schools twice in the Quarter, and catechise the remote Children on the Evenings of those Days he preaches at the Chapels and every Easter. and Christmas Day will oblige the Masters to have their Negroe Scholars brought to the Church to be publickly and all together catechised and that he will take care to keep a publick Register of the Ages, Baptisms, and Times of Admission on the different Children.

The Schoolmasters he woud recommend he says are such as already keep publick Schools for white Children to whom it wou'd be great Encouragement to have this small Bounty from the Associates.

He Saith he wrote to Governour Dobbs, who, he doubts not, will be an Encourager of the Design, but lives at too great a Distance

---

[1]Knight, *Documentary History of Education in the South before 1860*, I, 150– 53, 167–68, 170–73. The material is from the records of Dr. Bray's Associates.

to have any immediate Influence on a School in that or any of the neighbouring Parishes.

Agreed that Mr. Waring do return the Thanks of the Associates to Mr. Steward for his kind Letter and acquaint him that they refer it to him to make choice of the Method of promoting the Instruction of the Negroes, which to him may seem most likely to be attended with success, only they desire he will not exceed twenty pounds Sterling for teaching thirty Children and so in proportion for a greater or Less Number:

✿　✿　✿

Read a Letter dated at Williamsburgh Virginia 30th Sept. 1762 from the Revd. Mr. Yates and Robt. Nicholas Esq: wherein They say They have sent a List of the Black Children at present in the School, but can give no Satisfactory Account of those who have left the School the Mistress having kept no regular account. That at a late Visitation of the School they were pretty much pleased with the Scholars performances as they rather exceeded their Expectation, that They believe all the Children have been baptized and that it is general Practice in the Province for Negroe Parents to have their Children baptized that the many Difficulties They have to Struggle with in the Prosecution of the good Work made them Apprehensive that the Success might not answer the Expectation of the Associates but they shall think themselves Fortunate if any Endeavours of Theirs can contribute to the Spiritual Welfare and Happiness of the poor Negroes. They hope, notwithstanding the several obstacles to the Instruction and Reformation of the Negroes (which they enumerate) that this Scheme of Negro Schools properly conducted many have a good Effect. They say the People of that City were very willing to send their Young Negroes to School, and believe that double the present Number of Scholars might easily be procured, wou'd the Fund admit of it; but are fearful Many People do not send them upon right Motives, because They do not suffer them to continue at School long enough to be properly instructed, but keep them at Home as soon as they can be of the least Service in the Family. They add, that the Planters urge it a sin and politick to enlarge the understanding of their Slaves, which will render them more impatient of Slavery. They are apprehensive that the good Impressions made on the Childrens Mind whilst at School will afterwards be too easily effaced by the Examples of other

Slaves, especially of their Parents: howevery They are resolved not to be discouraged, but hope by the Blessing of God the undertaking will prosper—They think that Designs of this Nature cannot properly be conducted without certain Uniform Regulations, by which all parties concerned may know how to conduct themselves, and have therefore drawn up a Set of Rules for this Purpose a Copy of which They sent to be submitted to the Judgement of the Associates. They shall soon have Occasion for a few Testaments, Psalters Spelling Books for the use of the School and a Number of Baccu's Sermons to be dispersed among the Planters and conclude with wishing Success to the Associates in all their Designs.

Agreed that the Sincere and hearty Thanks of the Associates be returned to the Revd. Mr. Yates and Mr. Nicholas for their full and very Satisfactory Account of the present State of the Negroe School, and for their generous assurances that notwithstanding the manifold Difficulties and Discouragements they have to contend with, They are resolved to persevere in the Prosecution of this pious and charitable Undertaking.

Agreed that hearty Thanks be returned also for their Care in drawing up Rules and Regulations for the Better Government of the School and that They be made acquainted that the Associates do entirely approve thereof as Judiciously calculated to answer the good End proposed

Agreed that 25 Spelling Books 25 Psalters 20 Testaments and 25 Baccus Sermons be sent for the Use of the Negroe Schools at Williamsburgh.

LETTER FROM DANIEL EARL,
EDENTON, NORTH CAROLINA,
OCTOBER 3, 1761

No. Carolina Edenton 3 October 1761

Sir

Mr. Hazelwood Merchant in this Town Shewed me a Letter from you, wherein you signified to him, that a Society called Dr.

Brays Associates were desirous that a School may be opened here for the Education of Negroe Children: under the Care of him, Mr. Child, and myself; but as Mr. Child, some time ago, moved from here into Virga., neither Mr. Hazelwood or myself could learn the Societys Plan 'till very lately, when I waited upon him myself for that Purpose: Since which Time I have used my utmost Endeavour to recommend their beneficient and charitable Design to the Inhabitants of this Town; and to Represent it in that Light that it ought to Appear to all who Profess our Holy Religion: But am sorry to Acquaint you, that my Exhortations and Remonstrances have not as yet had the desired Effect; but hope they will consider better of it, and not suffer so fair an Opportunity of having their young Slaves instructed in the Principles of Christianity fall to the ground. They all Allow of the great Expediency of the Design, but say, that as their Circumstances are low and Depressed, (which is generally the Case) they can't spare their Negroes from their Service at the Age that they are susceptible of Education: And those that are in Affluent Circumstances are so very few, that the Number of Children sent by them would be so inconsiderable, as not be worth any Person's Acceptance; and as the teaching of Negroes precludes the taking of White Children, the Parents not Allowing their Children to be Educated among such.

If it should be proposed by your worthy Society to Allow any Sallary for the Education of white Children, it would be readily Embraced, and would be productive of great Utility to this poor and ignorant Colony, as the greatest part of them is brought up in profound Ignorance of every Kind of Literature, occasioned chiefly by the Poverty and Indigence of the Inhabitants.

I sometime ago signified to the Incorporated Society for Propagating the Gospel in foreign Parts, the want of Education in this Province as I have the Honour of being in their Service; but have not as yet received any Answer.

The Society may rest assured that as I have hitherto, so I shall hereafter incessantly Endeavour that their Munificient, laudable, and charitable Design may Answer all the good Purposes thereby intended.

LETTER FROM ALEXANDER
RHONNALD, NORFOLK, VIRGINIA,
SEPTEMBER 27, 1762

Revd. Sir

On the 21st of this current the Revd. Mr. Charles Smith my Predecessor waited on me at my School, where he produced a Letter from you, intending a School for Negroes in Norfolk. I was agreeably surprized at it, but when I had read your letter, I was likewise heartily sorry that in the Method and manner proposed it will not answer here for many reasons, as — 1st I find that a School Mistress is rather desired than a Master, for which reason it is obvious, that more girls are to be benefited than Boys, as they are to be educated in Affairs more proper for that Sex. — which thing will answer exactly the Ladies of this place who have many such to send, and will hinder others, so that this Charity must consequently be wrong applied.

2dly If a mistress must be had, qualified with such accomplishments, but especially with the Fear of GOD, the only Principle Qualification, such a One may be found Super valuable, who might instruct in some measure about five or Six, but there is not that Woman in this County young or old who could manage Thirty negro Children at one and the same time, however worthy or wicked she may be, which I can attest by Experience, who have had but a few under my Care, within these last Twenty Years of my Life.

3dly Supposing that such a Mistress could be found in this or any other Govermt. with all due Accomplishments, the Salary of £ 20 is not much above half the Trouble, or what is paid here for Whites, which is little more respected Employment as there are 24 Sterl. paid for each, and proportionably more according as girls are taught in the Branches of Work, or Boys at Arithmetic, etc., so that the Salary must be equal, at least, with what is given for White Children, otherwise, no woman, however gracious, would undertake the Charge. I myself would be will to add £ 5 of this Currency to the £ 20 Sterl. which will make it exactly £ 30 a Year, but I can perceive none willing under £ 50 and a House found for that purpose which will be about Ten pounds. So that this must be a great Bar in this pious proposal.

4. If these Difficulties could be happily Surmounted, There is one Obstacle which I can plainly foresee, would attend it, and that would be, That the gentlemen and their Ladies would fill up the number with their Negroes first, in spite of all Opposition here, otherwise endeavour by Insinuations either to ruin a School in the place, or by Misrepresentations to inform the honourable Society of the Minister of the parish [not clear] who would be only for promoting all he could the pious and worthy Dr. Bray's intentions, and that there was no need for such a School here. To that at last, finding nothing in his favour, it would drop of course, which would exactly be the Case with me, so that there is a necessity of adding more Trustees to that School, and in my humble Opinion, appointing Mr. Commissary the chief Trustee, to whom the Minister of this parish is to answer and account from limited Time to Time, concerning the number of Scholars, whose they are, and what progress they make, that he may place or remove any as he sees most convenient, but not to depend on the Minister of the parish as chief Visitor, only, as it would occasion him the Unwill of most of his parish, if he insisted on a charity School for poor Negroes, and not for the great and powerful of this place.

5^{thly} There are many poor Free Negroes and Mulattoes in this Borough and Parish, who could not be the better of this School, by reason of the Gentlemen insisting that their small Negroe Boys, whom they perhaps design for Domesticks or Livery Men, shall be preferred before them, and so of the girls who are to be brought up in Needlework or Knitting, fitting them for the House, when at the same time, I can plainly discern, That these girls will be more instructed for the latter Employment, than in that which may conduce to the Saving of the Souls, if well applied, and for that reason I am not a proper Person to be chief Manager of that School here, because

6^{thly} If I could not without offence, I would go through the Borough Parish among such free Negroes, or poor people who cannot afford to teach them themselves and if I could find any Young hopeful Lad or gentleman of that Colour, who after good Education at a School, would [word not clear] a Visit Such a School I would not only place but promote them all that lay in my power by boarding some of them, or giving them what I thought might the more encourage them, altho' I am poor and just entering on the World in an Age when many are above Want, having a large family of children and servants in my house, and other Necessities abounding which I would never mention, had I not thought that the society might conceive that I trifled with them and truckled to Interest here, I have no ends of my own to Serve, being above all things willing to serve my master in whose work I am now more particularly engaged, but still it is my Endeavour to follow peace with all men, and to cut off Occasion from them who Seek Occasion.

I observed in the end of Mr. Smith's Letter, a Small List of Books sent for that purpose, which he says, he hath distributed almost to such whites as he pleased, but that he has a few remaining on his hands that he has not yet given away. He might have sent them to my house not being above 30 yards from his house, when he had them, as he does not design to bring the People about his Ears, but he was careful enough not to mention any thing of that kind till he moved out of his place about 6 Weeks ago from his dwelling House to his Glebe in Portsmouth parish.

I also assure the honourable Society That if the great ones here have the sole property and privilege of the Schools, no Master nor Mistress will undertake it for Negro Children in general are very dull and stupid, and they will always be for telling Tales to the prejudice of the Teacher, to which, I have all along experienced that Masters or Mistresses will most greedily listen, and then Such Persons are ruin'd for ever from that time, if they stay any longer there, so that in Seven Years space, there possibly may be a Change of a Dozen of Teachers unless some barefaced convict, an old undaunted Soldier, or an impudent Sailor, who are all void of Shame or Fear, should happen to have the Charge. Three sorts of people I should always be careful not to encourage, those I dare to affirm, none could match the People better, but GOD forbid that I should be the Witness of either, as I want youth instructed only be the good and praise worthy where they may be found. And now if I may be allowed to add my own sentiment to the end of this long Epistle, I would not undertake such a Charge tho' I had nothing else to support my Consideration of money, neither as I have before said, should I be willing to be the chief Trustee of the School, lest I might find it worse than it was when I had a Charity

School in a neighbouring County where the gentlemens children were many years Educated, and the objects of Charity disdained till I was oblig'd to leave the School and lodge a Complaint in the Assembly, which has presented the grandees to-reign longer, but from that time they use one with the most invidious Terms of ill or abuse for my pains, and because I baptize more Negroes than other Brethren here and instruct them from the Pulpit, out of the common road, and encourage the good among them to come to the Communion after a due sense of the matter, I am criticised and branded by such as a Negro Parson, for which reason and many more might be offered, I do not chuse to throw myself out of the respect of my Parish altogether for unholding a Thing where I have none to stand by me, but shall most readily do it, if supported by the honorable Society and the Worthy Revd. Mr. Commissary Robinson.

All I have now to add is That considering my Years, and the sorry circumstance of my family, the honourable Society will be pleased to pity my case, who mean nothing but the good and spiritual Advantage of those poor unhappy illiterate Creatures, and if the honourable Society will insist on me to be an Inspector, to regulate the School, they would be good enough to find out a proper Expedient to strengthen my hands that with the Strength of GOD, I may be Instrumental in their eternal Happiness, which is the earnest prayer and hearty desire of. . . .

8. Of the Original Design, Rise, Progress and Present State of the Indian Charity-School in Lebanon, Connecticut. (1762)[1]

ELEAZAR WHEELOCK

Understanding there are numbers of religious and charitably disposed persons, who only wait to know where their charities may be bestowed in the best manner for the advancement of the kingdom of the great Redeemer; and supposing there may also be in some, evil surmisings about, and a disposition to discredit a cause which they don't love, and have no disposition to promote; I have, to gratify the one, and prevent the mischiefs of the other, thought it my duty to give the publick a short, plain, and faithful narrative of the original design, rise, progress, and present state of the Charity-School here, called Moor's Indian-Charity School, etc. And I hope there is need of little or nothing more than a plain and faithful relation of facts, with the grounds and reasons of them, to justify the undertaking, and all the pains and expence there has been, in the prosecution thereof. And to convince all persons of ability, that this school is a proper object of their charity; and that whatever they shall contribute for the furtherance of it, will be an offering acceptable to God, and properly bestowed for the promoting a design which the heart of the great Redeemer is infinitely set upon.

The considerations first moving me to enter upon the design of educating the children of our heathen natives were such as these; viz.

The great obligations lying upon us, as God's covenant-people, who have all we have better than they in a covenant way, and consequently are under covenant-bonds to improve it in the best

---

[1]Eleazer Wheelock, "Of the Original Design, Rise, Progress and Present State of the Indian Charity-School in Lebanon, Connecticut," [1762], *Old South Leaflets,* I (Boston, n.d.), No. 22.

manner for the honour and glory of our liberal Benefactor. And can such want of charity to those poor creatures, as our neglect has shewn; and our neglect of that which God has so plainly made to be the matter of our care and duty; and that which the heart of the great Redeemer is so set upon, as they he never desired any other compensation for all the travail of his soul, can it, I say, be without great guilt on our part?

It has seem'd to me, he must be stupidly indifferent to the Redeemer's cause and interest in the world; and criminally deaf and blind to the intimations of the favour and displeasure of God in the dispensations of his providence, who could not perceive plain intimations of God's displeasure against us for this neglect, inscribed in capitals, on the very front of divine dispensations, from year to year, in permitting the savages to be such a sore scourge to our land, and make such depredations on our frontiers, inhumanly butchering and captivating our people: not only in time of war, but when we had good reason to think (if ever we had) that we dwelt safely by them.

And there is good reason to think, that if one half which has been, for so many years past expended in building forts, manning and supporting them, had been prudently laid out in supporting faithful missionaries, and school-masters among them, the instructed and civilized party would have been a far better defence than all our expensive fortresses, and prevented the laying waste so many towns and villages: Witness the consequence of sending Mr. Sergeant to Stockbridge, which was in the very road by which they most usually came upon our people, and by which there has never been one attack made upon us since his going there; and this notwithstanding there has been, by all accounts, less appearance of the saving effects of the gospel there than in any other place, where so much has been expended for many years past.

And not only our covenant bonds, by which we owe our all to God, and our divine Redeemer—our pity to their bodies in their miserable, needy state—our charity to their perishing souls—and our own peace, and safety by them, should constrain us to it; but also gratitude, duty, and loyalty to our rightful sovereign. How great the benefit which would hereby accrue to the Crown of Great Britain, and how much the interests of His Majesty's dominions, especially in America, would be promoted hereby, we can hardly conceive.

And the Christianizing the natives of this land is expressly mentioned in the royal charter granted to this colony, as a motive inducing His Majesty to grant that royal favour to our fathers. And since we are risen up in their stead, and enjoy the inestimable favour granted to them, on this consideration; What can excuse our not performing to our utmost, that which was engaged by, and reasonably expected from, them? But that which is of greatest weight, and should powerfully excite and perswade us hereto, are the many commands, strong motives, precious promises, and tremendous threatenings, which fill so great a part of the sacred pages and are so perfectly calculated to awaken all our powers, to spread the knowledge of the only true God, and Saviour, and make it as extensive and common as possible. It is a work, in which every one in his place, and according to his ability, is under sacred bonds to use his utmost endeavours. But for brevity sake, I omit a particular mention of them, supposing none have read their Bibles attentively, who do not know, that this is a darling subject of them; and that enough is there spoken by the mouth of God himself, to obviate and silence all the objections which sloth, covetousness, or love of the world can suggest against it.

These were some of the considerations which, I think, had some influence to my making an attempt in this affair; though I did not then much think of any thing more than only to clear myself, and family, or partaking in the public guilt of our land and nation in such a neglect of them.

And as there were few or none who seemed so much to lay the necessity and importance of the case to heart, as to exert themselves in earnest, and lead the way therein, I was naturally put upon consideration and enquiry what methods might have the greatest probability of success; and upon the whole was fully perswaded that this, which I have been pursuing, had by far the greatest probability of any that had been proposed, viz. by the mission of their own sons in conjunction with the English; and that a number of girls shoud also be instructed in whatever should be necessary to render them fit to perform the female part, as house-wives, school-mistresses, tayloresses, etc. and to go and be with these youth, when they shall be hundreds of miles distant from the English on the business of their mission: And prevent a necessity of their turning savage in their manner of living, for want of those who may do those offices for them, and by this means support the reputation of their mission, and also recommend to the savages a more rational and decent manner of living, than that which they are in—and thereby, in time, remedy and remove that great, and hitherto insuperable difficulty, so constantly complained of by all our missionaries among them, as the great impediment in the way to the success of their mission, viz. their continual rambling about; which they can't avoid so long as they depend so much upon fishing, fowling, and hunting for their support. And I am more and more perswaded, that I have sufficient and unanswerable reasons to justify this plan.

As,

1. The deep rooted prejudices they have so generally imbibed against the English, that they are selfish, and have secret designs to incroach upon their lands, or otherwise wrong them in their interests. This jealousy seems to have been occasioned, nourished, and confirmed by some of their neighbours, who have got large tracts of their lands for a very inconsiderable part of their true value, and, it is commonly said, by taking the advantage of them when they were intoxicated with liquor. And also, by unrighteous dealers, who have taken such advantage to buy their skins and furrs at less than half price, etc. And perhaps these jealousies may be, not a little, increased by a conciousness of their own perfidy and inhumanity towards the English. And it seems there is no way to avoid the bad influence and effects of these prejudices, at present, unless it be by the mission of their own sons. And it is reasonable to suppose their jealousies are not less, since the late conquest in this land, by which they are put into our power, than they were before.

2. An Indian missionary may be supported with less than half the expence, that will be necessary to support an Englishman, who can't conform to their manner of living, and who will have no dependence upon them for any part of it. And an Indian who speaks their language, it may reasonably be supposed, will be at least four times as serviceable among them, supposing he be otherwise equally qualified as one who can communicate to or receive nothing from them, but by an interpreter: He may improve all opportunities not only in public, but, "when he sits in the house, walks by the way, when he lies down, and when he rises

up:" And speak with as much life and spirit as the nature and importance of the matter require, which is very much lost when communicated by an interpreter.

3. Indian missionaries may be supposed better to understand the tempers and customs of Indians, and more readily to conform to them in a thousand things than the English can; and in things wherein the nonconformity of the English may cause disgust, and be construed as the fruit of pride, and an evidence and expression of their scorn and disrespect.

4. The influence of their own sons among them will likely be much greater than of any Englishman whatsoever. They will look upon such an one as one of them, his interest the same with theirs; and will naturally esteem him as an honour to their nation, and be more likely to submit patiently to his instructions and reproofs than to any English missionary. . . .

5. The acquaintance and friendship which Indian boys from different and distant tribes and places, will contract and cultivate, while together at school, may, and if they are zealously affected will, be improved much for the advantage and furtherance of the design of their mission; while they send to, hear from, or visit one another, confirming the things which have been spoken. And this without so much ceremony to introduce one another, as will be necessary in the case of English missionaries; and without the cumber and expence of interpreters.

6. Indian missionaries will not disdain to own English ones, who shall be associated with them, (where the English can be introduced) as elder brethren; nor scorn to be advised or reproved, counselled or conducted by them; especially so long as they shall be so much dependent upon the English for their support; which will likely be till God has made them his people; and then, likely, they will not stand in such need of English guides and counsellors. And they will mutually help one another, to recommend the design to the favourable reception and good liking of the pagans, remove their prejudices, conciliate their friendship, and induce them to repose due confidence in the English.

7. In this school, children of different nations may, and easily will learn one another's language, and English youth may learn of them; and so save the vast expence and trouble of interpreters; and their ministry be much more acceptable and edifying to the Indians.

58

8. There is no such thing as sending English missionaries, or setting up and maintaining the English schools to any good purpose, in most places among them, as their temper, state and condition have been and still are. It is possible a school may be maintained to some good purpose, at Onoboquagee, where there have been heretofore several faithful missionaries, by the blessing of God upon whose labours the Indians are in some measure civilized, some of them baptized, a number of them in a judgment of charity, real Christians; and where they have a sachem, who is a man of understanding, virtue, steadiness, and entirely friendly to the design of propagating the gospel among them, and zealous to promote it. And where the Hon. Scotch Commissioners, I hear, have sent two missionaries, and have made some attempt to set up a school. But at Jeningo, a little beyond, they will by no means admit an English missionary to reside among them. And tho' they were many of them under great awakenings and concern, by God's blessing on the labours of a Christian Indian from these parts; yet such was the violent opposition of numbers among them, that it was thought by no means safe for any Englishman to go among them, with design to tarry with them. And like to this is the case with the parties of Indians, for near an hundred miles together, on the west side of Susquehanah River. Another school or two may possibly be set up with success among the Mohawks, where Mr. Ogilvie and other Episcopal missionaries have bestowed much labour, to good purpose; and where they have got into the way of cultivating their lands for a living, and so have more ability to support their children, and less occasion to ramble abroad with them. But even in these places we may find it more difficult than we imagine before the trial be made (though I would by no means discourage the trial of every feasible method for the accomplishing this great design) but by acquaintance with the schools which the Hon. London Commissioners have with pious zeal, set up and maintained among the several tribes in these parts, I am much confirmed in such sentiments. These parties live amongst, and are encompassed by the English, have long had good preaching, and numbers of them appear to be truly godly. Yet such is the savage temper of many, their want of due esteem for learning, and gratitude to their benefactors, and especially their want of government, that their school-masters, tho' skilful and faithful men, constantly complain they can't keep the children in any measure constant at

school. Mr. Clelland the school-master at Mohegan has often told me what unwearied pains he has taken by visiting, and discoursing with their parents, etc. to remedy this evil, and after all can't accomplish it. The children are suffered to neglect their attendance on instruction, and waste much time, by which means they don't learn so much in several years as they might, and others do in one, who are taken out of the reach of their parents, and out of the way of Indian examples, and are kept to school under good government and constant instruction. I rather mention this instance, because of the well-known fidelity and skill of that good gentleman, and because that tribe are as much civilized, and as many of them Christianized, as perhaps any party of them in this government. And by all I can learn, it is no better in this respect with any other. They are so disaffected towards a good and necessary government, that as gentle an exercise of it as may be, and answer the design of keeping up order and regularity in any measure among them, will likely so disgust them as to render the case worse rather than better. Captain Martin Kellog complain'd of this as his great discouragement in the school at Stockbridge, notwithstanding he understood as well as any man the disposition of Indians, and had the advantage of knowing their language and customs, having been so long a captive among them, and was high in their affection and esteem; yet he was obliged to take the children home to Weathersfield with him, quite away from their parents, before he could exercise that government which was necessary in order to their profiting at school. But as to most places, there is no such thing at present as introducing either English school-masters or missionaries to continue with them; such are their prejudices in general, and such the malevolent, and ungovernable temper of some, that none but an Indian would dare venture his life among them.

And besides all this, they are so extremely poor, and depend so much upon hunting for a livelihood, that they are in no capacity to support their children at school, if their disposition for it were ever so good. . . .

9. There are very few or no interpreters, who are suitable and well-accomplished for the business, to be had. . . . I suppose the interpreters now employed by the Hon. Commissioners are the best that are to be had at present. But how many nations are there for whom there is no interpreter at all, except, it may be,

some ignorant and perhaps vicious person, who has been their captive, and whom it is utterly unsafe to trust in matters of such eternal consequence. And how shall this difficulty be remedied? It seems it must be by one of these two ways, viz. either their children must come to us, or ours go to them. But who will venture their children with them, unless with some of the civilized parties, who have given the strongest testimonies of their friendship? If it be said, that all the natives are now at peace with us: It may be, their chiefs, and the better-temper'd part of them are so. But who does not know that their leagues and covenants with us are little worth, and like to be so till they become Christians? And that the tender mercies of many of them are cruelty? Who is so unacquainted with the history of them, as not to know, there is reason to think, there are many among their lawless herds, who would gladly embrace an opportunity to commit a secret murder on such English youth?—Even Mr. Occom, though an Indian, did not think it safe for him, being of another tribe and language, and in such connections with the English, to go among the numerous tribe of the Seneca's, where he had no avenger of his blood for them to fear.

When, as soon as the method proposed by the Rev'd. Mess. Sergeant and Brainerd, can be put into execution, viz. to have land appropriated to the use of Indian schools, and prudent skilful farmers, or tradesmen, to lead and instruct the boys, and mistresses to instruct the girls in such manufactures as are proper for them, at certain hours, as a diversion from their school exercises, and the children taken quite away from their parents, and the pernicious influence of Indian examples, there may be some good prospect of great advantage of schools among them.

And must it be esteemed a wild imagination, if it be supposed that well-instructed, sober, religious Indians, may with special advantage be employed as masters and mistresses in such schools; and that the design will be much recommended to the Indians thereby; and that there may be special advantage by such, serving as occasional interpreters for visitors from different nations from time to time; and they hereby receive the fullest conviction of the sincerity of our intentions and be confirmed and established in friendly sentiments of us, and encouraged to send their children, etc.?

I am fully perswaded from the acquaintance I have had with

them, it will be found, whenever the trial shall be made, to be very difficult if not impossible, unless the arm of the Lord should be revealed in an eminent manner, to cure them of such savage and sordid practices, as they have been inured to from their mother's virtue, decency and humanity, while they are daily under the pernicious influence of their parents example, and their many vices made familiar thereby.

10. I have found by experience, there may be a thorough and effectual exercise of government in such a school, and as severe as shall be necessary, without opposition from, or offence taken by, any. And who does not know, that evils so obstinate as those we may reasonably expect to find common in the children of savages, will require that which is severe? Sure I am, they must find such as have better natures, or something more effectually done to subdue their vicious inclinations, than most I have been concerned with, if it be not so. And moreover, in such a school, there will be the best opportunity to know what has such a genius and disposition, as most invite to bestow extraordinary expence to fit them for special usefulness.

11. We have the greatest security we can have, that when they are educated and fitted for it, they will be employed in that business. There is no likelihood at all that they will, though ever so well qualified, get into business, either as school-masters or mistresses, among the English; at least till the credit of their nations be raised many degrees above what it is now, and consequently they can't be employed as will be honorable for them, or in any business they will be fit for, but among their own nation. And it may reasonably be supposed, their compassion towards their "bretheren according to the flesh" will most naturally incline them to, and determine them upon such an employment as they were fitted and designed for. And besides all this, abundant experience has taught us, that such a change of diet, and manner of living as missionaries must generally come into, will not consist with the health of many Englishmen. And they will be obliged on that account to leave the service, though otherwise well disposed to it. Nor can this difficulty be avoided at present (certainly not without great expence.) But there is no great danger of difficulty in this respect as to Indians, who will only return to what they were used to from their mother's womb.

And there may also be admitted into this school, promising English youth of pregnant parts, and who from the best principles, and by the best motives, are inclined to devote themselves to that service; and who will naturally care for their state.

Divine skill in things spiritual, pure and fervent zeal for the salvation of souls, shining examples of piety and godliness, by which pagans will form their first notions of religion, rather than from any thing that shall be said to them, are most necessary qualifications in a missionary; and promise more real good than is to be expected from many times the number who have never "known the terrors of the Lord," and have no experimental, and therefore no right understanding of the nature of conversion and the way wherein it is wrought. Such were never under the governing influence of a real sense of the truth, reality, greatness and importance of eternal things, and therefore will not be likely to treat them suitable to the nature and eternal consequences of them, surely they will not naturally do it. And how sad are like to be the consequences to those who are watching to see whether the preacher himself does really believe the things which he speaks.

In such a school their studies may be directed with a special view to the design of their mission. Several parts of learning which have no great subserviency to it, and which will consume much time, may be less pursued, and others most necessary made their chief study. And they may not only learn the pagan languages, but will naturally get an understanding of their tempers, and many of their customs, which must needs be useful to missionaries. And instead of a delicate manner of living, they may by degrees, as their health will bear, enure themselves to such a way of living as will be most convenient for them to come into when on their mission.

And if the one half of the Indian boys thus educated shall prove good and useful men, there will be no reason to regret our toil and expence for the whole. And if God shall deny his blessing on our endeavours, as to the general design, it may be these particular youth may reap eternal advantage by what we do for them; and if but one in ten does so, we shall have no cause to think much of the expence. And if a blessing be denied to all, "we shall notwithstanding be unto God a sweet favour of Christ in them that perish."

63

CHAPTER 5

EDUCATION FOR THE MIDDLE CLASS

Good Education . . . the Surest Foundation of Happiness.

Benjamin Franklin, 1749

9. Proposals Relating to the Education of Youth in Pennsylvania (1749)[1]

BENJAMIN FRANKLIN

The good Education of Youth has been esteemed by wise Men in all Ages, as the surest Foundation of the Happiness both of private Families and Common-wealths. Almost all Governments have therefore made it a principal Object of their Attention, to establish and endow with proper Revenues, such Seminaries of Learning, as might supply the succeeding Age with Men qualified to serve the Publick with Honour to themselves, and to their Country.

Many of the first Settlers of these Provinces, were Men who had received a good Education in Europe, and to their Wisdom and good Management we owe much of our present Prosperity. But their Hands were full, and they could not do all Things. The present Race are not thought to be generally of equal Ability: For though the American Youth are allow'd not to want Capacity; yet the best Capacities require Cultivation, it being truly with them, as with the best Ground, which unless well tilled and sowed with profitable Seed, produces only ranker Weeds.

That we may obtain the Advantages arising from an Increase of Knowledge, and prevent as much as may be the mischievous Consequences that would attend a general Ignorance among us, the following *Hints* are offered towards forming a Plan for the Education of the Youth of Pennsylvania, viz.

It is propos'd,

THAT some Persons of Leisure and publick Spirit, apply for a CHARTER, by which they may be incorporated, with Power to

---

[1]L. W. Labaree (Ed.), *The Papers of Benjamin Franklin* (Yale University Press 1961), III, 399–419. The essay was first printed in 1749 to get public support for the planned academy.

erect an ACADEMY for the Education of Youth, to govern the same, provide Masters, make Rules, receive Donations, purchase Lands, etc. and to add to their Number, from Time to Time such other Persons as they shall judge suitable.

That the Members of the Corporation make it their Pleasure, and in some Degree their Business, to visit the Academy often, encourage and countenance the Youth, countenance and assist the Masters, and by all Means in their Power advance the Usefulness and Reputation of the Design; that they look on the Students as in some Sort their Children, treat them with Familiarity and Affection, and when they have behav'd well, and gone through their Studies, and are to enter the World, zealously unite, and make all the Interest that can be made to establish them, whether in Business, Offices, Marriages, or any other Thing for their Advantage, preferably to all other Persons whatsoever even of equal Merit.

And if Men may, and frequently do, catch such a Taste for cultivating Flowers, for Planting, Grafting, Inoculating, and the like, as to despise all other Amusements for their Sake, why may not we expect they should acquire a Relish for that *more useful* Culture of young Minds. . . .

That a House be provided for the ACADEMY, if not in the Town, not many Miles from it; the Situation high and dry, and if it may be, not far from a River, having a Garden, Orchard, Meadow, and a Field or two.

That the House be furnished with a Library (if in the Country, if in the Town, the Town Libraries may serve) with Maps of all Countries, Globes, some mathematical Instruments, and Apparatus for Experiments in Natural Philosophy, and for Mechanics; Prints, of all Kinds, Prospects, Buildings, Machines, etc.

That the RECTOR be a Man of good Understanding, good Morals, diligent and patient, learn'd in the Languages and Sciences, and a correct pure Speaker and Writer of the English Tongue; to have such Tutors under him as shall be necessary.

That the boarding Scholars diet together, plainly, temperately, and frugally.

That to keep them in Health, and to strengthen and render active their Bodies, they be frequently exercis'd in Running, Leaping, Wrestling, and Swimming, etc.

That they have peculiar Habits to distinguish them from other

Youth, if the Academy be in or near the Town; for this, among other Reasons, that their Behaviour may be the better observed.

As to their STUDIES, it would be well if they could be taught *every Thing* that is useful, and *every Thing* that is ornamental: But Art is long, and their Time is short. It is therefore propos'd that they learn those Things that are likely to be *most useful* and *most ornamental*, Regard being had to the several Professions for which they are intended.

All should be taught to write a *fair Hand*, and swift, as that is useful to All. And with it may be learnt something of *Drawing*, by Imitation of Prints, and some of the first Principles of Perspective.

Arithmetick, Accounts, and some of the first Principles of *Geometry* and *Astronomy.*

The English Language might be taught by Grammar; in which some of our best Writers, as Tillotson, Addison, Pope, Algernon Sidney, Cato's Letters, etc. should be Classicks: The *Stiles* principally to be cultivated, *being the clear* and the *concise.* Reading should also be taught, and pronouncing, properly, distinctly, emphatically; not with an even Tone, which *under-does* nor a theatrical, which *over-does* Nature.

To form their Stile, they should be put on Writing Letters to each other, making Abstracts of what they read; or writing the same Things in their own Words; telling or writing Stories lately read, in their own Expressions. All to be revis'd and corrected by the Tutor, who should give his Reasons, explain the Force and Import of Words, etc.

To form their Pronunciation, they may be put on making Declamations, repeating Speeches, delivering Orations, etc. The Tutor assisting at the Rehearsals, teaching, advising, correcting their Accent, etc.

But if HISTORY be made a constant Part of their Reading, such as the Translations of the Greek and Roman Historians, and the modern Histories of antient Greece and Rome, etc. may not almost all Kinds of useful Knowledge be that Way introduc'd to Advantage, and with Pleasure to the Student? As

GEOGRAPHY, by reading with Maps, and being required to point out the Places *where* the greatest Actions were done, to give their old and new Names, with the Bounds, Situation, Extent of the Countries concern'd, etc.

CHRONOLOGY, by the Help of Helvicus or some other Writer of the Kind, who will enable them to tell *when* those Events happened; what Princes were Cotemporaries, what States or famous Men flourish'd about that Time, etc. The several principal Ephochas to be first well fix'd in their Memories.

ANTIENT CUSTOMS, religious and civil, being frequently mentioned in History, will give Occasion for explaining them; in which the Prints of Medals, Basso Relievo's, and antient Monuments will greatly assist.

MORALITY, by descanting and making continual Observations on the Causes of the Rise or Fall of any Man's Character, Fortune, Power, etc. mention'd in History; the Advantages of the Temperance, Order, Frugality, Industry, Perseverence, etc. etc. Indeed the general natural Tendency of Reading good History, must be, to fix in the Minds of Youth deep Impressions of the Beauty and Usefulness of Virtue of all Kinds, Publick Spirit, Fortitude, etc.

History will show the wonderful Effects of ORATORY, in governing, turning and leading great Bodies of Mankind, Armies, Cities, Nations. When the Minds of Youth are struck with Admiration at this, then is the Time to give them the Principles of that Art, which they will study with Taste and Application. Then they may be made acquainted with the best Models among the Antients, their Beauties being particularly pointed out to them. Modern Political Oratory being chiefly performed by the Pen and Press, its Advantages over the Antient in some Respects are to be shown; as that its Effects are more extensive, more lasting, etc.

History will also afford frequent Opportunities of showing the Necessity of a *Publick Religion,* from its Usefulness to the Publick; the Advantage of a Religious Character among private Persons; the Mischiefs of Superstition, etc. and the Excellency of the CHRISTIAN RELIGION above all others antient or modern.

History will also give Occasion to expatiate on the Advantage of Civil Orders and Constitutions, how Men and their Properties are protected by joining in Societies and establishing Government; their Industry encouraged and rewarded, Arts invented, and Life made more comfortable: The Advantages of *Liberty,* Mischiefs of *Licentiousness,* Benefits arising from good Laws and a due Execution of Justice, etc. Thus may the first Principles of sound *Politicks* be fix'd in the Minds of Youth.

On *Historical* Occasions, Questions of Right and Wrong, Justice and Injustice, will naturally arise, and may be put to Youth, which they may debate in Conversation and in Writing. When they ardently desire Victory, for the Sake of the Praise attending it, they will begin to feel the Want, and be sensible of the Use of *Logic*, or the Art of Reasoning to *discover* Truth, and of Arguing to *defend* it, and *convince* Adversaries. This would be the Time to acquaint them with the Principles of that Art. Grotius, Puffendorff and some other Writers of the same Kind, may be used on these Occasions to decide their Disputes. Publick Disputes warm the Imagination, whet the Industry, and strengthen the natural Abilities.

When Youth are told, that the Great Men whose Lives and Actions they read in History, spoke two of the best Languages that ever were, the most expressive, copious, beautiful; and that the finest Writings, the most correct Compositions, the most perfect Productions of human Wit and Wisdom, are in those Languages, which have endured Ages, and will endure while there are Men; that no Translation can do them Justice, or give the Pleasure found in Reading the Originals; that those Languages contain all Science; that one of them is become almost universal, being the Language of Learned Men in all Countries; that to understand them is a distinguishing Ornament, etc. they may be thereby made desirous of learning those Languages, and their Industry sharpen'd in the Acquisition of them. All intended for Divinity should be taught the Latin and Greek; for Physick, the Latin, Greek and French; for Law, the Latin and French; Merchants the French, German, and Spanish: And though all should not be compell'd to learn Latin, Greek, or the modern foreign Languages; yet none that have an ardent Desire to learn them should be refused; their English, Arithmetick, and other Studies absolutely necessary, being at the same Time not neglected.

If the new *Universal History* were also read, it would give a *connected* Idea of human Affairs, so far as it goes, which should be follow'd by the best modern Histories, particularly of our Mother Country; then of these Colonies; which should be accompanied with Observations on their Rise, Encrease, Use to Great-Britain, Encouragements, Discouragements, etc. the Means to make them flourish, secure their Liberties, etc.

With the History of Men, Times and Nations, should be read at proper Hours or Days, some of the best *Histories of Nature,* which would not only be delightful to Youth, and furnish them with Matter for their Letters, etc. as well as other History; but afterwards of great Use to them, whether they are Merchants, Handicrafts, or Divines; enabling the first the better to understand many Commodities, Drugs, etc. the second to improve his Trade or Handicraft by new Mixtures, Materials, etc. and the last to adorn his Discourses by beautiful Comparisons, and strengthen them by new Proofs of Divine Providence. The Conversation of all will be improved by it, as Occasions frequently occur of making Natural Observations, which are instructive, agreeable, and entertaining in almost all Companies. *Natural History* will also afford Opportunities of introducing many Observations, relating to the Preservation of Health, which may be afterwards of great Use. Arbuthnot on Air and Aliment, Sanctorius on Perspiration, Lemery on Foods, and some others, may now be read, and a very little Explanation will make them sufficiently intelligible to Youth.

While they are reading Natural History, might not a little *Gardening, Planting, Grafting, Inoculating,* etc. be taught and practised; and now and then Excursions made to the neighbouring Plantations of the best Farmers, their Methods observ'd and reason'd upon for the Information of Youth. The Improvement of Agriculture being useful to all, and Skill in it no Disparagement to any.

The History of *Commerce,* of the Invention of Arts, Rise of Manufactures, Progress of Trade, Change of its Seats, with the Reasons, Causes, etc. may also be made entertaining to Youth, and will be useful to all. And this, with the Accounts in other History of the prodigious Force and Effect of Engines and Machines used in War, will naturally introduce a Desire to be instructed in *Mechanicks,* and to be inform'd of the Principles of that Art by which weak Men perform such Wonders, Labour is sav'd, Manufactures expedited, etc. etc. This will be the Time to show them Prints of antient and modern Machines, to explain them, to let them be copied, and to give Lectures in Mechanical Philosophy.

With the whole should be constantly inculcated and cultivated, that *Benignity of Mind,* which shows itself in *search for* and *seizing* every Opportunity *to serve* and *to oblige;* and is the Foundation of what is called GOOD BREEDING; highly useful to the Possessor, and most agreeable to all.

The Idea of what is *true Merit*, should also be often presented to Youth, explain'd and impress'd on their Minds, as consisting in an *Inclination* join'd with an *Ability* to serve Mankind, one's Country, Friends and Family; which *Ability* is (with the Blessing of God) to be acquir'd or greatly encreas'd by *true Learning*; and should indeed be the great *Aim* and *End* of all Learning.

10. IDEA OF THE ENGLISH SCHOOL (1751)[1]

BENJAMIN FRANKLIN

Idea of the English School,
Sketch'd out for the Consideration of the Trustees
of the Philadelphia Academy

It is expected that every Scholar to be admitted into this School, be at least able to pronounce and divide the Syllables in Reading, and to write a legible Hand. None to be receiv'd that are under [ ] Years of Age. [2]

First or Lowest CLASS

Let the first Class learn the *English Grammar* Rules, and at the same time let particular Care be taken to improve them in *Orthography*. Perhaps the latter is best done by *Pairing* the Scholars, two of those nearest equal in their Spelling to be put together; let these strive for Victory, each propounding Ten Words every Day to the other to be spelt. He that spells truly most of the other's Words, is Victor for that Day; he that is Victor most Days in a Month, to obtain a Prize, a pretty neat Book of some Kind useful in their future Studies. This Method fixes the Attention of Children extreamly to the Orthography of Words, and makes them good Spellers very early. 'Tis a Shame for a Man to be so ignorant of this little Art, in his own Language, as to be perpetually confounding Words of like Sound and different Significations; the Consciousness of which Defect, makes some Men, otherwise of good Learning and Understanding, averse to Writing even a common Letter.

---

[1]Labaree, *The Papers of Benjamin Franklin*, IV, 101–8.
[2]Franklin suggested that boys between the ages of eight and sixteen should be admitted to the English School.

Let the Pieces read by the Scholars in this Class be short, such as Croxall's Fables, and little Stories. In giving the Lesson, let it be read to them; let the Meaning of difficult Words in it be explained to them, and let them con it over by themselves before they are called to read to the Master, or Usher; who is to take particular Care that they do not read too fast, and that they duly observe the Stops and Pauses. A Vocabulary of the most usual difficult Words might be formed for their Use, with Explanations; and they might daily get a few of those Words and Explanations by Heart, which would a little exercise their Memories; or at least they might write a Number of them in a small Book for the Purpose, which would help to fix the Meaning of those Words in their Minds, and at the same Time furnish every one with a little Dictionary for his future Use.

The Second CLASS To Be Taught

Reading with Attention, and with proper Modulations of the Voice according to the Sentiments and Subject.

Some short Pieces, not exceeding the Length of a *Spectator,* to be given this Class as Lessons (and some of the easier *Spectators* would be very suitable for the Purpose.) These Lessons might be given over Night as Tasks, the Scholars to study them against the Morning. Let it then be required of them to give an Account, first of the Parts of Speech, and Construction of one or two Sentences; this will oblige them to recur frequently to their Grammar, and fix its principal Rules in their Memory. Next of the *Intention* of the Writer, or the *Scope* of the Piece; the Meaning of each Sentence, and of every uncommon Word. This would early acquaint them with the Meaning and Force of Words, and give them that most necessary Habit, of Reading with Attention.

The Master then to read the Piece with the proper Modulations of Voice, due Emphasis, and suitable Action, where Action is required; and put the Youth on imitating his Manner.

Where the Author has us'd an Expression not the best, let it be pointed out; and let his Beauties be particularly remarked to the Youth.

Let the Lessons for Reading be varied, that the Youth may be made acquainted with good Stiles of all Kinds in Prose and Verse, and the proper Manner of reading each Kind. Sometimes a well-told Story, a Piece of a Sermon, a General's Speech to his Soldiers, a Speech in a Tragedy, some Part of a Comedy, and Ode, a Satyr, a Letter, Blank Verse, Hudibrastick, Heroic, etc. But let such Lessons for Reading be chosen, as contain some useful Instruction, whereby the Understandings or Morals of the Youth, may at the same Time be improv'd.

It is requir'd that they should first study and understand the Lessons, before they are put upon reading them properly, to which End each Boy should have an English Dictionary to help him over Difficulties. When our Boys read English to us, we are apt to imagine *they* understand what *they* read because *we* do, and because 'tis their Mother Tongue. But they often read as Parrots speak, knowing little or nothing of the Meaning. And it is impossible a Reader should give the due Modulation to his Voice, and pronounce properly, unless his Understanding goes before his Tongue, and makes him Master of the Sentiment. Accustoming Boys to read aloud what they do not first understand, is the Cause of those even set Tones so common among Readers, which when they have once got a Habit of using, they find so difficult to correct: By which Means, among Fifty Readers we scarcely find a good One. For want of good Reading, Pieces publish'd with a View to influence the Minds of Men for their own or the publick Benefit, lose Half their Force. Were there but one good Reader in a Neighbourhood, a publick Orator might be heard throughout a Nation with the same Advantages, and have the same Effect on his Audience, as if they stood within the Reach of his Voice.

The Third CLASS To Be Taught

Speaking properly and gracefully, which is near of Kin to good Reading, and naturally follows it in the Studies of Youth. Let the Scholars of this Class begin with learning the Elements of Rhetoric from some short System, so as to be able to give an Account of the most usual Tropes and Figures. Let all their bad Habits of Speaking, all Offences against good Grammar, all corrupt or foreign Accents, and all improper Phrases, be pointed out to them.

Short Speechs from the Roman or other History, or from our *Parliamentary Debates,* might be got by heart, and deliver'd with the proper Action, etc. Speeches and Scenes in our best Tragedies and Comedies (avoiding every Thing that could injure the Morals of Youth) might likewise be got by Rote, and the Boys exercis'd in delivering or acting them; great Care being taken to form their Manner after the truest Models.

For their farther Improvement, and a little to vary their Studies, let them now begin to read *History,* after having got by Heart a short Table of the principal Epochas in Chronology. They may begin with Rollin's *Antient and Roman Histories,* and proceed at proper Hours as they go thro' the subsequent Classes, with the best Histories of our own Nation and Colonies. Let Emulation be excited among the Boys by giving, Weekly, little Prizes, or other small Encouragements to those who are able to give the best Account of what they have read, as to Times, Places, Names of Persons, etc. This will make them read with Attention, and imprint the History well in their Memories. In remarking on the History, the Master will have fine Opportunities of instilling Instruction of various Kinds, and improving the Morals as well as the Understandings of Youth.

The Natural and Mechanic History contain'd in *Spectacle de la Nature,* might also be begun in this Class, and continued thro' the subsequent Classes by other Books of the same Kind: For next to the Knowledge of *Duty,* this Kind of Knowledge is certainly the most useful, as well as the most entertaining. The Merchant may thereby be enabled better to understand many Commodities in Trade; the Handicraftsman to improve his Business by new Instruments, Mixtures and Materials; and frequently Hints are given of new Manufactures, or new Methods of improving Land, that may be set on foot greatly to the Advantage of a Country.

The Fourth CLASS *To Be Taught*

Composition. Writing one's own Language well, is the next necessary Accomplishment after good Speaking. 'Tis the Writing-Master's Business to take Care that the Boys make fair Characters, and place them straight and even in the Lines: But to *form their*

Stile, and even to take Care that the Stops and Capitals are properly disposed, is the Part of the English Master. The Boys should
be put on Writing Letters to each other on any common Occurences, and on various Subjects, imaginary Business, etc. containing little Stories, Accounts of their late Reading, what Parts of
Authors please them, and why. Letters of Congratulation, of Com-
pliment, of Request, of Thanks, of Recommendation, of Admonition, of Consolation, of Expostulation, Excuse, etc. In these they
should be taught to express themselves clearly, concisely, and
naturally, without affected Words, or high-flown Phrases. All their
Letters to pass through the Master's Hand, who is to point out the
faults, advise the Corrections, and commend what he finds right.
Some of the best Letters published in our own Language, as Sir
William Temple's, those of Pope, and his Friends, and some
others, might be set before the Youth as Models, their Beauties
pointed out and explained by the Master, the Letters themselves
transcrib'd by the Scholar.

Dr. Johnson's *Ethices Elementa,* or first Principles of Morality, may now be read by the Scholars, and explan'd by the Master,
to lay a solid Foundation of Virtue and Piety in their Minds. And
as this Class continues the Reading of History, let them now at
proper Hours receive some farther Instructions in Chronology,
and in that Part of Geography (from the Mathematical Master)
which is necessary to understand the Maps and Globes. They
should also be acquainted with the modern Names of the Places
they find mention'd in antient Writers. The Exercises of good
Reading and proper Speaking still continued at suitable Times.

Fifth CLASS

To improve the Youth in *Composition*, they may now, besides
continuing to write Letters, begin to write little Essays in Prose;
and sometimes in Verse, not to make them Poets, but for this
Reason, that nothing acquaints a Lad so speedily with Variety of
Expression, as the Necessity of finding such Words and Phrases as
will suit with the Measure, Sound and Rhime of Verse, and at the
same Time will express the Sentiment. These Essays should all
pass under the Master's Eye, who will point out their Faults, and

put the Writer on correcting them. Where the Judgment is not ripe enough for forming new Essays, let the Sentiments of a *Spectator* be given, and requir'd to be cloath'd in a Scholar's own Words; or the Circumstances of some good Story, the Scholar to find Expression. Let them be put sometimes of abridging a Paragraph of a diffuse Author, sometimes on dilating or amplifying what is wrote more closely. And now let Dr. Johnson's *Noetica*. or first Principles of human Knowledge, containing a Logic, or Art of Reasoning, etc. be read by the Youth, and the Difficulties that may occur to them be explained by the Master. The Reading of History, and the Exercises of good Reading and just Speaking still continued.

Sixth CLASS

In this Class, besides continuing the Studies of the preceding, in History, Rhetoric, Logic, Moral and Natural Philosophy, the best English Authors may be read and explain'd; as Tillotson, Milton, Locke, Addison, Pope, Swift, the higher Papers in the *Spectator* and *Guardian,* the best Translations of Homer, Virgil and Horace, of *Telemachus, Travels of Cyrus,* etc.

Once a Year, let there be publick Exercises in the Hall, the Trustees and Citizens present. Then let fine gilt Books be given as Prizes to such Boys as distinguish themselves, and excell the others in any Branch of Learning; making three Degrees of Comparison; giving the best Prize to him that performs best; a less valuable One to him that comes up next to the best; and another to the third. Commendations, Encouragement and Advice to the rest; keeping up their Hopes that by Industry they may excell another Time. The Names of those that obtain the Prizes, to be yearly printed in a list.

The Hours of each Day are to be divided and dispos'd in such a Manner, as that some Classes may be with the Writing-Master, improving their Hands, others with the Mathematical Master, learning Arithmetick, Accompts, Geography, Use of the Globes, Drawing, Mechanicks, etc. while the rest are in the English School, under the English Master's Care.

Thus instructed, Youth will come out of this School fitted for learning any Business, Calling or Profession, except such wherein

Languages are required; and tho' unacquainted with any antient or foreign Tongue, they will be Masters of their own, which is of more immediate and general Use; and withal will have attain'd many other valuable Accomplishments; the Time usually spent in acquiring those Languages, often without Success, being here employ'd in laying such a Foundation of Knowledge and Ability, as properly improv'd, may qualify them to pass thro' and execute the several Offices of civil Life, with Advantage and Reputation to themselves and Country.   B.F.

CHAPTER 6

TRAINING FOR THE ARISTOCRACY

The education of children requires constant unremitting attention.

Philip V. Fithian, 1774

11. JOURNAL AND LETTERS (1773–1774)[1]

PHILIP VICKERS FITHIAN

MONDAY NOVEMR 1st
We began School—The School consists of eight—Two of Mr Carters Sons—One Nephew—And five Daughters—The eldest Son is reading Salust; Gramatical Exercises, and latin Grammer—The second Son is reading english Grammar Reading English: Writing, and Cyphering in Subtraction—The Nephew is Reading and Writing as above; and Cyphering in Reduction—The eldest daughter is Reading the Spectator; Writing; and beginning to Cypher—The second is reading next out of the Spelling-Book, and beginning to write—The next is reading in the Spelling-Book—The fourth is Spelling in the beginning of the Spelling-Book—And the last is beginning her letters—
TEUSDAY 2. [sic]
Busy in School—begun to read Pictete—

LETTER OF PHILIP V. FITHIAN TO THE REVEREND ENOCH GREEN

Westmoreland. Novr 2d 1773.

Revd Sir.

According as I appointed I take this early oppertunity of acquainting you that I am arrived safe; and I am to assure you that I

---

[1]Selections from the *Journal and Letters of Philip Fithian, 1773–1774: A Plantation Tutor of the Old Dominion*, edited by Hunter D. Farish (Williamsburg: Colonial Williamsburg, Inc., 1943), pp. 25–222. Fithian returned to New Jersey and was licensed as a Presbyterian minister. He served in the Continental Army and died of dysentery and exposure during the Revolutionary War.

find the place fully equal to my highest expectations — I am situated in the *Northern-Neck,* in a most delightful Country; in a civil, polite neighbourhood; and in a family remarkable for regularity, and oeconomy, tho' confessedly of the highest quality and greatest worth of any in *Virginia.* I teach only Mr Carters children, and only one of them is to learn Languages, and he is reading Salust and the Greek grammer, is seventeen years old, and seems to be a Boy of Genius — the other two learn writing and Arithmetic — But he has four Daughters, young Misses that are at times to be taught writing and English — I have the terms as I expected, and find the place wholly agreeable — and am strongly solicited to stay many years — But money nor conveniency shall detain me long from my most important connections at home — You may expect me in may at the *Synod.* Please to have my compliments to Mrs Green, to Miss Betsy if at Deerfield, and to my acquaintances that shall enquire and accept to yourself the

Respect of your humble Servt

PHILIP V FITHIAN

JOURNAL

WEDNESDAY 3.
Busy in School —

THURSDAY 4.
Busy in School — To day the two eldest Daughters, and second Son attended the Dancing School.

FRYDAY 5.
Busy in School —

SATURDAY 6.
Catechised in School til twelve — the Children. And dismiss'd them. Afternoon rode with Ben Carter to the Bank of Potowmack — 8 Miles — Returned in the evening — Expence Ferriage I/.

SUNDAY 7.
Rode to Ucomico Church—8 miles—Heard Parson Smith. He shewed to us the uncertainty of Riches, and their Insufficiency to make us happy—Dined at Captain Walkers; With Parson Smith, his Wife; her Sister, a young Lady; etc.—Returned in the Evening.

MONDAY 8.
Busy in School—Finished reading the first, and begun to read the Second Book of Pictetes Theology. Expence to Boy/4.

WEDNESDAY 10.
Busy in School—The eldest Daughter taken off by her Teacher in Music; Mr Stadley who is learning her to play the *Forte-piano*—

THURSDAY 11.
Rose by seven—Busy in School—Miss Carter still absent—

FRYDAY 12.
Rose by Seven—Ben begun his Greek Grammer—Three in the Afternoon Mr Carter returned from *Williamsburg*. He seems to be agreeable, discreet, and sensible—He informed me more particularly concerning his desire as to the Instruction of his Children—

SATURDAY 13.
Catechised the Children and dismissed them about Eleven—Read in Pictete—and proceeded in writing my Sermon for the Presbytery—Expence for my Horse I/3.

MONDAY 29.
All our Scholars present—Mr Carter has put into my hands; Tyre's Dictionary, and the pronouncing Dictionary, to improve his Sons in Grammar classically, both latin and English. and he has given me Fenning in Arrithmetic.

TEUSDAY 30.
Busy in School—I was solicited the other Day at the Race by one Mr *Gorden,* to take and instruct two of his Sons, Saturday also I was again solicited by Mr Fantleroy to take two of his Sons—But I must decline it—

LETTER OF PHILIP V. FITHIAN TO THE REVEREND ENOCH GREEN

Decemr 1st 1773.

Revd Sir.

As you desired I may not omit to inform you, so far as I can by a letter, of the business in which I am now engaged, it would indeed be vastly agreeable to me if it was in my power to give you particular intelligence concerning the state and plan of my employment here.

I set out from home the 20th of Octr and arrived at the Hon: Robert Carters, of Nominy, in Westmorland County, the 28th I began to teach his children the first of November. He has two sons, and one Nephew; the oldest Son is turned of seventeen, and is reading Salust and the greek grammer; the others are about fourteen, and in english grammer, and Arithmetic. He has besides five daughters which I am to teach english, the eldest is turned of fifteen, and is reading the spectator; she is employed two days in every week in learning to play the Forte-Piana, and Harpsicord— The others are smaller, and learning to read and spell. Mr Carter is one of the Councellors in the general court at Williamsburg, and possest of as great, perhaps the clearest fortune according to the estimation of people here, of any man in Virginia: He seems to be a good scholar, even in classical learning, and is remarkable one in english grammar; and notwithstanding his rank, which in general seems to countenance indulgence to children, both himself and Mrs Carter have a manner of instructing and dealing with children far superior, I may say it with confidence, to any I have every seen, in any place, or in any family. They keep them in perfect subjection to themselves, and never pass over an occasion of reproof; and I blush for many of my acquaintances when I say that the children are more kind and complaisant to the servants who constantly attend them than we are to our superiors in age and condition. Mr Carter has an overgrown library of Books of which he allows me the free use. It consists of a general collection of law books, all the Latin and Greek Classicks, vast number of Books on Divinity chiefly by writers who are of the established Religion; he has the works of almost all the late famous writers, as Locke, Addison, Young, Pope, Swift, Dryden, etc. in Short, Sir, to speak moderately, he has more than eight times your number—His eldest Son, who seems to be a Boy of genius and application is to be sent to Cambridge University, but I believe will go through a course either in Philadelphia or Princeton College first. As to what is commonly said concerning Virginia that it is difficult to avoide being corrupted with the manners of the people, I believe it is founded wholly in a mistaken notion that persons must, when here frequent all promiscuous assemblies; but this is so far from truth that any one who does practise it, tho' he is accused of no crime, loses at once his character; so that either the manners have been lately changed, or the report is false, for he seems now to be best esteemed and most applauded who attends to his business, whatever it be, with the greatest diligence. I believe the virginians have of late altered their manner very much, for they begin to find that their estates by even small extravagance, decline, and grow involved with debt, this seems to be the spring which induces the People of fortune who are the pattern of all behaviour here, to be frugal, and moderate. You may expect me at home by the permission of Providence the latter end of april next, or the beginning of May; and as I proposed I shall present my exercises for the examination of the Presbytery; and if they think proper I shall gladly accept of a licence in the fall: I must beg your favour to mention me to such of my acquaintances in Deerfield as you think proper, but especially to Mrs Green, Miss *Betsy,* your family, and Mrs Pecks — I must also beg you to transmit so much of this intelligence to Mr Hunter as that my relations in Greenwich may know that I am through the mercy of heaven in good health. I beg, Sir, you will not fail to write, and let it be known to Mr Hunter, that a letter will come as secure by the Post as from Cohansie to Philadelphia; the Letters are to be directed to me thus, To Mr Philip V. Fithian at Mr *Carters* of Nominy, to be left at Hobes Hole

I am, Sir, yours
PHILIP V FITHIAN

MONDAY 13.
Mr Carter is preparing for a Voyage in his Schooner, the Hariot, to the Eastern Shore in Maryland, for Oysters: there are of the party, Mr *Carter,* Captain *Walker* Colonel *Richd Lee,* and Mr *Lancelot Lee.* With Sailors to work the vessel — I observe it is a general custom on Sundays here, with Gentlemen to invite one another

home to dine, after Church; and to consult about, determine their common business, either before or after Service—It is not the Custom for Gentlemen to go into Church til Service is beginning, when they enter in a Body, in the same manner as they come out; I have known the Clerk to come out and call them in to prayers.—They stay also after the Service is over, usually as long, sometimes longer, than the Parson was preaching—Almost every Lady wears a red Cloak; and when they ride out they tye a white handkerchief over their Head and face, so that when I first came into Virginia. I was distress'd whenever I saw a Lady, for I thought She had the tooth-Ach!—The People are extremely hospitable, and very polite both of which are most certainly universal Characteristics of the Gentlemen in Virginia—some swear bitterly, but the practise seems to be generally disapproved—I have heard that this Country is notorious for Gaming, however this be, I have not seen a Pack of *Cards,* nor a *Die,* since I left home, nor gaming nor Betting of any kind except at the Richmond-Race. Almost every Gentleman of Condition, keeps a Chariot and *Four;* many drive with six Horses—I observe that all the Merchants and shopkeepers in the Sphere of my acquaintance and I am told it is the Case through the Province, are young Scotch-Men; several of whom I know, as *Cunningham, Jennings, Hamilton, Blain;*—And it has been the custom heretofore to have all their Tutors, and Schoolmasters from Scotland, tho' they begin to be willing to employ their own Countrymen—Evening Ben Carter and myself had a long dispute on the practice of fighting—He thinks it best for two persons who have any dispute to go out in good-humour and fight manfully, and says they will be sooner and longer friends than to brood and harbour malice—Mr *Carter* is practising this Evening on the *Guittar* He begins with the *Trumpet Minuet.* He has a good Ear for Music; a vastly delicate Taste: and keeps good Instruments, he has here at Home a *Harpsichord, Forte-Piano, Harmonica, Guittar, Violin,* and *German Flutes,* and at Williamsburg, has a good Organ, he himself also is indefatigable in the Practice.

WEDNESDAY 15.

Busy in School—To day Dined with us Mrs Turburville, and her Daughter Miss Letty Miss Jenny Corbin, and Mr Blain. We dined at three. The manner here is different from our way of living in Cohansie—In the morning so soon as it is light a Boy knocks at my Door to make a fire; after the Fire is kindled, I rise which now in the winter is commonly by Seven, or a little after, By the time I am drest the Children commonly enter the School-Room, which is under the Room I sleep in; I hear them round one lesson, when the Bell rings for eight o-Clock (for Mr Carter has a large good Bell of upwards of 60 Lb. which may be heard some miles, and this is always rung at meal Times;) the Children then go out; and at half after eight the Bell rings for Breakfast, we then repair to the Dining-Room; after Breakfast, which is generally about half after nine, we go into School, and sit til twelve, when the Bell rings, and they go out for noon; the dinner-Bell rings commonly about half after two, often at three, but never before two.—After dinner is over, which in common, when we have no Company, is about half after three we go into School, and sit till the Bell rings at five, when they separate til the next morning; I have to myself in the Evening, a neat Chamber, a large Fire, Books, and Candle and my Liberty, either to continue in the school room, in my own Room or to sit over at the great House with Mr and Mrs Carter—We go into Supper commonly about half after eight or at nine and I usually go to Bed between ten and Eleven. Altho the family in which I live, is certainly under as good political Regulations, and every way as suitable and agreeable as I can expect, or even could desire; and though the Neighbourhood is polite, and the Country pleasant, yet I cannot help reflecting on my situation last winter, which was near the lovely Laura for whom I cannot but have the truest, and the warmest Esteem! possibly, If Heaven shall preserve my life, in some future time, I may again enjoy her good society.

Mr Carter heard this Evening that Captain *Walker* cannot go to Maryland, he is thus stop'd.

SUNDAY 2.

The weather warm and Damp—The Family rode to Church to-day and are to dine out. Mr Carter at my request, gave me the Keys of his Book-Cases and allowed me to spend the Day alone in his Library.

The place seems suitable for Study, and the Day ought to be spent in serious contemplation; therefore, as I proposed Yesterday, I shall collect together and write down what I have been

doing in the last Year. But will my Life bear the review? Can I look upon my Actions and not Blush! And shall I be no less careful, or have no better Success, in the prosecution of my Duty the Year to come, if I shall be kept alive to the Close of it?—
In the Beginning of the last year I was in Deerfield, in Cumberland County New-Jersey, with the Rev'd Mr Green; Under him I studied the Hebrew-Language and Divinity. I left the college the last of September 1772. After having setled my business at Home, I entered upon the Study of Divinity with the Rev'd Andrew Hunter; I was with him about a Month, and on the first of December I went to Mr *Green* with a design to acquaint myself with the Hebrew Tongue; he put me to the Grammar, which I learn'd through, and read some Chapters in the Psalter in the Course of the Winter: In Divinity, he advised me to read Ridgeleys body of Divinity for a System: And he gave me several separate treatisses on Repentance, Regeneration, Faith, etc., and towards spring gave me subjects to consider in the Sermon-Way. Yet how barren am I still? It is an arduous task to bring the Mind to close application; and still greater to lay up and retain useful Knowledge. I continued with Mr *Green* and pursued my studies, I hope with some Success till August 1773, when I was solicited by Dr *Witherspoon* to go into *Virginia* and teach in a Gentlemans Family—The Offer seem'd profitable; I was encouraged by the Dr and was to have his Recommendation—I had likewise myself a strong inclination to go—Yet I was in great Doubt, and Wholly undetermined for some Weeks, because many of my friends, and some of my near Relations opposed my leaving Home, and all seem'd utterly unwilling to advise to go—It is time, according to the Course of my Life they said that I was settling to some constant Employment, and they told me I ought especially to enter with as great speed as convenient into that plan of Life for which I have in particular had my Education—That Virginia is sickly—That the People there are profane, and exceeding wicked—That I shall read there no Calvinistic Books, nor hear any Presbyterian Sermons—That I must keep much Company, and therefore spend as much, very probably much more Money than my Salary—These considerations unsettled for a while my mind—On the other hand I proposed to myself the following advantages by going—A longer opportunity for Study than my friends would willingly allow me If I should remain at home—A more general acquaintance with the

manners of Mankind; and a better Knowledge of the Soil and Commerce of these neighbouring Provinces—And a more perfect acquaintance with the Doctrines, and method of Worship in the established Church in these Colonies, and especially with the Conduct of the Clergy of which there have been so many bad reports—All these however, when I had laid them together, seem'd to overbear the others, so that I determined at last to break through and go!—Here now I am in a strange Province; But I am under no more nor stronger temptations to any kind of vice, perhaps not so great as at Cohansie,—unless sometimes when I am solicited to dance I am forc'd to blush, for my Inability—I have the opportunity of living with Credit perfectly retired—in a well regulated family—With a man of Sense—May God help me to walk in his fear and Gloryfy his Name!

MONDAY 10th

The Morning very cold—Dined with us to-day Mr *Sanford* a Captain of a Sloop which trades out of *Potowmack* to *Norfolk*—I wrote out some Exercises for *Bob* and *Harry*—In the Evening the Colonel began with a small Still to disstill some Brandy from a Liquor made of Pisimmonds. I set Ben this Evening to writing. I likewise gave *Catalines* Speech in *Salust* to commit to memory in Latin, which he is to pronounce Extempore. In the Evening I borrowed of *Ben Carter* 15s.—I have plenty of Money with me, but it is in Bills of Philadelphia currency and will not pass at all here.

TEUSDAY 11.

The morning very cold—As cold I think, and the Frost seems to be as intense and powerful as I have ever known it either at Cohansie or at Princeton. This morning I put Ben to construe some Greek, he has yet no Testament, I gave him therefore Esops Fables in Greek, and Latin. I also took out of the Library, and gave him to read Gordon, upon Geography. Ben seem'd scared with his Greek Lesson, he swore, and wished for Homer that he might kick Him, as he had been told Homer invented Greek.

TEUSDAY 15.

This morning, as Ben and Bob were agreeing on the price of a Rudiman Grammar, which *Bob* wanted to purchase of *Ben;* after

88

some time when Bob would not give 2/10. Bens great demand for a Book almost worn out, which when new, may, by thousands be had in Philadelphia for 2/. that Currency—He threw his Book into the fire, and destroy'd it at once!—An Instance of two ruling Foibles which I discover in Ben viz. obstinacy, and avarice. And another I mentioned the other day, of his agreeing, for half a Bit, or 3½d a week, to play the flute for a limited time, every night after I am in Bed; of this however he has grown tired, and given up his wages on account of the Labour, or Confinement of the Task—And I should be deceived, if a very little money would not excite him to submit to almost any menial service—Bob however; for the present is frustrated in his purpose of learning Grammer, and it seems to chagrin him as much, as tho' he actually believed in what Mrs Taylor told him last Sunday, that without he understands Latin, he will never be able to win a young Lady of Family and fashion for his Wife.—At the Noon play-Hours *Bob* and *Nelson* the Boy who waits on the School had a fight, I know not on what account; it was Bobs misfortune in the course of the Battle to receive a blow on his cheek near his Eye, which is visible, and brought the intelligence of the Quarrel to me, for all were wholly silent till I made inquiry, when all in a moment seem'd to turn and try to convict him—In the Evening, after School, I took them both to my Room and examined them of the reason, Place, and manner of their fighting; from themselves it seem'd plain that they fought for mere Diversion I therefore dismiss'd Nelson, and kept Bob til near Supper and then gave him a smart correction and dismiss'd him.

LETTER OF PHILIP V. FITHIAN TO JOHN PECK

Nomini Hall August 12th 1774.
"Si bene moneo, attende."—

Sir.

I never reflect, but with secret, and peculiar pleasure, on the time when I studied in *Deerfield* with you, and several other pleasant Companions, under our common, and much respected instructor, Mr *Green*. And I acknowledge now, with a thankful heart, the many favours, which I received from your family while I was a member of it. This sense of obligation to your Family, And personal friendship for you, have excited me, when it was in my power, to introduce you to the business which I now occupy; into a family, where, if you be prudent and industrious, I am confident you will speedily acquire to yourself both Honour and Profit—But inasmuch as you are wholly a stranger to this Province; and have had little or no Experience in the business which you ar shortly to enter upon; and lest, from common Fame, which is often erroneous, you shall have entertained other notions of the manners of the People here, and of your business as a Tutor, than you will find, when you come, to be actually true; I hope you will not think it *vain* or *untimely*, if I venture to lay before you some Rules for your direction which I have collected from a year's observation. I shall class what I have to say in the following order. First. I shall attempt to give you some direction for the plan of your Conduct among your neighbours, and the People in General here, so long as you sustain the character of a Tutor. Then I shall advise you concerning the rules which I think will be most profitable and convenient in the management of your little lovely charge, the School. Last of all. I shall mention several Rules for your personal conduct. I choose to proceed in the order I have laid down, as well that you may more fully and speedily receive my mind, as that you may also the more readily select out and apply what you shall find to be most necessary.

✿   ✿   ✿

2. You will act wisely, if, from the beginning, you convince all your Scholars which you may easily do, of your abilities in the several branches, which you shall profess to teach; you are not to tell them, totidem Verbis, "that you understand, perhaps as well as any man on the Continent both the Latin and Greek Classicks"; "and have gone through the usual Course in the noted College of New-Jersey, under Dr Witherspoon, so universally known and admired, where you have studied Criticism, Oratory, History, not to mention Mathematical and philosophical Studies, and dipt a good way into the French-Language, and that you have learn'd a smattering of Dancing, Cards, etc. etc. etc." For Dun-p or Hack—n or the most profound dunce in your College or School would have

too much sense to pass such impudence by, and not despise and reproach it; but you may speedily and certainly make them think you a "Clever Fellow" (which is a phrase in use here for a good Scholar) if you never mention any thing before them, only what you seem to be wholly master of—This will teach them never to dispute your determination, and always to rely upon your Judgment; two things which are most essential for your peace, and their advantage. That you may avoid yourself of this with certainty I shall recommend for your practice the following method, as useful at least, if not intirely necessary. Read over carefully, the lessons in Latin and Greek, in your leisure hours, that the story and Language be fresh in your memory, when you are hearing the respective lessons; for your memory is treacherous, and I am pretty certain it would confound you if you should be accosted by a pert School-Boy, in the midst of a blunder, with "Physician heal thyself"!—You ought likewise to do this with those who are working Figures; probably you may think that because the highest Cypherer is only in decimal arithmetic, it is not there fore worth your critical attention to be looking previously into the several Sums. But you are to consider that a sum in the Square-Root, or even in the Single Rule of three direct, is to your Pupils of as great importance, as the most abstruse problem in the Mathematicks to an able artist; and you may lay this down for a Maxim, that they will reckon upon your abilities, according as they find you acquainted and expert in what they themselves are studying. If therefore you have resolution (as I do not question your ability) to carry this plan which I have laid down into execution; you will thereby convince them of the propriety of their Subordination to you, and obedience to your instructions, so that you may lead them, without any resistance, and fix them to the Study of whatever Science you think proper, in which they will rise according to their respective Capacities. I have said that you ought to strive "from the beginning" in fixing this very material article in the minds of your Scholars, Viz a Sense of your authority; for one error of Judgment, or false determination will diminish your Ability with them more than doing forty things with truth would increase your authority—They act in this case as you would do in the company of a number of Strangers—A whole evenings conversation, if it was tolerable good Sense, would perhaps make little or no

impression on you; But if through hast[e] in speaking, or inattention, any one should let fall a sentence either remarkably foolish,
or grossly wicked, it would be difficult if not impossible to per-
suade you presently that the author was not either a *thick-Scull,* or
a *Villain!* — The education of children requires constant unremitting attention. The meanest qualification you can mention in a
useful teacher is *diligence* And without diligence no possible
abilities or qualifications can bring children on either with speed
or profit. There must be a Combination of qualifications which
must all operate strongly and uniformly. In short, give this said
Pedagogizing the softest name you will, it is still a "difficult Task."
You will meet with numberless difficulties, in your new imploy-
ment, which you never dreamt had yet existence. All these you
must endeavour to resist and Subdue. This I have seen compared
to a Man swimming against a current of Water. But I am mistaken
if you will agree, after having six months practice, that the comparison be strong as the truth: You will add to the figure, I am
certain, and throw into the Current sharp fragments of *Ice,* and
Blocks, which would make swimming not only difficult but dangerous! I am not urging these things to discourage you; they are
hints for your direction, which, if you will attend to, tho' at first the
practice seem rough and unpleasant, shall yet make the remainder
of your task pleasing, and the whole of it useful, I will mention
several of these Obstacles that you may the more easily guard
against them. You will, in the first place, be often solicited, probably oftner that you would wish, to ride abroad; this, however, if
you do it moderately, and in seasonable time, and go to proper
company, I recommend as conducive to health to one in your
sedentary manner of living. But if you go much into company, you
will find it extremely difficult to break away with any many of
credit till very late at night or in most cases for several days, and if
you are wanting to your School, you do manifest injury to your
Imployer. In this case, I advise you to copy Mr *Carter.* Whenever
he invites you, ride. You may *stay,* and talk, and drink, and ride to
as great excess as he; and may with safety associate yourself with
those whom you find to be his intimates. In all other Cases, except
when you ride to Church, at least till you are very intimate in the
Colony, you had better ride to a certain Stump, or to some noted
plantation, or pretty landscape; you will have in this every advan-

tage of exercise, the additional advantage of undisturbed Meditation, and you will be under no Jealous apprehension in point of
behaviour, nor any restraint as to the time of your return.

Another current difficulty will be petitions for holidays. You
must have good deal of steadiness if you are able to evade cleverly
this practice which has grown so habitual to your little charge from
a false method in their early education that they absolutely claim
it as a necessary right.

You must also as much as you can, avoid visible partiality. At
least you must never suffer your fondness for one Scholar to grow
so manifest, as that all your School shall see you look over a fault
in him or her which same fault, if commited by another, you se-
verly chastise. This will certainly produce in the others hatred and
contempt. A fourth difficulty, and the last I shall mention, consists
in knowing when, and in what measure to give the Boys Liberty to
go from Home. The two younger Boys are wholly under your
inspection; so that not only the progress they make in learning,
but their moral Conduct (for both of these are critically observed
and examined) either justifies or condemns your management to
the World. If you keep them much at home, and close to business,
they themselves will call you unfeeling and cruel; and refuse to be
industrious; if you suffer them to go much abroad they are certainly
out of the way of improvement by Study, probably, by discovering
their gross Ignorance, they will expose to ridicule both themselves
and all their former instructors, and possibly they may commit
actual Crimes so as very much to injure themselves and scandalize
their family; but in each of these you will have a large share of
blame, perhaps more than the parents, or even the Boys themselves
— It will be said that the parents gave them no licence relying
wholly on your Judgment and prudence, this will in good measure
Justify them to the world. And as to the Boys they are full of
youthful impetuosity and vigour, and these compel them, when
they are free of restraint, to commit actions which with proper
management they had surely avoided. I say, when you lay these
things together, and view them on every side you will find so
many perplexities arising in your mind, from a sense of ignorance
of your duty, that you will proceed with caution and moderation,
and will be careful to examine with some precision into the circumstances of *time, company,* and *Business* when you license

them to go out entirely at the risk of your Reputation—But the practice of three or four Weeks will give you a more full notion of these and many other incidents than I am able now either to recollect or express; I shall have gained my End if these hints prevent you from setting off wrong, and doing inadvertantly at first what your Scholars will assert to be precedents for your after conduct. I go on, therefore, in the third place as I proposed,

3. To mention several Rules for your personal conduct. The happy Education which you have had in point of religion, you ought to consider as an important and distinguishing Blessing of Heaven. That train of useful *Instruction, Advice* and *Example* to which you have been accustomed from your infancy is a more perfect, and will be a safer guide in your future walk, than any directions I am able to give you. You have taken notice of a method for Assistance in Composition, which Longinus recommends.

Place, says he, in imagination, several eminent ancient Authors before your Eyes, and suppose that they inspect your Work, a Sense of inferiority would make you diligent, and your composition accurate. Perhaps the same advice when transferr'd to Morality, would be equally salutary. Unless it be objected that a Belief of Gods presence at all times in every place is the strongest possible restraint against committing Sin. This I constantly admit; but when I consider how easily our minds are put in motion, and how strongly they are sometimes agitated merely by the senses, and that the senses are affected most by things which fall under their immediate notice, I am fully convinced that if some such plan as I have just mentioned should be fallen upon, and practised, it would make a visible and useful change in our behaviour—In this place I think it needful to caution you against hasty and ill founded prejudices. When you enter among a people, and find that their manner of living, their *Eating, Drinking, Diversions, Exercises* etc., are in many respects different from any thing you have been accustomed to, you will be apt to fix your opinion in an instant, and (as some divines deal with poor Sinners) you will condemn all before you without any meaning or distinction what seems in your Judgment disagreeable at first view, when you are smitten with the novelty. You will be making ten thousand Comparisons. The face of the Country, The *Soil*, the *Buildings*, the *Slaves*, the *Tobacco*, the method of spending *Sunday* among Christians; *Ditto*

94

among the Negroes; the three grand divisions of time at the Church on Sundays, Viz. before Service giving and receiving letters of business, reading Advertisements, consulting about the price of Tobacco, Grain etc., and settling either the lineage, Age, or qualities of favourite Horses 2. In the Church at Service, prayrs read over in haste, a Sermon seldom under and never over twenty minutes, but always made up of sound morality, or deep studied Metaphysicks. 3. After Service is over three-quarters of an hour spent in strolling round the Church among the Crowd, in which time you will be invited by several different Gentlemen home with them to dinner. The Balls, the Fish-Feasts, the Dancing-Schools, the Christnings, the Cock fights, the Horse-Races, the Chariots, the Ladies Masked, for it is a custom among the West-morland Ladies whenever they go from home, to muffle up their heads, and Necks, leaving only a narrow passage for the Eyes, in Cotton or silk handkerchiefs; I was in distress for them when I first came into the Colony, for every Woman that I saw abroad, I looked upon as ill either with the Mumps or Tooth-Ach! — I say, you will be often observing and comparing these things which I have enumerated, and many more that now escape me, with the manner of spending Money time and credit at Cohansie: You are young, and (you will allow me the Expression) in the morning of Life. But I hope you have plann'd off, and entered upon the work which is necessary to be performed in the course of your Day; if not, I think it my duty to acquaint you, that a combination of the amusements which I have just now mentioned, being always before your Eyes, and inviting your Compliance will have a strong tendency to keep you doubtful and unsetled, in your notions of Morality and Religion, or else will fix you in a false and dangerous habit of *thinking* and *acting,* which must terminate at length in Sorrow and despair. You are therefore, if you count any thing upon the value of my advice, to fix the plan in which you would spend your life; let this be done with deliberation, Candour, and precission, looking to him for direction, by fervent Prayr, who is the "Wonderful Counsellor"; and when you have done this, let no importunity of whatever kind prevail over you, and cause you to transgress your own Limitations. I have already exceeded the usual bounds of an Epistle. But you will easily pardon a little prolixity, when I assure you it flows from a heart deeply impressed

95

with a sense of the many difficulties which you must encounter, and the dangers which will surround you when you come first out from the peaceful recess of Contemplation, and enter, young and unexperienced, into the tumultuous undiscerning World. I submit these hints to your consideration, and have nothing more than sincere and ardent wishes for your present and perpetual Felicity.

I am, Sir,

yours.

PHILIP V. FITHIAN.

To Mr John Peck
On going to Virginia in
Character of a Tutor.

PART II:

THE REPUBLICAN IDEA
OF EDUCATION, 1776–1820

THE LAST years of the eighteenth century and early decades of the nineteenth stand out as a period of premature nationalism in which Americans concentrated on achieving a degree of cultural and economic independence and on furthering the political experiment of republicanism. Their efforts were deliberate, exaggerated, and often self-conscious, and the results at times were ludicrous. There were those who advocated such ridiculous ideas as Americanizing the Mother Goose rhymes and forbidding the importation of English-published books; name-changing along American and republican lines was a far more successful undertaking. All these notions were in keeping with the feeling of optimism and confidence and the belief in the promise of the American experiment and its accomplishments. Beneath the truculence and militancy and the ardent patriotism and boastfulness, was a deep commitment to the democratic ideal which was to take shape and form in the following decades.

In the realm of education, as in literature and the arts, the spirit of youthful nationalism is apparent. The actual achievements are not exceptional or outstanding, nor do they represent a break with the past; but the various new schemes for a system of national and universal education are revolutionary and significant milestones in the development of American education and the free school movement of a later generation. The production of new school books also reflects this nationalistic republicanism and self-conscious Americanism.

The traditional English readers, spellers, grammar and arithmetic books seemed unsuitable to the Young Americans, and in the period following the War for Independence, America's first important school books with a definite American slant began to appear; some of these were to remain the standard diet for school youths for almost a century. In general they were close imitations of the long-used English books, but with a strong dose of Americanism; in title, approach, and content the spirit of nationalism was blatantly displayed. Caleb Bingham, the New England school master, produced *American Preceptor* (1794) and the *Columbian Orator* (1797). Jedidiah Morse offered his nation *Geography Made Easy* (1784). The titles are indicative of the patriotism of the early American writers. The books, which were meant specifically for Americans, aimed at helping them learn quickly and easily and assisting them in achieving the national objectives of happiness and prosperity. Erastus Root in his *Introduction to Arithmetic* (1795) revealed his loyalty to his nation by rejecting "the British intricate mode of reckoning," which he considered "suited to the genius of their government." To him it was the "policy of tyrants, to keep their accounts as intricate and perplexing a method as possible." What could be more American than his offering the new nation a republican monetary system that was "simple and adapted to the meanest capacity?" The patriotic sting is sharp, but the dedication to republicanism is meaningful. The early American compilers of school books recognized that the printed word was a potent weapon in achieving cultural independence and in promoting learning among all classes. Root, like so many of his fellow writers, sought to help Americans learn.

The single individual who played the most important role in educating young America—frontiersman, city dweller, farmer, and foreigner—was Noah Webster, who rightly deserves the title of First Schoolmaster of the Republic. Intellectual pioneer and ardent patriot, Noah Webster devoted his energy, his fortune, and his life to helping America learn and to promoting American culture, American ideals, and American ways. Through his well-known speller which appeared in 1783 as the first part of *A Grammatical Institute of the English Language,* and finally through the famous *American Dictionary of the English Language* (1828), Noah Webster contributed immeasurably to the development of American education and culture. His purpose in preparing the speller was nationalistic, patriotic, and democratic; he wished to simplify the language and make it uniform, so that neither pronunciation nor spelling would differentiate the social classes (12). Furthermore, he saw that uniformity would bind the nation together by ridding the language of dialects, colloquialisms, and foreign phrases. It was to be an American language, as he expressed it somewhat prematurely in the title of his dictionary.

His speller was not original in its approach or organization; only in the introduction of spelling reforms and in the simplification of pronunciation was Webster revolutionary. And, with time, he steadily modified his more extreme ideas of language and spelling reform as well as his earlier democratic views. The overwhelming success and popularity of the famous blue-back speller in the schools in the nineteenth century, the acceptance of the American Dictionary, and the emergence of a uniform American language in spelling and pronunciation all attest to the impact of Webster's ideas and published works.

Webster was so much the preacher of nationalism that he even undertook to apply the same yardstick of Americanism to the Bible. Here too he sought to give the nation an American book, written in the language of the common man and devoid of the "antiquarian style." But the common man apparently recognized unconsciously the aesthetic greatness of the King James version, and Webster's American Bible was never a success, although he had already left a lasting imprint on American culture and education.

The school books became the immediate and practical instruments by which young Americans could be trained in loyalty, republican principles, and Christian virtues. What the new nation needed, however, as the intellectual as well as political leadership recognized, was a system of schools which would guarantee the fulfillment of the principles and ideology of the American Revolution, unify and bind the nation together, and promote cultural development. The state and the church had long accepted education as the most powerful means of inculcating youth in the doctrines of loyalty, responsibility, and orthodoxy. The church, through the various denominations, had dominated the educational scene throughout the colonial years, but now the leaders, in keeping with the spirit of secularism, turned to the state as the agent for promoting and furthering education in the new nation.

Numerous tracts and essays written on the subject appeared in the last decades of the eighteenth century, and the striking fact is that, although there was wide diversity of opinion on the methods of education, there was great similarity among the theorists on how the training was to be carried out, by whom, and for what purpose. Though not one of these many schemes came to be implemented in that era, they nonetheless stand out as superb examples of the spirit of the age: the belief in man's abilities, the faith in the American experiment, and the acceptance of education as a means of promoting reform and the welfare of the individual and of the nation. They express both the idealism of the new nation and the realism of the intellectual and political pioneers seeking to solve the peculiar educational problems of a diversified and widely scattered population. These writings provided the basic ideas and theories for educational reform and helped create the atmosphere that in the next generation could develop into the free school movement.

Throughout the writings runs the constant refrain of education as a means of binding the nation together, whether the plan is for a national university or for the creation of a system of schools by the federal government. George Washington, John Adams, Thomas Jefferson, and later John Quincy Adams were among those who advocated the establishment of a national university, which would keep Americans home as well as bring them together from the vast reaches of the growing nation. For a brief moment, Jefferson's and Adams' plans for the development of a national university on the foundations of the University of Geneva transplanted to the new nation seemed a possibility, but Washington rejected such a scheme in the hopes of creating a home-grown institution rather than transferring a foreign one. He even left a small bequest for such an undertaking. These were the high hopes and aspirations of the early national leaders.

Even more significant as examples of the early nationalistic spirit are the detailed educational schemes offered by such well-known figures as Jefferson, Webster, and Benjamin Rush, as well as such less famous men as Robert Coram, William Manning, Samuel Knox, and Samuel Smith whose significance in early American history rests largely on their untried but elaborate plans. Though their proposals varied in detail, all of them accepted the principles of education for all classes and of state responsibility.

To some, such as Jefferson, education rested with the state government and not the federal; and, as governor of Virginia in 1779, he proposed the Bill for the More General Diffusion of Learning based on the concept of public education for the talented (13). Jefferson envisioned a system which would permit free education on each level for a select few of ability until a handful of the brightest young men would enter the College of William and Mary at public expense. The scheme of education for the talented was fundamentally aristocratic, but nonetheless revolutionary in the fact that the state did assume responsibility and that at the rudimentary level free education was provided for all classes.

Neither in 1779 nor in 1802 was Virginia prepared to accept such a plan.

To others education was a matter for the national government, and various individuals drew up elaborate plans for a national system of schools. The need to draw the nation together, to reinforce political independence, and to produce a loyal and capable citizenry were the arguments ably presented by these educational reformers. Interwoven into these nationalistic views was the democratic theme that only through state responsibility could everyone in the nation have equal opportunity to learn, and only through an enlightened populus could democracy develop.

These theorists showed a keen interest not only in the objectives of education but also in the kind of training to be provided at state expense (14) (15). Here many of the ideas advocated by Benjamin Franklin in the mid-eighteenth century received full development. The note of practicality is sounded again and again. These theorists seriously questioned the usefulness of Latin and Greek, described by Dr. Rush as "two dead languages." The demand was for a new kind of education that concerned itself with promoting the welfare of the classes rather than promoting knowledge of the classics, that met the needs of the new nation, and that helped promote its cultural, economic, and political potentiality.

In 1797 the American Philosophical Society, itself an organization devoted to the promotion of learning and knowledge, offered a prize of one hundred dollars "for the best System of liberal Education and literary instruction, adapted to the genius of the Government of the United States." Though none of the many schemes appeared suitable to the existing conditions of the nation, the Society judged two essays to be of exceptional merit and awarded fifty dollars each to Samuel Knox of Blandenburg, Maryland, and Samuel H. Smith of Philadelphia(16) (17). Both were men of affairs, dedicated to scholarship and education. Knox was a teacher, physician and minister, and his essay provided a detailed plan for a national system of education from the lowest level of parish or primary schools to a national university. Smith, a writer and editor, presented the philosophical argument for education by relating virtue to wisdom. He, too, offered an "ideal" scheme for national education with emphasis on practical training and its usefulness to the individual, the nation, and the world. As excerpts from their essays reveal, Knox and Smith were men of the Enlightenment and enlightened individuals of their times, well aware of the new nation's shortcomings. Their ideas are representative of the views held by the spokesmen for educational reform. Their high idealism, their demand for practical and useful training, their criticism of the existing order, their concern for the nation's welfare, and their keen awareness of the national need all express the spirit of nationalism and republicanism.

Despite the widespread interest in promoting public education among the intellectual leadership, a great distance separated theory and practice. The federal constitution was silent about education, and the new state constitutions did not reflect the equalitarian principles advocated by these men. Of the sixteen states in the union in 1800, nine did not mention education in their constitutions, and the others expressed vague sentiments about furthering learning; or in the case of the New England states, the common school through the township system was continued. In general, the separate states followed the colonial precedent of providing free education for the dependent classes only (18). The old system prevailed everywhere.

Not until Indiana came into the union in 1816, did a state constitution incorporate the principle of public responsibility for education from the lowest to the highest level. But a generation was to pass before Indiana's lofty constitutional provisions were put into practice. Not until the free school movement forced the states and local communities to fulfill the constitutional promises and democratic hopes of the citizens did America begin to develop a system of free public education. It was the state as a political unit that assumed responsibility, not the federal government. The idea of a national system of schools had passed in the first wave of early nationalism which came at the turn into the nineteenth century.

Chapter 7

Educational Schemes and Constitutional Provisions

To establish an uniform system of national education.

Samual Knox, 1799

12. An Essay on the Necessity, Advantages and Practicality of Reforming the MODE of Spelling (1789)[1]

NOAH WEBSTER

The question now occurs; ought the Americans to retain these faults which produce innumerable inconveniencies in the acquisition and use of the language, or ought they at once to reform these abuses, and introduce order and regularity into the orthography of the AMERICAN TONGUE? . . .

The principal alterations, necessary to render our orthography sufficiently regular and easy, are these:

1. The Omission of all superfluous or silent letters; as a in bread. . . . Would this alteration produce any inconvenience, any embarrassment or expense? By no means. On the other hand, it would lessen the trouble of writing, and much more, of learning the language; it would reduce the true pronunciation to a certainty; and while it would assist foreigners and our own children in acquiring the language, it would render the pronunciation uniform, in different parts of the country, and almost prevent the possibility of changes.

2. A substitution of a character that has a certain definite sound, for one that is more vague and indeterminate. Thus by

---

[1]Noah Webster, "An Essay on the Necessity, Advantages, and Practicality of Reforming the MODE of the Spelling and of Rendering the Orthography of Words Correspondent to Prounnunciations," *Dissertations on the English Language* (Boston: Isaiah Thomas, 1789), pp. 393–98. Webster's speller, part of *A Grammatical Institute of the English Language,* first appeared in 1783 containing some of the reform ideas presented in this essay, though the changes were not extreme. It served as an "Educational and Cultural Declaration of Independence," and its overwhelming popularity made it the most influential tool for standardizing spelling and creating an American language. In the early nineteenth century he devoted himself to compiling the American dictionary which appeared in 1825—another factor in reforming the language and standardizing spelling and pronunciation.

putting ee instead of ea or ie, the words mean, near, speak, grieve, zeal, would become meen, neer, speek, greev, zeel. This alteration could not occasion a moments trouble; at the same time it would prevent a doubt respecting the pronunciation; . . .

3. A trifling alteration in a character, or the addition of a point would distinguish different sounds, without the substitution of a new character. Thus a very small stroke across th would distinguish its two sounds. A point over a vowel, in this manner, à, or ò, or ī, might answer all the purposes of different letters. And for the dipthong ow, let the two letters be united by a small stroke, or both engraven on the same piece of metal, with the left hand line of the w united to the o.

These, with a few other inconsiderable alterations, would answer every purpose, and render the orthography sufficiently correct and regular.

The advantages to be derived from these alterations are numerous, great and permanent.

1. The simplicity of the orthography would facilitate the learning of the language. It is now the work of years for children to learn to spell; and after all, the business is rarely accomplished. A few men, who are bred to some business that requires constant exercise in writing, finally learn to spell most words without hesitation; but most people remain, all their lives, imperfect masters of spelling, and liable to make mistakes, whenever they take up a pen to write a short note. Nay, many people, even of education and fashion, never attempt to write a letter, without frequently consulting a dictionary.

But with the proposed orthography, a child would learn to spell, without trouble, in a very short time, and the orthography being very regular, he would ever afterwards find it difficult to make a mistake. It would, in that case, be as difficult to spell wrong, as it is now to spell right.

Besides this advantage, foreigners would be able to acquire the pronunciation of English, which is now so difficult and embarrassing, that they are either wholly discouraged on the first attempt, or obliged, after many years labor, to rest contented with an imperfect knowledge of the subject.

2. A correct orthography would render the pronunciation of the language, as uniform as the spelling in books. A general uniform-

ity thro the United States, would be the event of such a reformation as I am here recommending. All persons, of every rank, would
speak with some degree of precision and uniformity. Such a uniformity in these states is very desireable; it would remove prejudice, and conciliate mutual affection and respect.

3. Such a reform would diminish the number of letters about
one sixteenth or eighteenth. This would save a page in eighteen;
and a saving of an eighteenth in the expense of books, is an advantage that should not be overlooked.

4. But a capital advantage of this reform in these states would
be, that it would make a difference between the English orthography and the American. This will startle those who have not
attended to the subject; but I am confident that such an event is an
object of vast political consequence. For,

The alteration, however small, would encourage the publication of books in our own country. It would render it, in some
measure, necessary that all books should be printed in America.
The English would never copy our orthography for their own use;
and consequently the same impressions of books would not answer for both countries. The inhabitants of the present generation
would read the English impressions; but posterity, being taught a
different spelling, would prefer the American orthography.

Besides this, a national language is a band of national union.
Every engine should be employed to render the people of this
country national; to call their attachments home to their own
country; and to inspire them with the pride of national character.
However they may boast of Independence, and the freedom of their
government, yet their opinions are not sufficiently independent; an
astonishing respect for the arts and literature of their parent country, and a blind imitation of its manners, are still prevalent among
the Americans. Thus an habitual respect for another country, de-
served indeed and once laudable, turns their attention from their
own interests, and prevents their respecting themselves.

13. Bill for the More General Diffusion of Knowldege (1779) [1]

THOMAS JEFFERSON

Section I. Whereas it appeareth that however certain forms of government are better calculated than others to protect individuals in the free exercise of their natural rights, and are at the same time themselves better guarded against degeneracy, yet experience hath shewn that even under the best forms those intrusted with power have, in time, and by slow operations, perverted it into tyranny; and it is believed that the most effectual means of preventing this would be, to illuminate, as far as practicable, the minds of the people at large, and more especially to give them knowledge of those facts, which history exhibiteth, that, possessed thereby of the experience of other ages and countries, they may be enabled to know ambition under all its shapes, and prompt to exert their natural powers to defeat its purpose; And whereas it is generally true that that people will be happiest whose laws are best, and are best administered, and that laws will be wisely formed, and honestly administered, in proportion as those who form and administer them are wise and honest; whence it becomes expedient for promoting the publick happiness that those persons, whom nature hath endowed with genius and virtue, should be rendered by liberal education worthy to receive, and able to guard the sacred deposit of the rights and liberties of their fellow citizens, and that they should be called to that charge without regard to wealth, birth or other accidental condition or circumstance; but the indigence of the greater number disabling them from so educating, at their own expence, those of their children whom nature hath fitly formed and disposed to become

[1]Knight, *Documentary History of Education in the South before 1860* (1950), II, 142–50.

useful instruments for the public, it is better that such should be sought for and educated at the common expence of all, than that the happiness of all should be confined to the weak or wicked.

Sect. II. Be it therefore enacted by the General Assembly, that in every county within this commonwealth, there shall be chosen annually, by the electors qualified to vote for Delegates, three of the most honest and able men of their county, to be called the Aldermen of the county; and that the election of the said Aldermen shall be held at the same time and place, before the same persons, and notified and conducted in the same manner as by law is directed, for the annual election of Delegates for the county.

Sect. III. The person before whom such election is holden shall certify to the court of the said county the names of the Aldermen chosen, in order that the same may be entered of record, and shall give notice of their election to the said Aldermen within a fortnight after such election.

Sect. IV. The said Aldermen on the first Monday in October, if it be fair, and if not, then on the next fair day, excluding Sunday, shall meet at the court-house of their county, and proceed to divide their said county into hundreds, bounding the same by water courses, mountains, or limits, to be run and marked, if they think necessary, by the county surveyor, and at the county expence, regulating the size of the said hundreds, according to the best of their discretion, so as that they may contain a convenient number of children to make up a school, and be of such convenient size that all the children within each hundred may daily attend the school to be established therein, and distinguishing each hundred by a particular name; which division, with the names of the several hundreds, shall be returned to the court of the county and be entered of record, and shall remain unaltered until the increase or decrease of inhabitants shall render an alteration necessary, in the opinion of any succeeding Aldermen, and also in the opinion of the court of the county.

Sect. V. The electors aforesaid residing within every hundred shall meet on the third Monday in October after the first election of Aldermen, at such place, within their hundred, as the said Aldermen shall direct, notice thereof being previously given to them by such person residing within the hundred as the said

Aldermen shall require who is hereby enjoined to obey such requisition, on pain of being punished by amercement and imprisonment. The electors being so assembled shall choose the most convenient place within their hundred for building a school-house. If two or more places, having a greater number of votes than any others, shall yet be equal between themselves, the Aldermen, or such of them as are not of the same hundred, on information thereof, shall decide between them. The said Aldermen shall forthwith proceed to have a school-house built at the said place, and shall see that the same shall be kept in repair, and, when necessary, that it be rebuilt; but whenever they shall think necessary that it be rebuilt, they shall give notice as before directed, to the electors of the hundred to meet at the said school-house, on such a day as they shall appoint, to determine by vote, in the manner before directed, whether it shall be rebuilt at the same, or what other place in the hundred.

Sect. VI. At every of those schools shall be taught reading, writing, and common arithmetick, and the books which shall be used therein for instructing the children to read shall be such as will at the same time make them acquainted with Graecian, Roman, English, and American history. At these schools all the free children, male and female, resident within the respective hundred, shall be entitled to receive tuition gratis, for the term of three years, and as much longer, at their private expence, as their parents, guardians, or friends shall think proper.

Sect. VII. Over every ten of these schools (or such other number nearest thereto, as the number of hundreds in the county will admit, without fractional divisions) an overseer shall be appointed annually by the aldermen at their first meeting, eminent for his learning, integrity, and fidelity to the common wealth, whose business and duty it shall be, from time to time, to appoint a teacher to each school, who shall give assurance of fidelity to the commonwealth, and to remove him as he shall see cause; to visit every school once in every half year at the least; to examine the scholars; see that any general plan of reading and instruction recommended by the visiters of William and Mary College shall be observed; and to superintend the conduct of the teacher in everything relative to his school.

Sect. VIII. Every teacher shall receive a salary of _____ by the year, which, with the expences of building and repairing the school-houses, shall be provided in such manner as other county expences are by law directed to be provided and shall also have his diet, lodging, and washing found him, to be levied in like manner, save only that such levy shall be on the inhabitants of each hundred for the board of their own teacher only.

Sect. IX. And in order that grammar schools may be rendered convenient to the youth in every part of the commonwealth, be it therefore enacted, that on the first Monday in November, after the first appointment of overseers for the hundred schools, if fair, and if not, then on the next fair day, excluding Sunday, after the hour of one in the afternoon, the said overseer appointed for the schools in the counties of Princess Ann, Norfolk, Nansemond and Isle of Wight, shall meet at Nansemond court-house. . . [a list of counties and meeting places follows] and shall fix on such place in some one of the counties in their district as shall be most proper for situating a grammer school-house, endeavoring that the situation be as central as may be to the inhabitants of the said counties, that it be furnished with good water, convenient to plentiful supplies of provision and fuel, and more than all things that it be healthy. And if a majority of the overseers present should not concur in their choice of any one place proposed, the method of determining shall be as follows: If two places only were proposed, and the votes be divided, they shall decide between them by fair and equal lot; if more than two places were proposed, the question shall be put on those two which on the first division had the greater number of votes; or if no two places had a greater number of votes than the others, then it shall be decided by fair and equal lot (unless it can be agreed by a majority of votes) which of the places having equal numbers shall be thrown out of the competition, so that the question shall be put on the remaining two, and if on this ultimate question the votes shall be equally divided, it shall then be decided finally by lot.

Sect. X. The said overseers having determined the place at which the grammer school for their district shall be built, shall forthwith (unless they can otherwise agree with the proprietors of the circumjacent lands as to location and price) make application to the clerk of the county in which the said house is to be situated, who shall thereupon issue a writ, in the nature of a writ of ad quod damnum, directed to the sheriff of the said county commanding him to summon and impannel twelve fit persons to meet at the place, so destined for the grammer school-house, on a certain day, to be named in the said writ, not less than five, nor more than ten, days from the date thereof; and also to give notice of the same to the proprietors and tenants of the lands to be viewed if they be found within the county, and if not, then to their agents therein if any they have. Which freeholders shall be charged by the sheriff impartially, and to the best of their skill and judgment to view the lands round about the said place, and to locate and circumscribe, by certain meets and bounds, one hundred acres thereof, having regard the rein principally to the benefit and convenience of the said school, but respecting in some measure also the convenience of the said proprietors, and to value and appraise the same in so many several and distinct parcels as shall be owned or held by several and distinct owners or tenants, and according to their respective interests and estates therein. And after such location and appraisement so made, the said sheriff shall forthwith return the same under the hands and seals of the said jurors, together with the writ, to the clerk's office of the said county and the right and property of the said proprietors and tenants in the said lands so circumscribed shall be immediately divested and be transferred to the commonwealth for the use of the said grammer school, in full and absolute dominion, any want of consent or disability to consent in the said owners or tenants notwithstanding. But it shall not be lawful for the said overseers so to situate the grammer school-house, nor to the said jurors so to locate the said lands, as to include the mansion-house of the proprietor of the lands, nor the offices, curtilage, or garden, thereunto immediately belonging.

Sect. XI. The said overseers shall forthwith proceed to have a house of brick or stone, for the said grammer school, with necessary offices, built on the said lands, which grammer school-house shall contain a room for the school, a hall to dine in, four rooms for a master and usher, and ten or twelve lodging rooms for the scholars.

Sect. XII. To each of the said grammer schools shall be allowed out of the public treasury, the sum of _____ pounds, out of which shall be paid by the Treasurer, on warrant from the Auditors, to the proprietors or tenants of the lands located, the value of their several interests as fixed by the jury, and the balance thereof shall be delivered to the said overseers to defray the expense of the said buildings.

Sect. XIII. In either of these grammer schools shall be taught the Latin and Greek languages, English Grammer, geography, and the higher part of numerical arithmetick, to-wit, vulgar and decimal fractions, and the extrication of the square and cube roots.

Sect. XIV. A visiter from each county constituting the district shall be appointed, by the overseers, for the county, in the month of October annually, either from their own body or from their county at large, which visiters, or the greater part of them, meeting together at the said grammer school on the first Monday in November, if fair, and if not, then on the next fair day, excluding Sunday, shall have power to choose their own Rector, who shall call and preside at future meetings, to employ from time to time a master, and if necessary, an usher, for the said school, to remove them at their will, and to settle the price of tuition to be paid by the scholars. They shall also visit the school twice in every year at the least, either together or separately at their discretion, examine the scholars, and see that any general plan of instruction recommended by the visiters, of William and Mary College shall be observed. The said masters and ushers, before they enter on the execution of their office, shall give assurance of fidelity to the commonwealth.

Sect. XV. A steward shall be employed, and removed at will by the master, on such wages as the visiters shall direct; which steward shall see to the procuring provisions, fuel, servants for cooking, waiting, house cleaning, washing, mending, and gardening on the most reasonable terms; the expense of which, together with the steward's wages, shall be divided equally among all the scholars boarding either on the public or private expence, and also the price of their tuitions due to the master or usher, shall be paid quarterly by the respective scholars, their parents, or guardians, and shall be recoverable, if withheld, together with costs, on motion in any Court of Record, ten days notice thereof being previously given to the party, and a jury impannelled to try the issue joined, or enquire of the damages. The said steward shall also, under the direction of the visiters, see that the houses be kept in repair, and necessary enclosures be made and repaired, the accounts for which shall, from time to time, be submitted to the Auditors, and on their warrant paid by the Treasurer.

Sect. XVI. Every overseer of the hundred schools shall, in the month of September annually, after the most diligent and impartial examination and inquiry, appoint from among the boys who shall have been two years at the least at some one of the schools under his superintendance, and whose parents are too poor to give them farther education, some one of the best and most promising genius and disposition, to proceed to the grammer school of his district; which appointment shall be made in the court-house of the county, and on the court day for that month if fair, and if not, then on the next fair day, excluding Sunday, in the presence of the Aldermen, or two of them at the least, assembled on the bench for that purpose, the said overseer being previously sworn by them to make such appointment, without favor or affection, according to the best of his skill and judgment, and being interrogated by the said Aldermen, either on their own motion, or on suggestions from the parents, guardians, friends, or teachers of the children, competitors for such appointment; which teachers the parents shall attend for the information of the Aldermen. On which interrogatories the said Aldermen, if they be not satisfied with the appointment proposed, shall have right to negative it; whereupon the said visiter may proceed to make a new appointment, and the said Aldermen again to interrogate and negative, and so toties quoties until the appointment is approved.

Sect. XVII. Every boy so appointed shall be authorized to proceed to the grammer school of his district, there to be educated and boarded during such time as is hereafter limited; and his quota of the expences of the house together with a compensation to the master or usher for his tuition, at the rate of twenty dollars by year, shall be paid by the Treasurer quarterly on warrant from the Auditors.

Sect. XVIII. A visitation shall be held, for the purpose of probation, annually at the said grammer school on the last Monday in September, if fair, and if not, then on the next fair day, excluding Sunday, at which one-third of the boys sent thither by appointment of the said overseers, and who shall have been there one year only, shall be discontinued as public foundationers, being those who, on the most diligent examination and enquiry, shall be thought to be the least promising genius and disposition; and of those who shall have been there two years, all shall be discontinued save one only the best in genius and disposition, who shall be at liberty to continue there four years longer on the public foundation, and shall thence forward be deemed a senior.

Sect. XIX. The visiters for the district which, or any part of which, be southward and westward of James River, as known by that name, or by the names of Fluvanna and Jackson's river, in every other year, to-wit, at the probation meetings held in the years, distinguished in the Christian computation by odd numbers, and the visiters for all the other districts at their said meetings to be held in those years, distinguished by even numbers, after diligent examination and enquiry as before directed, shall chuse one among the said seniors, of the best learning and most hopeful genius and disposition, who shall be authorized by them to proceed to William and Mary College; there to be educated, boarded, and clothed, three years; the expence of which annually shall be paid by the Treasurer on warrant from the Auditors.

14. Education Agreeable to a Republican Form of Government (1786)[1]

BENJAMIN RUSH

Before I proceed to the subject of this essay, I shall point out, in a few words, the influence and advantages of learning upon mankind.

I. It is friendly to religion, inasmuch as it assists in removing prejudice, superstition and enthusiasm, in promoting just notions of the Deity, and in enlarging our knowledge of his works.

II. It is favourable to liberty. Freedom can exist only in the society of knowledge. Without learning, men are incapable of knowing their rights, and where learning is confined to a few people, liberty can be neither equal nor universal.

III. It promotes just ideas of laws and government. "When the clouds of ignorance are dispelled (says the Marquis of Beccaria) by the radiance of knowledge, power trembles, but the authority of laws remains immovable."

IV. It is friendly to manners. Learning in all countries, promotes civilization, and the pleasures of society and conversation.

V. It promotes agriculture, the great basis of national wealth and happiness. Agriculture is as much a science as hydraulics, or optics, and has been equally indebted to the experiments and researches of learned men. The highly cultivated state, and the immense profits of the farms in England, are derived wholly from the patronage which agriculture has received in that country, from learned men and learned societies.

---

[1]Dagobert Runes (Ed.), *Selected Writings of Benjamin Rush* (New York: Philosophical Library, 1947), pp. 97–100. Rush, a Princeton graduate, received his medical degree from the University of Edinburgh in 1768 and became Professor of Chemistry of the College of Philadelphia the following year. As a man of affairs who concerned himself with medical science, politics, and social reform, Rush was a staunch advocate of a unified system of state education and of female training.

VI. Manufactures of all kinds owe their perfection chiefly to learning—hence the nations of Europe advance in manufactures, knowledge, and commerce, only in proportion as they cultivate the arts and sciences.

For the purpose of diffusing knowledge through every part of the state, I beg leave to propose the following simple plan.

I. Let there be one university in the state, and let this be established in the capital. Let law, physic, divinity, the law of nature and nations, economy, &c. be taught in it by public lectures in the winter season, after the manner of the European universities, and let the professors receive such salaries from the state as will enable them to deliver their lectures at a moderate price.

II. Let there be four colleges. One in Philadelphia; one at Carlisle; a third, for the benefit of our German fellow citizens, at Lancaster; and a fourth, some years hence at Pittsburgh. In these colleges, let young men be instructed in mathematics and in the higher branches of science, in the same manner that they are now taught in our American colleges. After they have received a testimonial from one of these colleges, let them, if they can afford it, complete their studies by spending a season or two in attending the lectures in the university. I prefer four colleges in the state to one or two, for there is a certain size of colleges as there is of towns and armies, that is most favourable to morals and good government. Oxford and Cambridge in England are the seats of dissipation, while the more numerous, and less crowded universities and colleges in Scotland, are remarkable for the order, diligence, and decent behaviour of their students.

II. Let there be free schools established in every township, or in districts consisting of one hundred families. In these schools let children be taught to read and write the English and German languages, and the use of figures. Such of them as have parents that can afford to send them from home, and are disposed to extend their educations, may remove their children from the free school to one of the colleges.

By this plan the whole state will be tied together by one system of education. The university will in time furnish masters for the colleges, and the colleges will furnish masters for the free schools, while the free schools, in their turns, will supply the colleges and the university with scholars, students and pupils. The same systems of grammar, oratory and philosophy, will be taught in every part of the state, and the literary features of Pennsylvania will thus designate one great, and equally enlightened family.

But, how shall we bear the expense of these literary institutions?—I answer—These institutions will *lessen* our taxes. They will enlighten us in the great business of finance—they will teach us to increase the ability of the state to support government, by increasing the profits of agriculture, and by promoting manufactures. They will teach us all the modern improvements and advantages of inland navigation. They will defend us from hasty and expensive experiments in government, by unfolding to us the experience and folly of past ages, and thus, instead of adding to our taxes and debts, they will furnish us with the true secret of lessening and discharging both of them.

But, shall the estates of orphans, bachelors and persons who have no children, be taxed to pay for the support of schools from which they can derive no benefit? I answer in the affirmative, to the first part of the objection, and I deny the truth of the latter part of it. Every member of the community is interested in the propagation of virtue and knowledge in the state. But I will go further, and add, it will be true economy in individuals to support public schools. The bachelor will in time save his tax for this purpose, by being able to sleep with fewer bolts and locks to his doors—the estates of orphans will in time be benefited, by being protected from the ravages of unprincipled and idle boys, and the children of wealthy parents will be less tempted, by bad company, to extravagance. Fewer pillories and whipping posts, and smaller gaols, with their usual expenses and taxes, will be necessary when our youth are properly educated, than at present; I believe it could be proved, that the expenses of confining, trying and executing criminals, amount every year, in most of the counties, to more money than would be sufficient to maintain all the schools that would be necessary in each county. The confessions of these criminals generally show us, that their vices and punishments are the fatal consequences of the want of a proper education in early life.

I submit these detached hints to the consideration of the legislature and of the citizens of Pennsylvania. The plan for the free schools is taken chiefly from the plans which have long been used with success in Scotland, and in the eastern states of America, where the influence of learning, in promoting religion, morals, manners and good government, has never been exceeded in any country.

The manner in which these schools should be supported and governed—the modes of determining the characters and qualifications of schoolmasters, and the arrangement of families in each district, so that children of the same religious sect and nation, may be educated as much as possible together, will form a proper part of a law for the establishment of schools, and therefore does not come within the limits of this plan.

15. Of the Mode of Education Proper in a Republic (1798)[1]

BENJAMIN RUSH

The BUSINESS of education has acquired a new complexion by the independence of our country. The form of government we have assumed, has created a new class of duties to every American. It becomes us, therefore, to examine our former habits upon this subject, and in laying the foundations for nurseries of wise and good men, to adapt our modes of teaching to the peculiar form of our government.

The first remark that I shall make upon this subject is, that an education in our own, is to be preferred to an education in a foreign country. The principle of patriotism stands in need of the reinforcement of prejudice, and it is well known that our strongest prejudices in favour of our country are formed in the first one and twenty years of our lives. The policy of the Lacedemonians is well worthy of our imitation. When Antipater demanded fifty of their children as hostages for the fulfillment of a distant engagement, those wise republicans refused to comply with his demand, but readily offered him double the number of their adult citizens, whose habits and prejudices could not be shaken by residing in a foreign country. Passing by, in this place, the advantages to the community from the early attachment of youth to the laws and constitution of their country, I shall only remark, that young men who have trodden the paths of science together, or have joined in the same sports, whether of swimming, skating, fishing, or hunting, generally feel, thro' life, such ties to each other, as add greatly to the obligations of mutual benevolence.

I conceive the education of our youth in this country to be peculiarly necessary in Pennsylvania, while our citizens are com-

---

[1]Runes, *Selected Writings of Benjamin Rush*, pp. 87–96.

posed of the natives of so many different kingdoms in Europe. Our schools of learning, by producing one general, and uniform system of education, will render the mass of the people more homogeneous, and thereby fit them more easily for uniform and peaceable government.

I proceed in the next place, to enquire, what mode of education we shall adopt so as to secure to the state all the advantages that are to be derived from the proper instruction of youth; and here I beg leave to remark, that the only foundation for a useful education in a republic is to be laid in Religion. Without this there can be no virtue, and without virtue there can be no liberty, and liberty is the object and life of all republican governments.

Such is my veneration for every religion that reveals the attributes of the Deity, or a future state of rewards and punishments, that I had rather see the opinions of Confucius or Mahomed inculcated upon our youth, than see them grow up wholly devoid of a system of religious principles. But the religion I mean to recommend in this place, is that of the New Testament.

It is foreign to my purpose to hint at the arguments which establish the truth of the Christian revelation. My only business is to declare, that all its doctrines and precepts are calculated to promote the happiness of society, and the safety and well being of civil government. A Christian cannot fail of being a republican. The history of the creation of man, and of the relation of our species to each other by birth, which is recorded in the Old Testament, is the best refutation that can be given to the divine right of kings, and the strongest argument that can be used in favor of the original and natural equality of all mankind. A Christian, I say again, cannot fail of being a republican, for every precept of the Gospel inculcates those degrees of humility, self-denial, and brotherly kindness, which are directly opposed to the pride of monarchy and the pageantry of a court. A Christian cannot fail of being useful to the republic, for his religion teacheth him, that no man "liveth to himself." And lastly, a Christian cannot fail of being wholly inoffensive, for his religion teacheth him, in all things to do to others what he would wish, in like circumstances, they should do to him.

I am aware that I dissent from one of those paradoxical opinions with which modern times abound; and that it is improper to fill the minds of youth with religious prejudices of any kind, and that they should be left to choose their own principles, after they have arrived at an age in which they are capable of judging for themselves. Could we preserve the mind in childhood and youth a perfect blank, this plan of education would have more to recommend it; but this we know to be impossible. The human mind runs as naturally into principles as it does after facts. It submits with difficulty to those restraints or partial discoveries which are imposed upon it in the infancy of reason. Hence the impatience of children to be informed upon all subjects that relate to the invisible world. But I beg leave to ask, why should we pursue a different plan of education with respect to religion, from that which we pursue in teaching the arts and sciences? Do we leave our youth to acquire systems of geography, philosophy, or politics, till they have arrived at an age in which they are capable of judging for themselves? We do not. I claim no more then for religion, than for the other sciences, and I add further, that if our youth are disposed after they are of age to think for themselves, a knowledge of one system, will be the best means of conducting them in a free enquiry into other systems of religion, just as an acquaintance with one system of philosophy is the best introduction to the study of all the other systems in the world.

Next to the duty which young men owe to their Creator, I wish to see a regard to their country, inculcated upon them. When the Duke of Sully became prime minister to Henry the IVth of France, the first thing he did, he tells us, "Was to subdue and forget his own heart." The same duty is incumbent upon every citizen of a republic. Our country includes family, friends and property, and should be preferred to them all. Let our pupil be taught that he does not belong to himself, but that he is public property. Let him be taught to love his family, but let him be taught, at the same time, that he must forsake, and even forget them, when the welfare of his country requires it. He must watch for the state, as if its liberties depended upon his vigilance alone, but he must do this in such a manner as not to defraud his creditors, or neglect his family. He must love private life, but he must decline no station, however public or responsible it may be, when called to it by the suffrages of his fellow citizens. He must love popularity, but he must despise it when set in competition with the dictates of his judgement, or the real interest of his country. He must love character, and have a due sense of injuries, but he must be taught to appeal only to the laws of the state, to defend the one, and punish the other. He must love family honor, but he must be taught that neither the rank nor antiquity of his ancestors, can command respect, without personal merit. He must avoid neutrality in all questions that divide the state, but he must shun the rage, and acrimony of party spirit. He must be taught to love his fellow creatures in every part of the world, but he must cherish with a more intense and peculiar affection, the citizens of Pennsylvania and of the United States. I do not wish to see our youth educated with a single prejudice against any nation or country; but we impose a task upon human nature, repugnant alike to reason, revelation and the ordinary dimensions of the human heart, when we require him to embrace, with equal affection, the whole family of mankind. He must be taught to amass wealth, but it must be only to encrease his power of contributing to the wants and demands of the state. He must be indulged occasionally in amusements, but he must be taught that study and business should be his principal pursuits in life. Above all he must love life, and endeavour to acquire as many of its conveniences as possible by industry and economy, but he must be taught that this life "is not his own," when the safety of his country requires it. These are practicable lessons, and the history of the commonwealths of Greece and Rome show, that human nature, without the aids of Christianity, has attained these degrees of perfection.

While we inculcate these republican duties upon our pupil, we must not neglect, at the same time, to inspire him with republican principles. He must be taught that there can be no durable liberty but in a republic, and that government, like all other sciences, is of a progressive nature. The chains which have bound this science in Europe are happily unloosed in America. Here it is open to investigation and improvement. While philosophy has protected us by its discoveries from a thousand natural evils, government has unhappily followed with an unequal pace. It would be to dishonor human genius, only to name the many defects which still exist in the best systems of legislation. We daily see matter of a perishable nature rendered durable by certain chemical operations. In like manner, I conceive, that it is possible to combine power in such a way as not only to encrease the happiness, but to promote the duration of republican forms of government far beyond the terms limited for them by history, or the common opinions of mankind.

To assist in rendering religious, moral and political instruction more effectual upon the minds of our youth, it will be necessary to subject their bodies to physical discipline. To obviate the inconveniences of their studious and sedentary mode of life, they should live upon a temperate diet, consisting chiefly of broths, milk and vegetables. The black broth of Sparta, and the barley broth of Scotland, have been alike celebrated for their beneficial effects upon the minds of young people. They should avoid tasting spirituous liquors. They should also be accustomed occasionally to work with their hands, in the intervals of study, and in the busy seasons of the year in the country. Moderate sleep, silence, occasional solitude and cleanliness, should be inculcated upon them, and the utmost advantage should be taken of a proper direction of those great principles in human conduct,—sensibility, habit, imitations and association.

The influence of these physical causes will be powerful upon the intellects, as well as upon the principles and morals of young people.

To those who have studied human nature, it will not appear paradoxical to recommend, in this essay, a particular attention to vocal music. Its mechanical effects in civilizing the mind, and thereby preparing it for the influence of religion and government, have been so often felt and recorded, that it will be unnecessary to mention facts in favour of its usefulness, in order to excite a proper attention to it.

I cannot help bearing a testimony, in this place, against the custom, which prevails in some parts of America, (but which is daily falling into disuse in Europe) of crowding boys together under one roof for the purpose of education. The practice is the gloomy remains of monkish ignorance, and is as unfavorable to the improvements of the mind in useful learning, as monasteries are to the spirit of religion. I grant this mode of secluding boys from the intercourse of private families, has a tendency to make them scholars, but our business is to make them men, citizens and Christians. The vices of young people are generally learned from each other. The vices of adults seldom infect them. By separating them from each other, therefore, in their hours of relaxation from study, we secure their morals from a principal source of corruption, while we improve their manners, by subjecting them to those restraints which the difference of age and sex, naturally produce in private families.

From the observations that have been made it is plain, that I consider it is possible to convert men into republican machines. This must be done, if we expect them to perform their parts properly, in the great machine of the government of the state. That republic is sophisticated with monarchy or aristocracy that does not revolve upon the wills of the people, and these must be fitted to each other by means of education before they can be made to produce regularity and unison in government.

Having pointed out those general principles, which should be inculcated alike in all the schools of the state, I proceed now to make a few remarks upon the method of conducting, what is commonly called, a liberal or learned education in a republic.

I shall begin this part of my subject, by bearing a testimony against the common practice of attempting to teach boys the learned languages, and the arts and sciences too early in life. The first twelve years of life are barely sufficient to instruct a boy in reading, writing and arithmetic. With these, he may be taught those modern languages which are necessary for him to speak. The state of the memory, in early life, is favorable to the acquisition of languages, especially when they are conveyed to the mind, through the ear. It is, moreover, in early life only, that the organs of speech yield in such a manner as to favour the just pronunciation of foreign languages.

Too much pains cannot be taken to teach our youth to read and write our American language with propriety and elegance. The study of the Greek language constituted a material part of the literature of the Athenians, hence the sublimity, purity and immortality of so many of their writings. The advantages of a perfect knowledge of our language to young men intended for the professions of law, physic, or divinity are too obvious to be mentioned, but in a state which boasts of the first commercial city in America, I wish to see it cultivated by young men, who are intended for the compting house, for many such, I hope, will be educated in our colleges. The time is past when an academical education was thought to be unnecessary to qualify a young man for merchandize. I conceive no profession is capable of receiving more embellishments from it. The French and German languages should likewise be carefully taught in all our colleges. They abound with useful books upon all subjects. So important and necessary are those languages, that a degree should never be conferred upon a young man who cannot speak or translate them.

Connected with the study of languages is the study of eloquence. It is well known how great a part it constituted of the Roman education. It is the first accomplishment in a republic, and often sets the whole machine of government in motion. Let our youth, therefore, be instructed in this art. We do not extol it too highly when we attribute as much to the power of eloquence as to the sword, in bringing about the American Revolution.

With the usual arts and sciences that are taught in our American colleges, I wish to see a regular course of lectures given upon History and Chronology. The science of government, whether it relates to constitutions or laws, can only be advanced by a careful selection of facts, and these are to be found chiefly in history. Above all, let our youth be instructed in the history of the ancient republics, and the progress of liberty and tryanny in the different states of Europe. I wish likewise to see the numerous facts that relate to the origin and present state of commerce, together with the nature and principles of money, reduced to such a system, as to be intelligible and agreeable to a young man. If we consider the commerce of our metropolis only as the avenue of the wealth of the state, the study of it merits a place in a young man's education; but, I consider commerce in a much higher light when I recommend the study of it in republican seminaries. I view it as the best security against the influence of hereditary monopolies of land, and, therefore, the surest protection against aristocracy. I consider its effects as next to those of religion in humanizing mankind, and, lastly, I view it as the means of uniting the different nations of the world together by the ties of mutual wants and obligations.

Chemistry by unfolding to us the effects of heat and mixture, enlarges our acquaintance with the wonders of nature and the mysteries of art; hence it has become, in most of the universities of Europe, a necessary branch of a gentleman's education. In a young country, where improvements in agriculture and manufactures are so much to be desired, the cultivation of this science, which explains the principles of both of them, should be considered as an object of the utmost importance.

Again, let your youth be instructed in all the means of promoting national prosperity and independence, whether they relate to improvements in agriculture, manufactures, or inland navigation. Let him be instructed further in the general principles of legislation, whether they relate to revenue, or to the preservation of life, liberty or property. Let him be directed frequently to attend the courts of justice, where he will have the best opportunities of acquiring habits of comparing, and arranging his ideas by observing the discovery of truth, in the examination of witnesses, and where he will hear the laws of the state explained, with all the advantages of that species of eloquence which belongs to the bar. Of so much importance do I conceive it to be, to a young man, to attend occasionally to the decisions of our courts of law, that I wish to see our colleges established, only in county towns.

But further, considering the nature of our connection with the United States, it will be necessary to make our pupil acquainted with all the prerogatives of the national government. He must be instructed in the nature and variety of treaties. He must know the difference in the powers and duties of the several species of ambassadors. He must be taught wherein the obligations of individuals and of states are the same, and wherein they differ. In short, he must acquire a general knowledge of all those laws and forms, which unite the sovereigns of the earth, or separate them from each other.

I beg pardon for having delayed so long to say any thing of the separate and peculiar mode of education proper for women in a republic. I am sensible that they must concur in all our plans of education for young men, or no laws will ever render them effectual. To qualify our women for this purpose, they should not only be instructed in the usual branches of female education, but they should be taught the principles of liberty and government; and the obligations of patriotism should be inculcated upon them. The opinions and conduct of men are often regulated by the women in the most arduous ennterprizes of life; and their approbation is frequently the principal reward of the hero's dangers, and the patriot's toils. Besides, the first impressions upon the minds of children are generally derived from the women. Of how much consequence, therefore, is it in a republic, that they should think justly upon the great subject of liberty and government!

The complaints that have been made against religion, liberty and learning, have been, against each of them in a separate state. Perhaps like certain liquors, they should only be used in a state of mixture. They mutually assist in correcting the abuses, and in improving the good effects of each other. From the combined and reciprocal influence of religion, liberty and learning upon the morals, manners and knowledge of individuals, of these, upon government, and of government, upon individuals, it is impossible to measure the degrees of happiness and perfection to which mankind may be raised. For my part, I can form no ideas of the golden age, so much celebrated by the poets, more delightful, than the contemplation of that happiness which it is now in the power of the legislature of Pennsylvania to confer upon her citizens, by establishing proper modes and places of education in every part of the state.

16. An Essay on the Best System of Liberal Education (1799)[1]

SAMUEL KNOX

SECTION SECOND
ON THE QUESTION, WHETHER PUBLIC BE PREFERABLE TO PRIVATE EDUCATION

Convinced of the great advantage and importance of education, in proportion as any nation or society, of which we have any knowledge from historical records, improved in the arts of civilization and refinement, so have they been forward in encouraging and patronising seminaries of learning and systems of literary instruction. The enlightened part of the ancient world were no less sensible of the great advantages of public education, than those of the same description in the modern. And though they sometimes encouraged private tuition; yet we find from the reputation of the famous academy at Athens, that public education was most approved. Many are the illustrious characters of antiquity that bear witness to the truth of this observation. Most of those, indeed, who, at any period of the world, have made a figure in literature, acquired their knowledge under the direction of some academical institution. The justly celebrated Cicero, was so conscious of the advantage to be acquired at Athens, that he sent his son there to compleat his studies; though it is probable, that, at that time, Rome was not deficient in the means of private literary instruction.

In modern times, also, we find few of those who have distinguished themselves in the higher walks of science, but have been educated on some similar plan. Indeed, the superior advantages of academical education are sufficiently obvious. As they bid fairest for being furnished with tutors or professors of the most general

---

[1]Samuel Knox, *An Essay on the Best System of Liberal Education Adapted to the Genius of the Government of the United States* (Baltimore, 1799), Sections 2 and 3.

approved merit; and in whole abilities and character the greatest confidence may be reposed; they, thus, prevent the student from being exposed to the pedantic caprice of any tutor, whom chance, favour or necessity may have thrown in his way.

In such institutions, also, the means and apparatus for acquiring a competent knowledge of the arts and sciences, may be supposed to be more liberal and extensive, than could be expected, or indeed obtained in a domestic or private situation.

Education would diffuse its happy influence to a very contracted extent, indeed, were there no public schools or universities established by national or public encouragement.

Independent of these important considerations, *emulation,* which hath so powerful an influence on the human mind, especially in the season of youth, would lose its effects in promoting improvement, and the love of excellence, on any other plan than that of the academical. Indeed this consideration alone ought to be sufficiently decisive in its favour.

Love of excellence predominates in every uncorrupted youthful breast; and where this principle is under the conduct of impartial and skilful directors, it is observed to have the happiest effects in promoting that intensity of application and persevering industry, which the more abstruse and arduous departments of science necessarily require.

Granting that something resembling emulation may be excited even on a private plan of education, yet it is manifest that the great variety of abilities and genius which the university or academy exhibits must afford a much greater field for competition; as well as such public and flattering prospects of reward as are the principal incitements to a laudable emulation and love of excellence.

It is commonly observed, and perhaps, with some share of justice, that the man of the world has, in many respects, the advantage of the mere scholar; and that though a long and close attention to books and study may render him master of arts and sciences; yet he may still remain ignorant of many accomplishments, without which it is scarce profitable to pass through the world with safety, satisfaction or advantage. This is obviously the effect of the scholar's having his mind or ideas habitually applied to the same objects; and it is undeniable that this consequence of a close application to literary acquisition may be much more effectually checked or prevented by a course of public, than private

131

education. That diversity of character and variety of manners and conduct, together with other observations, which the former affords, tends, in a high degree, to wear off that studious and aukward air which is apt to be rather confirmed than diminished by the latter.

Another argument in favour of an academical education is, that such as are tutored in private are apt to form too high an opinion of their own attainments or abilities. Owing to the want of an opportunity of observing the abilities or exertions of others, it is easy to conceive that such may most probably be the consequence of that mode of instruction. It is but just to observe that to this cause we may assign that arrogance, pedantry, dogmatism and conceit that too often disgrace the scholar, who, without rivalship or competition, hath been accustomed to listen only to his own praise.

The academic school has, also, the peculiar means of affording youth an opportunity of forming such friendships and connections as often in a literary and interested view contribute eminently to their future prosperity and happiness. In that season, the youthful breast glowing with every generous, friendly and benevolent feeling is generally most attached to those who discover the same amiable qualities and disposition. Hence friendships have been formed and cemented, which no circumstance or accident, during their future lives, could intirely dissolve. The story of the two Wesminster scholars, in the civil war between Charles the first of England and the parliament is well known.

It is true that many object to public plans of education, because that from their situation in populous towns, and the various complexion of the many students who attend, opportunites are thereby given for corruption, by scenes of vice and example of debauchery.

It may with equal truth, however, be replied to this that, there are few domestic situations so private as not to admit of ground for the same objections. The first of these, as far as situation is concerned might be easily remedied – But it requires no very elaborate proof to manifest that the most dangerous temptations to vice more effectually succeed in the private and retired shades of bad example, and domestic indulgence, than in the social scene, bustling croud or public assembly.

Another objection to an academical plan of education, has been suggested, on account of the division that must necessarily take place in the attention of the tutors or professors, from the great number of students that may be under their care. But it has been already shewn that in faithful and skilful hands this may rather tend to forward their proficiency than otherwise. The partial abuse of any system by one or more individuals ought certainly to bring no discredit to the plan or institution; neither ought it, in justice, to furnish any argument against its merits, or even excellence.

The celebrated Locke himself not excepted, we find very few who have attempted to offer any plausible objections to a public education; or in preference to a private any argument in its favour, who were not themselves indebted to some academical institution even for being qualified to reason upon the subject. The good effects of the one they had experienced, of which Locke, in particular, affords an illustrious testimony; those they would ascribe to the other could be but little better than mere theory, or fanciful speculation. Upon the whole, it appears that there are many and various arguments in favour of an academical, as preferable to a private education; and that any objections that can be offered against the former, are almost all, in an equal degree, applicable to the latter. One conclusive argument, however, in favour of public education, arises from its becoming an object of national patronage and encouragement, on some uniform and approved plan or institution. It is from this view that education might be made to assume a still higher degree of importance in its influence on human happiness, in those advantages which it holds out to individuals or the nation in general. It is hence too that the best means would be furnished for distinguishing literary genius and merit; and consequently pointing out to public view such talents as are best fitted to fill the various stations and offices which the different exigences of the state, and the many departments of society require.

SECTION THIRD
THE IMPORTANCE OF ESTABLISHING
A SYSTEM OF NATIONAL EDUCATION

When we take into consideration the many great exertions, and laudable institutions which various commonwealths or nations have devised and adopted for the general benefit, in framing and

133

maintaining wholesome laws and government, it would appear, in some degree, unaccountable that little hath yet been done in promoting some general plan of education equally suitable and salutary to the various citizens of the same state of community.

It is true that in the history of some of the most celebrate commonwealths of antiquity we find some such plans were adopted for the improvement of youth; but so circumscribed was the state of literature in those times; and such the circumstances of those commonwealths that their plans of education were rather military schools preparing them for the camp, either for self defence, or for butchering the human species, than seminaries suited to literary acquisition; the conduct of life; or the improvement of the human mind. This observation, however, extends no farther than as it applies to institutions of national education; and is by no means considered as applicable to the schools of the philosophers; or of many celebrated orators, grammarians and rhetoricians of the ancient world. If some of the states or nations of antiquity had been possessed of the means which we enjoy, since the invention of printing, of diffusing literary knowledge, it is more than probable, from what they have done, that they would have availed themselves of them in a manner superior to what we have yet accomplished.

In our own times and language, we have been favoured by ingenious men with several excellent treatises on the subject of education. The greater part of these, however, are rather speculative theories, adapted to the conduct of life and manners; than applicable to the practical diffusion of literary knowledge. What has lately been done in France excepted, I know of no plan devised by individuals, or attempted by any commonwealth in modern times, that effectually tends to the establishment of any uniform, regular system of nation education. Universities or colleges hitherto instituted by the pride or patronage of princes or other individuals, are in general too partial either in their situation or their regulations to extend the necessary advantages of literature to the more remote parts of the community for which they were intended. Immense revenues and donations have, indeed, been applied to the founding of such seminaries, while the poor, and such as most wanted literary instruction, or the means of acquiring it, have been left almost totally neglected. A few, indeed, whom wealth and leasure enabled, might drink deep of the Pierian spring, while the diffusion of its salutary streams through every department of the commonwealth has been either neglected, or considered as of inferior importance.

It must be allowed that these remarks may, in some measure, apply to any plan of public education that can possibly be formed. It is not, perhaps, possible to establish any system that can render education equally convenient and equally attainable by every individual of a nation in all their various situations and circumstances.

This observation must be particularly applicable to the condition of the *United States* of America and the widely dispersed situations of their citizens. In undertakings, however, of the first national importance, difficulties ought not to discourage. It does not appear more impracticable to establish an uniform system of national education, than a system of legislation or civil government; provided such a system could be digested as might justly merit, and meet with general approbation.

The good effects of such a system are almost self-evident. In the present state of education however ably and successfully conducted in particular local situations, the nation is, in a great measure, incapable of judging its condition or effects. Diversity of modes of education, also, tend, not only to confound and obstruct its operation and improvement; but also give occasion to many other inconveniences and disagreeable consequences that commonly arise in the various departments of civil society; or even the polished enjoyments of social intercourse. But were an approved system of national education to be established, all these imperfections of its present state, would, in a great measure, be remedied, and at the same time accompanied with many peculiar advantages, hitherto unexperienced in the instruction and improvement of the human mind.

Great, surely, must be the difference between two communities, in the one of which, good laws are executed only in some particular situations, while in others they are almost totally neglected; and in the other are universally established with equal and impartial authority. Such, surely, must be difference between the effects of education when abandoned to the precarious uncertainty of casual, partial or local encouragement; and of that which has been established uniformly and generally by the united wisdom and exertions of a whole nation. In such a state it is elevated to no more than that importance to which it is justly intitled; and it is to be hoped that the close of the eighteenth century will be so enlightened as to see education encouraged and established, as well by this as other nations, in such a manner as to be considered next to the administration of just and wholesome laws, the first great object of national patronage and attention.

The history of human society informs us, what have been the effects of nations uniting their zealous exertions for the accomplishment of any great object to which they were directed. The happiest effects, then, might surely be expected from the united public exertions of this country in the combined cause of public virtue and literary improvement. The patronage or encouragement of the one, has certainly a very intimate connection with that of the other, more especially if it be allowed that in the same system may be comprehended the institutes of morals and the principles of civil liberty.

In a country circumstanced and situated as the United States of America, a considerable local diversity in improvement, whether with respect to morals or literature, must be the consequence of such a wide extent of territory, inhabited by citizens blending together almost all the various manners and customs of every country in Europe. Nothing, then, surely, might be supposed to have a better effect towards harmonizing the whole in these important views than an *uniform system of national education.*

The late much celebrated Doctor Price, in a discourse delivered before the trustees of the academy at Hackney, on the evidences of a future period of improvement in the state of mankind, earnestly urges an improvement in the state of education. He observes that it is a subject with which the world is not yet sufficiently acquainted; and believes there may remain a secret in it yet to be discovered which will contribute more than any thing to the amendment of mankind; and adds, that he who would advance one step towards making this discovery would deserve better of the world than all the learned scholars and professors who have hitherto existed.

It requires, then, little demonstration, I think, to prove, that if a justly approved plan of national education constitute not the secret alluded to by the Doctor, it is at least the most important step towards it that hath ever yet been taken. National exertions directed to this important object could not fail to have the happiest effects on society. The rays of knowledge and instruction would then be enabled to disipate every partial and intervening cloud from our literary hemisphere, and the whole community receive a more equal distribution, as well as a more effectual and salutary display of their enlightening influence. . . .

17. REMARKS ON EDUCATION (1798)[1]

SAMUEL HARRISON SMITH

II. SHOULD EDUCATION BE PUBLIC OR PRIVATE?

The most distinguished talents have been engaged in the discussion of this subject; and here, as in most controversies of a speculative cast, we find a great diversity of sentiment. Quintillian and Milton are warm in their eulogium on a public, while Locke is equally animated in his praise of a private system of education. The great argument, which may be called the centre of all others urged, is the production of emulation by a public education; while the great objection made to public education, is the sacrifice, alleged to be produced, of morality and honesty.

As there is, undoubtedly, truth on both sides, it becomes necessary to consider what weight the alleged advantages and disadvantages ought to possess in determining the preference of the judgment to one over the other system. It will, perhaps, be possible to reconcile the apparently conflicting ideas, in such a way, as to make the result of benefit produced infinitely larger than the risque of injury sustained.

The early period of life is under parental and especially maternal control. The solicitude of a mother is now the best, the only protection, which the child can receive. Some years elapse, before the mind seems capable of being impressed with true or false knowledge in a degree sufficient to influence its future expansion, and during this period, it is fortunate that we have not occasion to regret the unenlightened state of the female mind. But though these years do not mark much strength of mind, yet they rapidly unfold and form the disposition, which seldom fails to receive a virtuous bias from a mother, who, however vicious herself, feels

---

[1] Samuel Harrison Smith, *Remarks on Education: Illustrating the Close Connection Between Virtue and Wisdom* (Philadelphia, 1798), Part II.

138

deeply interested in the virtue of her offspring. Hence those amiable affections are excited which are the ornament of human nature. Before the age of five the child seldom feels a disposition to do an immoral thing; and even if it should exhibit such a symptom, the temper is so flexible, that it easily yields to a more virtuous direction.

The young mind, having passed five years of its existence, free from much corruption, and a plan of education being now commenced, it becomes an object of consideration whether the child should remain with its parents, or be separated from them.

As a large portion of parental solicitude still exists, which alone seems capable of securing a vigilant attention to those little indications of temper and mind which now so profusely appear, it seems highly important that the child should still remain under the immediate control of parental authority. That affection which, on the part of the child, is but half formed, will have time and opportunity to gain strength, a love of domestic tranquility will be produced, and both these principles will form a firm shield to virtue.

On the other hand, the daily attendance at school will withdraw the mind of the child from an *entire* dependence on its parents; will place it in situations demanding the exercise of its faculties; and will strengthen, instead of weakening, its attachment to domestic scenes. To be deprived of that which we love is in some degree painful to us all; to children it is painful in the highest degree. Yet a habit of voluntary or compulsory abstinence from pleasure is absolutely necessary to human happiness.

The child, in this situation, having its time divided between school, the hours of diversion, and those spent in the house of its parents, will, perhaps, remain as free from a prostration of morals, as can be expected in infancy. This, indeed, is the plan, which universally prevails in the civilized world, and its universality is certainly some argument in its favour.

Let this plan, partly domestic and partly public, be pursued till the mind begins bodly to expand itself, and to indicate an ability and an inclination to think for itself. The commencement of this capacity of combining ideas takes place about the age of ten. We have now reached the period which claims the closest attention. The mind now feels its vigour, and delights in displaying it. Ambition is kindled, emulation burns, a desire of superiority and distinction are roused.

This, then, appears to be the era, if ever, of public education. The indulgence of parental tenderness should now be exchanged for the patient and unobstructed exercise of the mental powers. Let us attend to the advantages of the two rival systems at this period.

With regard to the plan of public Education;

1. Emulation is excited. Without numbers there can be no emulation. It is founded on the love of distinction. In a private family this distinction cannot be acquired.

2. An attention to study, when the child is removed from the house of its parent, may be uninterrupted; whereas while it resides with him a thousand trifling, menial avocations, will always take precedence. From this results the conviction in the mind of the child that study is altogether subordinate to the objects to which it is compelled to attend.

3. But, above every other consideration, the system of public education, inspires a spirit of independent reflection and conduct. Removed from a scene, where it has little occasion to think, and less to act, the child now finds itself placed in a situation free from rigid parental authority. Placed in the midst of objects of pursuit, its preference of one object to another, is often determined by its own volition. Hence reflection is excited; and with children there is certainly no danger of too much thought; — the only apprehension is that there being too little.

Let a spirit of independent reflection animate a large number of even youthful minds, and the acquisition of useful truths will soon be rapid. This spirit, aided by the instruction of enlightened precepts, must give an undeniable ascendency to the public over the private plan.

Error is never more dangerous than in the mouth of a parent. The child, from the dawn of its existence, accustomed to receive as undoubted every idea from this quarter, seldom, if ever, questions the truth of what is told. Hence prejudices are as hereditary as titles; and you may almost universally know the sentiments of the son by those of the father. Now by education remote from parental influence, the errors of the father cease to be entailed upon the child — Still farther, the child, having acquired true ideas, very often, from the superior force of truth, dissipates the errors of his parent by the remonstrances of reason.

As education professes to improve the state and character of men, and not barely to oppose their declension, it must follow that domestic education is improper, as it does no more, even if successful, than secure the last at the expence of the first.

When we consider the argument urged against public education (for only one is urged with any tenacity) we shall find that the evil it deprecates arises from the imperfection of human nature, more than from any appropriate and exclusive property of public education.

"Whenever there are numbers of children assembled together, there will be mischief and immorality." This is true; but is it so extensively true as to countervail the numerous advantages which have been but partially stated? Is it equal to the injury sustained by the mechanical adoption of parental error or vice? More mischief, more immorality, have sprung from this source, than from the one complained of. On the other hand does not the conduct of children, in a public institution, in a considerable degree, resemble the actions of men in the world? The knowledge, therefore, thus acquired, though sometimes at the expence of honesty and truth, must be deemed of some importance. It is probable that it arose from the spirit of their plans of education, that Sparta was the last nation that fell a prey to the Macedonians, and Crete to the Romans. The Samnites, Montesquieu observes, had the same institutions, which furnished those very Romans with the subject of four and twenty triumphs. Indeed, though it be probable, that no plan can ever be devised, which shall admit all the advantages of an honorable and zealous competition, and exclude all the injuries heretofore so closely allied as to be deemed inseparable, yet some improvement ought not to be despaired of, amidst the universal tendency of every thing to amelioration.

The discussion of this subject appears in some measure superseded, and the preference unequivocally established of the public over the private plan, by the small expence of the first, compared with the impracticable expence of the last. If parents educated their children, the hours withdrawn from business would alone impoverish them.

Before a detail is given of the course of education proposed, it may be proper concisely to state the points, which it has been the object of the preceding remarks to establish.

In the first place, virtue and wisdom have been deemed to possess an inseparable connection, and the degree and efficiency of the one has been decided to depend on the measure and vigor of the other. From this proposition the inference is deduced that a nation cannot possibly be too enlightened, and that the most energetic zeal is necessary to make it sufficiently so for the great interests of virtue and happiness.

Secondly. That it is the duty of a nation to superintend and even to coerce the education of children, and that high considerations of expediency not only justify, but dictate the establishment of a system, which shall place under a control, independent of, and superior to, parental authority, the education of children.

Thirdly. The preference has been given at a certain age to public education over domestic education.

Fourthly. The period of education recommended has been fixed at an age so early, as to anticipate the reign of prejudice, and to render the first impressions made on the mind subservient to virtue and truth.

Guided by these principles it is proposed:

I. That the period of education be from 5 to 18.

II. That every male child, without exception, be educated.

III. That the instructor in every district be directed to attend to the faithful execution of this injunction. That it be made punishable by law in a parent to neglect offering his child to the preceptor for instruction.

IV. That every parent, who wishes to deviate in the education of his children from the established system, be made responsible for devoting to the education of his children as much time as the established system prescribes.

V. That a fund be raised from the citizens in the ratio of their property.

VI. That the system be composed of primary schools; of colleges; and of a *University*.

VII. That the primary schools be divided into two clases; the first consisting of boys from 5 to 10 years old; the second consisting of boys from 10 to 18. — And that these classes be subdivided, if necessary, into smaller ones.

VIII. That the instruction given to the first class be the rudiments of the English language, Writing, Arithmetic, the commission to memory and delivery of select pieces, inculcating moral duties, describing natural phenomena, or displaying correct fancy.

IX. Though this class is formed of boys between the age of 5 and 10 years, yet should rapid acquisitions be made in the above branches of knowledge at an earlier age than that of 10, the boy is to be promoted into the second class.

X. The most solemn attention must be paid to avoid instilling into the young mind any ideas or sentiments whose truth is not unequivocally established by the undissenting suffrage of the enlightened and virtuous part of mankind.

XI. That the instruction given to the second class be an extended and more correct knowledge of Arithmetic; of the English language, comprising plain rules of criticism and composition; the concise study of General History, and a more detailed acquaintance with the history of our own country; of Geography; of the laws of nature, practically illustrated. That this practical illustration consist in an actual devotion of a portion of time to agriculture and mechanics, under the superintendance of the preceptor. That it be the duty of this class to commit to memory, and frequently to repeat, the constitution, and the fundamental laws of the United States.

XII. That each primary school consist of 50 boys.

XIII. That such boys be admitted into the college as shall be deemed by the preceptor to be worthy, from a manifestation of industry and talents, of a more extended education. That one boy be annually chosen out of the second class of each primary school for this preferment.

XIV. That the students at college so promoted be supported at the public expence, but that such other students may be received, as shall be maintained by their parents.

XV. That the studies of the college consist in a still more extended acquaintance with the above stated branches of knowledge, together with the cultivation of polite literature.

XVI. That each college admit 200 students.

XVII. That an opportunity be furnished to those who have the ability, without interfering with the established studies, of acquiring a knowledge of the modern languages, music, drawing, dancing, and fencing; and that the permission to cultivate these accomplishments be held forth as the reward of diligence and talents.

XVIII. That a National University be established, in which the highest branches of science and literature shall be taught. That it consist of students promoted from the colleges. That one student out of ten be annually chosen for this promotion by a majority of the suffrages of the professors of the college to which he may belong.

*　*　*

The necessary expence must, then, be submitted to without reluctance. On an enquiry into the sources of taxation we shall find more encouragement than discouragement. When it is stated that the wealth of the state of Pennsylvania alone may be estimated at more than 400 million of dollars, it will at once be seen how little the most liberal sum, raised for the purpose of education, would partake of burthen or oppression. When on the other hand the greatness of the object is correctly estimated and truly felt, all prejudices ought at once to be annihilated; and it is only doing justice to the patriotism of our citizens to believe that they would be annihilated.

Two subjects connected with a general system of education, viz. female instruction, and that which has been called ornamental, have been avoided. Both of these certainly involve very important considerations. But in the existing diversity of opinion respecting the nature and extent of the first, such coincidence and agreement as to produce a system must absolutely be despaired of. It is sufficient, perhaps, for the present that the improvement of women is marked by a rapid progress, and that a prospect opens equal to their most ambitious desires. — With regard to ornamental instruction, it would seem to rest more on principles of expediency than of necessity. It may, also, be considered as a kind of mental luxury, which like that of a grosser nature, will imperceptibly, but surely, by the allurements and pleasures which its cultivation holds forth, insinuate itself into general acceptance. But as it is of some consequence, that a plan of instruction in the polite arts should be devised, which so far from being incompatible with, might aid the promotion of branches of knowledge more immediately necessary, it is proposed, that a limited opportunity be offered in the colleges, and a full one in the university, to become acquainted with the principles as well as execution of every polite
144

art. The effects of these elegant pursuits on the mind and temper are of the most beneficial nature. They may be emphatically denominated the finished offspring of civilization and refinement. Besides, a system of sufficient comprehensiveness should contain a department for every species of genius. Every spark of mental energy should be cherished. The mind should be left free to chuse its favourite object, and when chosen should find the means of prosecuting it with ardour.

Such is the system proposed. Its imperfections are beyond doubt numerous. Of this fact, no man can be more sensible than their author. In the discussion of a subject, which has ably employed the pens of the most distinguished writers, without producing a general conviction of the preference of one plan over another, it became the writer to exercise as much diffidence as consists with the exposition of truth. If he has manifested in any part of the preceding speculations the appearance of arrogant confidence in his own sentiments, he trusts it will be ascribed to his impressions of the importance of the subject, and not to a vain attachment to his peculiar ideas. He who is solemnly impressed with interesting truths, will think with energy, and express his thoughts with decision.

Notwithstanding the universal agreement of all men in this country as to the necessity of a reform in education, so essentially do their professions disagree with their actions, that nothing short of the commanding eloquence of truth, without cessation thundered on their ears, can produce that concurrence of action, that unity of effort, which shall give efficiency to a wise system of education. Let then the voice of the good man mingle with that of the wise in announcing the necessity of speedily adopting such a measure. Instead of one party denouncing another for equivocal political crimes, let all parties unite in attesting their patriotism by their cooperating efforts in so great a cause. Is it a question with any man whether our liberties are secure? Let him know that they depend upon the knowledge of the people, and that this knowledge depends upon a comprehensive and energetic system of education. It is true that some nations have been free without possessing a large portion of illumination; but their freedom has been precarious and accidental, and it has fallen as it rose.

The two things which we are most interested in securing are harmony at home, and respect abroad. By calling into active oper-

145

ation the mental resources of a nation, our political institutions will be rendered more perfect, ideas of justice will be diffused, the advantages of the undisturbed enjoyment of tranquillity and industry will be perceived by every one, and our mutual dependence on each other will be rendered conspicuous. The great result will be harmony. Discord and strife have always proceeded from, or risen upon, ignorance and passion. When the first has ceased to exist, and the last shall be virtuously directed, we shall be deprived of every source of misunderstanding. The sword would not need a scabbard, were all men enlightened by a conviction of their true interests.

Harmony at home must produce respect abroad. For the era is at hand when America may hold the tables of justice in her hand, and proclaim them to the unresisting observance of the civilized world. Her numbers and her wealth vie with each other in the rapidity of their increase. But the immutable wisdom of her institutions will have a more efficient moral influence, than her physical strength. Possessed of both she cannot fail to assume, without competition, the station assigned her by an overruling power.

Such is the bright prospect of national dignity and happiness, if America give to her youth the advantages of a liberal and just education. On the other hand, should avarice, prejudice, or malice, frustrate this great object, and should a declension of knowledge, gradually, but not the less decisively as to a future period, be suffered to triumph, the prospect is gloomy and dreadful. Gigantic power misapplied, towering ambition unsatiated with criminal gratification, avarice trampling poverty under foot, mark but a few of the dark shades which will, in all probability, envelop our political horizon. On such an event, we must expect the miseries of oppression at home, and conquest abroad.

It may interest the attention, as it certainly will amuse the fancy, to trace the effects of the preceding principles of education on a future age. It has been observed that however virtuous, enlightened and vigorous our first efforts to aggrandize the human character, it were, notwithstanding, folly to expect the celerity of preternatural agency. A system founded on true principles must gradually and cautiously eradicate error, and substitute truth. The period, will, therefore, be remote before the world is benefited by its complete developement. . . .

146

18. Constitutional Provisions for Education (1777 – 1819)[1]

CONSTITUTION OF GEORGIA, 1777

ARTICLE LIV. Schools shall be erected in each county, and supported at the general expense of the State, as the legislature shall hereafter point out.

CONSTITUTION OF MASSACHUSETTS, 1780

CHAPTER V, SECTION II. — The Encouragement of Literature, Etc.

Wisdom and knowledge, as well as virtue, diffused generally among the body of the people, being necessary for the preservation of their rights and liberties; and as these depend on spreading the opportunities and advantages of education in the various parts of the country, and among the different orders of the people, it shall be the duty of legislatures and magistrates, in all future periods of this commonwealth, to cherish the interests of literature and the sciences, and all seminaries of them; especially the university at Cambridge, public schools and grammar schools in the towns; to encourage private societies and public institutions, rewards and immunities, for the promotion of agriculture, arts, sciences, commerce, trades, manufactures, and a natural history of the country; to countenance and inculcate the principles of humanity and general benevolence, public and private charity, industry and frugality, honesty and punctuality in their dealings; sincerity, good humor, and all social affections, and generous sentiments, among the people.

AMENDMENTS. ARTICLE XVIII. All moneys raised by taxation in the

[1]Francis N. Thorpe (Ed.), *The Federal and State Constitutions, Colonial Charters, and Other Organic Laws of the States, Territories, and Colonies Now or Heretofore Forming the United States* (Washington: U.S. GPO, 1909), II, 784, 1068–69; III, 1161, 1907–08, 1918; V, 2911–12; VI, 3770–71.

towns and cities for the support of public schools, and all moneys which may be appropriated by the state for the support of common schools, shall be applied to, and expended in, no other schools than those which are conducted according to law, under the order and superintendence of the authorities of the town or city in which the money is to be expended; and such moneys shall never be appropriated to any religious sect for the maintenance, exclusively, of its own school.

CONSTITUTION OF VERMONT, 1793

CHAPTER II, SECTION 41. Laws for the encouragement of virtue and prevention of vice and immorality, ought to be constantly kept in force, and duly executed: and a competent number of schools ought to be maintained in each town, for the convenient instruction of youth: and one or more grammar schools be incorporated and properly supported, in each County in this State.

CONSTITUTION OF OHIO, 1802

ARTICLE VIII, SECTION 25. That no law shall be passed to prevent the poor in the several counties and townships within this State, from an equal participation in the schools, academies, colleges, and universities within this State, which are endowed, in whole or in part, from the revenues arising from the donations made by the United States for the support of schools and colleges; and the doors of the said schools, academies, and universities shall be open for the reception of scholars, students, and teachers of every grade, without any distinction or preference whatever, contrary to the intent for which the said donations were made.

CONSTITUTION OF INDIANA, 1816

ARTICLE IX. SECTION 1. Knowledge and learning, generally diffused through a community, being essential to the preservation of a free government, and spreading the opportunities and advantages of education through the various parts of the country being highly conducive to this end, it shall be the duty of the General Assembly to provide, by law, for the improvement of such lands as are or hereafter may be granted by the United States to this State for the use of schools, and to apply any funds which may be raised from such lands or from any other quarter to the accomplishment of the grand object for which they are or may be intended. But no lands granted for the use of schools or seminaries of learning shall be sold by authority of this State prior to the year 1820; and the moneys which may be raised out of the sale of any such lands, or otherwise obtained for the purposes aforesaid, shall be and remain a fund for the exclusive purpose of promoting the interest of literature and the sciences, and for the support of seminaries and public schools. The General Assembly shall, from time to time, pass such laws as shall be calculated to encourage intellectual, scientifical and agricultural improvements, by allowing rewards and immunities for the promotion and improvement of arts, sciences, commerce, manufacture and natural history; and to countenance and encourage the principles of humanity, honesty, industry and morality.

SECTION 2. It shall be the duty of the General Assembly, as soon as circumstances will permit, to provide, by law, for a general system of education, ascending in a regular gradation from township schools to a State University, wherein tuition shall be gratis, and equally open to all.

SECTION 3. And for the promotion of such salutary end, the money which shall be paid, as an equivalent, by persons exempt from military duty, except in times of war, shall be exclusively, and in equal proportion, applied to the support of County Seminaries; also, all fines assessed for any breach of the penal laws, shall be applied to said seminaries in the County wherein they shall be assessed. . . .

CONSTITUTION OF MAINE, 1819

ARTICLE VIII. Literature. A general diffusion of the advantages of education being essential to the preservation of the rights and liberties of the people; to promote this important object, the Legislature are authorized, and it shall be their duty to require, the several towns to make suitable provision, at their own expense, for the support and maintenance of public schools; and it shall further be their duty to encourage and suitably endow, from time to time, as the circumstances of the people may authorize, all academies, colleges and seminaries of learning within the State; provided, that no donation, grant or endowment shall at any time be made by the Legislature to any literary institution now established, or which may hereafter be established, unless, at the time of making such endowment, the Legislature of the State shall have the right to grant any further powers to alter, limit or restrain any of the powers vested in, any such literary institution, as shall be judged necessary to promote the best interests thereof.

PART III:

THE FREE SCHOOL MOVEMENT

BY THE mid-nineteenth century, the public school systems of modern America were taking shape and form. Free universal education on the elementary level existed in principle in most of the northern and western states. The triumph had come not suddenly but through the constant efforts of individuals, organizations, and societies determined to give youth, regardless of their social and economic origins and rank, the opportunity for free education. The free school movement is significant, not only because it established the idea of free universal education, but also because it exemplified the reform spirit that swept through the nation in the decades preceding the Civil War. And it is best described in terms of the intellectual milieu of that period.

The belief in progress, the desire for equalitarianism, and the fervor and zeal of the adherents of various causes all help to explain the amazing accomplishments in this fascinating era of hope and faith. No field of human activity was left untouched; no group of society was ignored in the humanitarian strivings of so many. The orphaned, the poor, the insane, the imprisoned, the females, the workingmen, the Negroes—freed and enslaved—all received the attention and labors of the reformers. And always the goal was improvement: remaking the man-made institutions, seeking solutions to the ills of life, attempting to create the best of all worlds. The world was their field, and mankind was their immediate concern. The widely diversified group of reformers were dedicated missionaries working for a higher, though secular, cause: the improvement of society and its institutions.

No other era in American history was so charged with militancy, so intense with enthusiasm, and so dedicated to causes as this one. In such an atmosphere transcendentalism could take hold and flourish among the intelligentsia, and frontier revivalism with its promises of equality to all men in achieving salvation could spread. Andrew Jackson, symbol of the common man, could attain the highest office in the land; and Robert Owen, Bronson Alcott, George Ripley, and a host of other visionaries could carry on their Utopian experiments in living. The individual states could undergo a second revolution in revising and rewriting their constitutions in an effort to fulfill the democratic promise of an earlier age; and reformers and reform groups could give their time, their energies, their leadership, even their wealth in an effort to rid society of its ills and evils and to achieve for man equal opportunities and fair and humane treatment. Ralph Waldo Emerson, the philosopher of the romantic ideal and himself an ardent reformer, expressed both the spirit of the age and the means of achieving heaven on earth: "What is man born for but to be a Reformer, a Remaker of what man has made."

Such was the spirit of the age which nurtured equalitarianism in education and brought it to fulfillment by the middle years of the century. The idea of the necessity of education for the welfare of the individual, the society, and the nation was a well established and accepted concept among many of the political and intellectual leaders. The free school movement was the implementation of theories that had long been expressed and even experimented with for several decades. The movement evolved not from the colonial heritage, which emphasized class differences and parental responsibility, but rather from the ideas of the revolutionary decades and the enlightenment as they developed into the early nineteenth century's faith, optimism, and belief in progress.

To describe and analyze the free school movement in detail would require a study of the developments in each state over a thirty- or forty-year period. Free public education came in stages, and the basic victory of this period was in the eradication of pauper education long practiced in the colonies and in the states, and in the establishment by legislative or constitutional means of a system of free schools open to all classes. The refinements of American public education were to evolve slowly in these and subsequent decades through the development of the district system, the creation of state boards to supervise local institutions, the improvement of teacher training, and compulsory school attendance laws. But the principle existed: Americans were to receive elementary education at public expense.

Despite the high degree of decentralization in the evolution of American public education, a striking similarity among states did develop. This was in large part because the new midwestern states imitated the systems taking shape in the older northeastern states, which had been among the first to practice theories long discussed by reformers and other leaders. Massachusetts, which had experimented with the common school in colonial times, set

154

the pace under the leadership of James Carter and Horace Mann in establishing a state system of free schools under a central agency. Pennsylvania and New York joined Massachusetts as models for other states, so that in time there was a degree of uniformity in educational organization and practices among the various states.

In analyzing the factors which promoted the free school movement, it is necessary to consider both the general acceptance of free public education as a universal panacea and the specific conditions which demanded educational change and reform. Everything about the reform spirit—its faith in man, its belief in progress and in the perfectability of institutions, its desire to elevate and dignify man—rested on the premise that education was the most effective and efficient means of improving American society and preserving and promoting democratic values and ideals. Such was the philosophical and ideological basis for the free school movement, but of equal importance were the existing practices that brought forth the leadership and the organization which made possible the improvement in education.

Certainly educational conditions themselves were out of step with the growing equalitarianism. Class differentiation in education flourished everywhere. Practically every state constitution had incorporated the colonial system of providing education only for the dependent classes. Thus public and free education was equivalent to pauper education, a stigma strenuously resisted and criticized. Even in such progressive states as Pennsylvania, the number of children not attending schools was astonishingly high. With the growing complexities of social organization, the family and church could no longer play a dominant educational role, and the apprenticeship system had ceased to provide training in the letters. Through the years formal education provided by the schools had steadily gained in importance; yet existing practices were completely inadequate and contradictory to the ideals of an aggressive, democratic society who demanded equality of opportunity in the educational realm as they were achieving such equality in the political world. Vox populi played a determining role in the evolution of the free school system. With the extension of the franchise to the nonpropertied, the working class could use the ballot box to seek those reforms and innovations which would eventually contribute to their rise and prosperity. Education—free schooling of good quality with no stigma of pauperism attached —was to the nineteenth-century man the most important avenue for improving his lot and rising in the social and economic world.

The composition of the supporters of the free school movement is diversified and varied, but the role played by the working class is of utmost significance. And that part was played not so much by the class as a whole—except in terms of voting strength—as it was by the famous, though short-lived, workingmen's organizations, institutions, and finally political parties.

The urban centers of Boston, New York, Philadelphia, and Washington were the nuclei out of which the workingmen's reform movement would emanate. Here the number of mechanics was steadily increasing; here the social and economic problems connected with urban development were becoming severe; here the leadership that could bind the workingmen into organizations for improvement, for social and economic reform, and for political action was emerging. The premature flowering of the early trade unions left little imprint on American labor developments, but the activity of the workingmen's associations in the realm of social, educational, and economic reform is of great importance. Through their voting strength, through organization as political parties, through constant agitation in newspapers, through publication of special studies, through petitions and memorials to the state legislatures—these groups conformed to the pattern of humanitarian and social reform and exemplified the democratic impulse in the political realm. Their demands ranged widely: reform in taxation, direct elections, abolition of imprisonment for debt, and above all free universal education and the improvement of education. "Next to life and liberty, we consider education the greatest blessing to mankind," was the fundamental principle of the workingmen's movement.

To select representative items from this movement to promote education is a difficult matter, because of the overwhelming amount of material available. The newspapers sponsored by the associations, the numerous petitions and memorials, the special reports, and the writings of the leaders form a superb and extensive source of information for the free school movement and reforms in general. These writings are full of fervor and hope and

156

occasionally are militant and aggressive (20). *The Working Man's Advocate* (New York) is a fine example of the both lofty and immediate goals of the Association for the Protection of Industry and for the Promotion of National Education (19). The article reveals the methods used by the organization and explains its ultimate purpose. The tone throughout is highly democratic; the fight is for equality, against privilege of any kind.

The selection reprinted from *The Philadelphia Mechanics Free Press* is a report of the Committee of Philadelphia in 1829 on the educational situation in the state (21). Here the approach is factual: a black picture of "the degraded state of education in Pennsylvania" as a result of the law of 1809 which granted free training to children whose parents' status was that of poverty as determined by the assessors. The newspaper strenuously attacks "pauperism in education" and demands reforms, using both idealistic and practical arguments. There is "no real liberty without diffusion of real intelligence." This is a popular theme that runs throughout the workingmen's efforts to attain free public education.

An excerpt from Stephen Simpson's *Working Man's Manual,* a handbook of the movement, is a statement of the wage-earners' outlook on education (22). The essay presents the entire range of arguments for a system of free schools. Simpson, as spokesman for the workingmen's movement, first demands education as a right; he then strengthens his viewpoint by pointing out the importance and value of an educated citizenry to society. He sees education as a means of preserving republican government, of achieving human happiness and promoting virtue, and of increasing the moral energies of the nation through the development of human character. He caps his argument by emphasizing the value of education in eliminating the evils existing in society, such as intemperance. Education, as Simpson presents it, is the universal panacea to all society's ills and the stepping-stone toward a more perfect social order. "The odious system of charity schools" had to be eliminated if this new world was to be achieved. A nationalistic tone is apparent in his insistence that the states establish a system suited to the needs of the American people rather than imitating English and European types.

Simpson's *Manual* is a superb summary of the various arguments and attitudes of the workingmen's groups. It is emotional and stirring in its demands for freedom and equality for the worker. It is noteworthy, however, that Simpson's main concern was for the working class as future citizens of the commonwealth. He is an ardent reformer in these terms, but represents the conservative and traditional viewpoint in regard to another reform movement of this era, that of educational equality for the female. He even goes to the extent of rejecting the idea of common school education for girls, a practice that was fairly widespread. He regards the female's position in society to be outside the realm of public duties; therefore her education need not be a public responsibility.

The close relationship between the workingmen's groups and the accomplishments in free education in Massachusetts, Pennsylvania, and New York is apparent, but the question remains as to what role these groups actually played in the final victories. Were the wage-earners' organizations the principal force behind the educational achievements, or were they simply the agitators and advertisers for reform? Were the workingmen's groups and parties responsible for legislative action, or were they largely the educators of public opinion which the political and intellectual leaders could then use to mastermind the legislative battles? The final answer to these complex and controversial questions of cause and effect lies in an intensive investigation of the public school movement in the separate states.

Regardless which side one argues, it is obvious that the workingmen's groups did play an important role in the free school movement, but they were only one arm of it. There were a host of other associations dedicated to the improvement of society through free education: the Philadelphia Association for the Instruction of the Poor, the Association for the Education of Negroes, the Pennsylvania Society for the Promotion of Public Schools, the Free School Society of New York City, the Public School Society of New York City; the list could go on and on. These were organizations of interested and public-spirited citizens, professional reformers, and leading intellectuals who sought to educate the public, to pressure the governing bodies, and to establish institutions of instruction in conformity with their beliefs in free education. There information-gathering activities, their fervent crusading, their role in educating the public and influencing politicians, and their actual accomplishments in sponsoring schools were of invaluable service to the states and local communities in which they worked. These various societies established bridgeheads of free schooling in Philadelphia and New York City and eventually helped conquer the states as a whole. Like the workingmen's groups, the organizations were instrumental in forcing the issue onto the public stage, and the free school systems they established in the cities became the pattern for free education throughout the states.

It rested with the political leadership to put into practice the ideals so many were seeking. Here again wide variation in the composition of political factions supporting the public school idea is apparent. No one party or no single political viewpoint was the nucleus of the free school movement. Edward Everett, the conservative politician from Massachusetts; DeWitt Clinton, philanthropist, mayor of New York City and later governor of the state; Thaddeus Stevens, violent anti-Jacksonian and ardent reformer of the Pennsylvania House; George Wolf, Democratic governor of Pennsylvania during the crucial years of the school battle in the early 1830s—all advocated the idea of free education and public responsibility. Their arguments reflected their particular social, political, and economic orientations and philosophies. In general, however, their objectives were similar, and the speeches of DeWitt Clinton and Edward Everett, two extremes in the political scale, reveal both the similarities and differences in their support of free public education (23) (24).

The final establishment of free universal education came through legislative provision and state supervision, and each state offers a separate case study. The story is incomplete without recognizing the part professional educational reformers played in the political area. James Carter and Horace Mann of Massachusetts, Henry Barnard of Connecticut, and Walter Johnson of Pennsylvania provided the factual information, the intellectual stimulus, and the philosophical basis that helped educate the public to the free school ideas (25) (26). Through lectures, articles, and reports in the newly founded educational journals, they put across the ideas and offered the practical solutions for carrying out the educational ideals of a free society. And finally they helped implement the ideas into a working system.

A selection by Frances Wright—transplanted foreigner, zealous reformer, dedicated humanitarian—rounds out the diverse and often provocative and challenging arguments for free education (27). Here is a perfect example of the crusading spirit of those who joined their efforts to rid society of its ills and to create a better world for mankind. Education was but one field for Frances Wright, and she is militant and extreme in her demands for "a national education . . . a rational education." Her socialistic schemes go far beyond the plans of most of the reformers of the era; she calls for a wardship system and a parental tax to care for the children of the poor. Though her views were visionary, unrealistic, and impractical, they nonetheless hold a place in the spectrum of reform ideas of that age, as they represent the utopian dream of a planned, orderly, and effective society. Her ideas made no lasting imprint on American educational developments, but they reveal one more facet of the battle for reform.

The selection from Philadelphia's *The National Gazette* deals with the opposition to the free school movement in Pennsylvania, usually considered a progressive state in the evolution of public education (28). Yet, here as elsewhere, opposition was widespread and strong and at times well organized and successful in hindering the movement. The opponents, like the supporters, represented a wide and varied segment of society, each group having its particular reasons for opposing public education. Various religious denominations did not favor the idea as they already provided adequate education for their children and genuinely feared the "Godless" public institutions. In the rural areas where location of a public school was a key problem the population seriously questioned the need for formal education beyond the mere rudiments for sons and daughters of the soil. Some of the propertied interests, who disliked the notion of being taxed to provide free schooling for the children of the masses, believed education was a parental rather than a public responsibility. The conservative leadership looked upon the intervention of the state in the matter of education as beyond its powers and rights, and feared the demand for equalitarianism as a threat to the status quo in political and economic as well as educational realms.

The National Gazette was the chief spokesman for the opposition and waged a constant battle, as did other newspapers in other states, against the free school movement. The editorial presented offers the traditional "aristocratic" argument that education is a private matter and that literary training could be acquired only by the wealthy, leisured class. The red herring of that day and age was "agrarianism" which sought through "compulsory equalitarianism" to put government in the hands of the non-propertied. Free education was only one aspect of the threat. Despite the strenuous opposition to the free school movement in such important states as Pennsylvania and New York, the tide of the 1830s and 1840s was in the direction of equalitarianism and democracy, and in stages state after state accepted the principle of free universal education. Out of this acceptance evolved the public school systems that became an integral part of the American ideal so strenuously sought after during the era of reform.

Though there was great variation among the states in the evolution of the public school system, the South as a regional entity deserves special attention in regard to the free school movement, which coincides with the development of southern nationalism. The southern states were experimenting with the idea of free education at public expense to replace the old system of parental instruction and pauper education just as the northern and western states were. The letter by President James H. Thornwell of South Carolina College to Governor Manning in 1853 reflects the high idealism and hopes of the enlightened citizens of the South in promoting education (29). Their arguments are similar in many respects to those circulating in New York, Massachusetts, Pennsylvania, and other northern and western states. And George Fitzhugh, the sociologist of the slave system, offers an economic view in favor of popular education but also reveals the peculiar problems of the South which hindered to a large extent the free school movement in the antebellum years (30).

The South as a region was moving along with the tide of educational reform in the early decades of the nineteenth century. The developments here, however, were considerably slower than in the other states, partly because the energy and thought of the southern political and intellectual leadership centered on the constitutional questions and also because the reform movements in general could not thrive in an area that lacked urban centers and urban reform groups. No well organized workingmen's societies existed here to agitate and demand educational equality or to use their political influence and popular press to achieve their aims. The peculiar social and economic order of the South and its defense of this system also served as a barrier to reform and change. Journals and newspapers displayed an intense interest in education, but more and more the call was less for free public education than it was for southern colleges, southern schools, southern books. The pull of southern nationalism was stronger than the more democratic reform movements.

Throughout the era, as enlightened leadership in the South struggled for public education, better quality of training, and equal opportunity for all white children, the actual system of education continued to reflect the class stratification so much a part of southern life and institutions. Private academies, especially military ones, flourished and served the needs of the upper and middle strata of society; free education was largely for the vast white pauper class (as it was in other regions); and the Negroes, freed and enslaved, were the forgotten class.

It was with regard to education of the Negroes that there was the greatest change in southern attitudes and practices from colonial times. Through most of the eighteenth century and the early nineteenth, the whites had accepted the idea of education in Christian knowledge and even in the rudiments as beneficial and worthwhile for the slave. With the conversion of slavery to an economic institution, enlightenment among the slaves came to be feared, and state after state passed stringent legislation to prohibit the education of the slaves and to restrict instruction even among the freedmen. The states continued to permit Christian education, but only through oral instruction. South Carolina had set the pace as early as 1740, but the others did not follow for almost a century. Several state laws are presented as examples of this restrictive movement in the South, just at the time the northeastern states were engaged in promoting learning among the Negroes of their area (31). The selection dealing with the arrest in 1854 of Mrs.

Margaret Douglass of Norfolk, Virginia, reveals the intense indignation of the community and its opposition to Mrs. Douglass' attempt to educate the free Negroes.

The crux of the educational problem in the South was the division of the intellectual leadership. On the one hand, the South involved itself in promoting education through the free school idea; yet achievements lagged far behind the other regions in the pre-war era, because the constitutional question, the need to protect southern ideals and institutions, and the attempt to control and discipline the vast slave population and freed Negro took precedence. Not until after the war did the South accept the principle of free elementary education at public expense for all classes — whites and Negroes.

CHAPTER 8

WORKING MEN'S ORGANIZATIONS

Equal knowledge, the only security for equal liberty.

Report of the joint committee
of the city and county of
Philadelphia, 1829

19. Association For The Protection Of Industry And For The Promotion Of National Education (1829)[1]

Reasons for the formation of the Association. Because industry is at present unprotected, oppressed, despised, and indirectly deprived of its just reward; and because there is in this republic no system of education befitting a republic; none which secures the equal maintenance, protection, and instruction of youth — of the children of the poor man as of the rich; none which is at once free from sectarian and clerical influences, and from aristocratical distinctions; none which is calculated to induce in the rising generation those habits of industry, those principles of sound morality, those feelings of brotherly love, together with those solid intellectual acquirements, which are necessary to secure to all the fair exercise of those equal political rights set forth in the institutions of the land.

Means by which the Association may attain the object. By procuring and publishing information as to the actual condition of the working class, and the actual remuneration for industry. By investigating the causes which depress industry and produce crime and suffering; and the measures which protect and favor industry, and which check oppression and vice.

By procuring information as to the state of public schools, as to the influence which rules them, and as to the value of the instruction they impart. By considering the practical means which are in the hands of the people to establish, through their representatives, a *state system of education.*

By printing and circulating tracts, calculated to give information to the people on these important subjects.

By corresponding regularly with similar societies in other towns and cities.

---

[1]*Working Man's Advocate* (New York City), Oct. 31, 1829.

By promoting the gradual extension of the Association through all the states of the Union.

And, generally, by watching over the great interests of the people — a most necessary and most neglected duty; and by noting and proclaiming the influence, and opposing the success, of every measure that tends to injure or oppress them.

Character of the Association. It shall be such as to exclude no honest man. All who sign their names as members, shall be considered as having thereby expressed "THEIR INTENTION TO ASSIST IN DEFENDING THE RIGHTS AND PROMOTING THE INTERESTS OF THE PEOPLE, AND IN CARRYING THROUGH THE STATE LEGISLATURES A SYSTEM OF EQUAL REPUBLICAN EDUCATION."

Although such an Association may expect to find the true friends of equal justice and popular instruction chiefly among the industrious classes, and may therefore reasonably be distrustful of others, it will not prejudge nor exclude any man, be his class what it may.

It will not meddle with speculative opinions; neither with religion, nor with irreligion. These are matters between each man and his own conscience. He who has faith, let him have it to himself; he who is religious, let him be religious in his closet when the door is shut, but not in public — not in an Association whose object is to discuss and reform temporal concerns. Plans for this world, and hopes of another, are two distinct things, that had better be kept separate; for men may agree about the one, while they will probably quarrel about the other.

State religion and monied ascendancy have done much harm to the people in every age and in every nation. It behoves an Association, therefore, which has in view the benefit of the people, to watch the political movements of the clergy and the rich. If the clergy, forgetting that they profess to be the servants of one whose kingdom is not of this world, intermeddle with temporal matters, a popular Association ought to thwart all such mischievous and unrepublican intermeddling. If the rich, presuming on their riches, attempt to carry measures *for* themselves and *against* the laboring classes, a popular Association ought to thwart all such mischievous and unrepublican attempts. But, though it be hard for a rich man, or for a clergyman, honestly to espouse the cause of the people against monied and clerical oppression, the Association will exclude neither. Let both join it, if they see fit. Let both speak, if they will. If they speak well and advise aright, the people will be the gainers. If otherwise, the people are neither blind nor asleep; their eyes are open and their tongues are free: they can judge what is said, and they can reply to it.

The character of the Association, then, is *not exclusive and not sectarian*. It is NATIONAL.

20. Working Men's Meeting (1829)[1]

At a meeting of the working men of Philipsburgh, Pa. held on Saturday evening, September 26, John Kinnear was called to the chair, and John Dale appointed secretary, when, on motion, the following preamble and resolutions were unanimously adopted:

In a free government, founded upon the authority of the people, and instituted for their peace, happiness, and safety, no artificial distinctions or inequalities ought to be tolerated by law, inasmuch as the first principle of nature as well as republicanism, is, that all men are born equally free and independent.

Natural inequalities among men does, and always will, exist to a certain extent; but it is the duty of a wise government to soften and modify them as much as possible, and in no case to increase them.

This, we believe to be the spirit and very essence of our excellent constitution, but yet when we look at the effect which many of our laws have upon the community, and compare the situation of the laboring classes with that of others, it would seem as if our legislatures were acting upon principles directly the reverse, and were endeavoring to increase these distinctions by throwing all the power and wealth of the country into the hands of the few, and leaving the many wholly unprotected, against the oppressive monopolies which have been established by law.

No system of education, which a freeman can accept, has yet been established, for the poor; whilst thousands of dollars of the public money have been appropriated for building colleges and academies for the rich.

No law has been passed, calculated to raise the price of the poor man's labor; but yet, the whole community has been taxed, by heavy tariff duties upon foreign importations, in order that rich men may build up manufactories.

---

[1]*Working Man's Advocate*, Oct. 31, 1829.

168

Banks, and other privileged corporations, are increasing without number throughout the land, all tending by their power to monopolize business and control the circulating medium, to strengthen the aristocracy, and reduce the power of the farmer, mechanic, and laborer.

The effect already is, that one half of society are the slaves of etiquette, and the other of excessive labor.

The hardest labor is made the least productive; and the most useless drones of society are the best paid.

One class is doomed to toil for bread, and another privileged to wanton in luxurious idleness.

The producers of wealth are poor and dependent, whilst the *consumers* are rich and powerful.

Therefore, *Resolved,* That in the opinion of this meeting, it is the duty of working men to unite their efforts, to have the laws made and administered more in conformity with the spirit of republican principles.

Resolved, That we form ourselves into a political association, similar to those already formed in other parts of the state, and that we make it a part of our duty to examine and discuss all the political questions, upon which we are called upon to pass judgment, by our votes at the general elections.

Resolved, That the *proceedings* of this meeting be signed by the chairman and secretary, and published in the Penn Banner.

JOHN KINNEAR, Ch'n.

John Dale, Sec'y.

21. Public Education (1830)[1]

A public meeting of the friends of general and equal education was held in the District Court room on the evenings of the 4th, 8th, and 11th, ult., M. M. Carll in the chair and John Thompson and Wm. Heighton secretaries. The proceedings of a joint committee appointed by the working men of the city and liberties of Philadelphia, consisting of a report, together with two public school bills, and other documents relating to public education, were presented. After much deliberation and some amendments made, the proceedings of the joint committee were unanimously adopted, and a committee appointed with instructions to procure their publication.

In pursuance of these instructions a resolution has been adopted by the committee to lay the whole proceedings before the public in the order in which they were presented to the meeting.

It was also resolved, by the committee, that all editors of journals, both in the German and English language, throughout the state, favorable to education, be respectfully requested to publish the same. Signed,

JOHN MITCHELL, Chairman.
WM. HEIGHTON, Secretary.

REPORT

Of the Joint Committees of the City and County of Philadelphia, appointed September, 1829, to ascertain the state of public instruction in Pennsylvania, and to digest and propose such improvements in education as may be deemed essential to the intellectual and moral prosperity of the people.

---

[1]*Working Man's Advocate*, March 6, 1830. Reprinted from the *Philadelphia Mechanic's Free Press*.

170

It is now nearly five months since the committees were appointed to cooperate on this arduous duty. But the importance of the subject; the time expended in research and enquiry, in order to procure information relative to it; and the multiplied discussions and deliberations necessary to reconcile and correct their own different and sometimes conflicting views, will, they believe, constitute a reasonable apology for this long delay.

After devoting all the attention to the subject, and making every enquiry which their little leisure and ability would permit, they are forced into the conviction, that there is great defect in the educational system of Pennsylvania; and that much remains to be accomplished before it will have reached that point of improvement which the resources of the state would justify, and which the intellectual condition of the people and the preservation of our republican institutions demand.

With the exception of this city and county, the city and incorporated borough of Lancaster, and the city of Pittsburgh, erected into "school districts" since 1818, it appears that the entire state is destitute of any provisions for public instruction, except those furnished by the enactment of 1809. This law requires the assessors of the several counties to ascertain and return the number of children whose parents are unable, through poverty, to educate them; and such children are permitted to be instructed at the most convenient schools at the expense of their respective counties.

The provisions of this act, however, are incomplete and frequently inoperative. They are, in some instances, but partially executed; in others, perverted and abused—and in many cases entirely and culpably neglected. The funds appropriated by the act, have, in some instances, been embezzled by fraudulent agents; and in others, partial returns of the children have been made, and some have been illegally and intentionally excluded from participating in the provisions of the law. From a parsimonious desire of saving the county funds, the cheapest, and consequently the most inefficient schools have, been usually selected by the commissioners of the several counties.

The elementary schools throughout the state are irresponsible institutions, established by individuals, from mere motives of private speculation or gain, who are sometimes destitute of character, and frequently, of the requisite attainments and abilities.

From the circumstance of the schools being the absolute property of individuals, no supervision or effectual control can be exercised over them; hence, ignorance, inattention, and even immorality, prevail to a lamentable extent among their teachers.

In some districts, no schools whatever exist! no means whatever of acquiring education are resorted to; while ignorance, and its never failing consequence, crime, are found to prevail in these neglected spots, to a greater extent than in other more favored portions of the state.

The "three school districts," however, which have been alluded to, are not liable to these objections. Much good, in particular, has resulted from the establishment of the first of these, comprising this city and county, and which owes its establishment to the persevering efforts of a few individuals, who, in order to succeed, even so far, were compelled to combat the ignorance, the prejudices, and the pecuniary interests of many active and hostile opponents.

But the principles on which these "school districts" are founded, are yet, in the opinion of the committees, extremely defective and inefficient. Their leading feature is pauperism!—They are confined exclusively to the children of *the poor*, while there are, perhaps, thousands of children whose parents are unable to afford for them, a good private education, yet whose standing, professions or connexions in society effectually exclude them from taking the benefit of a *poor law*. There are great numbers, even of the poorest parents, who hold a dependence on the public bounty to be incompatible with the rights and liberties of an American citizen, and whose deep and cherished consciousness of *independence* determines them rather to starve the intellect of their offspring, than submit to become the objects of public charity.

There are, also, many poor families, who are totally unable to maintain and clothe their children, while at the schools; and who are compelled to place them, *at a very early age,* at some kind of labor that may assist in supporting them, or to bind them out as apprentices to relieve themselves entirely of the burthen of their maintenance and education, while the practice formerly universal, of schooling apprentices, has, of late years, greatly diminished and is still diminishing.

172

Another radical and glaring defect in the existing public school system, is the very limited amount of instruction it affords, even to the comparatively small number of youth, who enjoy its benefits. It extends, in no case, further than a tolerable proficiency in reading, writing, and arithmetic, and sometimes to a slight acquaintance with geography. Besides these, the girls are taught a few simple branches of industry. A great proportion of scholars, however, from the causes already enumerated, acquire but a very slight and partial knowledge of these branches.

The present public school system, limited as it is to three solitary school districts, makes no provision for the care and instruction of children under five years old. This class of children is numerous, especially among the poor, and it frequently happens that the parents, or *parent*, (perhaps a widow) whose only resource for a livelihood is her needle or wash tub, is compelled to keep her elder children from the school to take charge of the younger ones, while her own hands are industriously employed in procuring a subsistence for them. Such instances are far from being rare, and form a very prominent and lamentable drawback on the utility of the schools in these districts. The care thus bestowed on infants, is insufficient and very partial. They are frequently exposed to the most pernicious influences and impressions. The seeds of vice, thus early scattered over the infant soil, are too often permitted to ripen, as life advances, till they fill society with violence and outrage, and yield an abundant harvest for magdalens and penitentiaries.

An opinion is entertained by many good and wise persons, and supported to a considerable extent, by actual experiment, that proper schools for supplying a judicious infant training, would effectually prevent much of that vicious depravity of character which penal codes and punishments are vainly intended to counteract. Such schools would, at least, relieve, in a great measure, many indigent parents, from the care of children, which in many cases occupies as much of their time as would be necessary to earn the childern a subsistence. They would also afford many youth an opportunity of participating in the benefits of the public schools, who otherwise must, of necessity, be detained from them.

From this view of the public instruction in Pennsylvania, it is manifest that, even to *"the school districts,"* to say nothing of the remainder of the state, a very large proportion of youth are either partially or entirely destitute of education.

It is true the state is not without its colleges and universities, several of which have been fostered with liberal supplies from the public purse. Let it be observed, however, that the funds so applied, have been appropriated exclusively for the benefit of the wealthy, who are thereby enabled to procure a liberal education for their children, upon *lower terms* than it could otherwise be afforded them. Funds thus expended, may serve to engender an aristocracy of talent, and place knowledge, the chief element of power, in the hands of the privileged *few;* but can never secure the common prosperity of a nation nor confer *intellectual* as well as political equality on a people.

The original element of *despotism* is a MONOPOLY OF TALENT, which consigns the multitude to comparative ignorance, and secures the balance of knowledge on the side of the rich and the rulers. If then the healthy existence of a free government be, as the committee believe, rooted in the WILL of the American people, it follows as a necessary consequence, of a government based upon that *will,* that this monopoly should be broken up, and that the means of equal knowledge, (the only security for equal liberty) should be rendered, by legal provision, the common property of all classes.

In a republic, the people constitute the government, and by wielding its powers in accordance with the dictates, either of their intelligence or their ignorance; of their judgment or their caprices, are the makers and the rulers of their own good or evil destiny. They frame the laws and create the institutions, that promote their happiness or produce their destruction. If they be wise and intelligent, no laws but what are just and equal will receive their approbation, or be sustained by their suffrages. If they be ignorant and capricious, they will be deceived by mistaken or designing rulers, into the support of laws that are unequal and unjust.

It appears, therefore, to the committees that there can be no real liberty without a wide diffusion of real intelligence; that the members of a republic, should all be alike instructed in the nature and character of their equal rights and duties, as human beings, and as citizens; and that education, instead of being limited as in our public poor schools, to a simple acquaintance with words and cyphers, should tend, as far as possible, to the production of a just disposition, virtuous habits, and a rational self governing character.

When the committees contemplate their own condition, and that of the great mass of their fellow laborers; when they look around on the glaring inequality of society, they are constrained to believe, that until the means of equal instruction shall be equasecured to all, liberty is but an unmeaning word, and equality an empty shadow, whose substance to be realized must first be planted by an equal education and proper training in the minds, in the habits, in the manners, and in the feelings of the community.

While, however, the committees believe it their duty to exhibit, fully and openly, the main features and principles of a system of education which can alone comport with the spitit [sic] of American liberty, and the equal prosperity and happiness of the people, they are not prepared to assert, that the establishment of such a system in its fullness and purity, throughout the state, is by any means attainable at a single step.—While they maintain that each human being has an equal right to a full development of all his powers, moral, physical, and intellectual; that the common good of society can never be promoted in its fullness till all shall be equally secured and protected in the enjoyment of this right, and that it is the first great duty of the states, to secure the same to all its members; yet, such is now the degraded state of education in Pennsylvania, compared with what, in the opinion of the committees, education for a free people should be, that they despair of so great a change as must be involved in passing from one to the other, being accomplished suddenly throughout the state. No new system of education could probably be devised with consequences so manifestly beneficial, as to awaken at once in the public mind, a general conviction and concurrence in the necessity of its universal adoption.

The committees are aware, also, that it is their duty to consult the views, the feelings, and the prejudices, not of a single district or county merely, but of the state in general. The measure which it is their business to propose, is one designed to be of universal extent and influence, and must, to be successful, be based upon the manifest wishes of nearly the whole commonwealth. It is not,

175

therefore, to what would constitute a perfect education only, but also, to what may be rendered practicable—it is not with a view, exclusively, to the kind of education every child of Pennsylvania *ought to have,* but likewise to what it is possible, under existing circumstances, views, and prejudices, every child of Pennsylvania *may* and *can* have, that they have drawn up a bill or outline of what they deem a system of public education, adapted to the present condition and necessities of the state in general.

The principal points in which the bill for establishing common schools, accompanying this report, differs from the existing system of free schools, are as follows:

1. Its provisions, instead of being limited to three single districts, are designed to extend throughout the commonwealth. 2d, It places the managers of the public schools, immediately under the control and suffrage of the people. 3d, Its benefits and privileges will not, as at present, be limited as an act of charity to the poor alone, but will extend equally and of right to all classes, and be supported at the expense of all. 4th, It lays a foundation for infantile, as well as juvenile instruction. And lastly, it leaves the door open to every possible improvement which human benevolence and ingenuity may be able to introduce.

While, however, the committees would urge the establishment of common elementary schools throughout the state, as comprising, perhaps, the best general system of education which is at present attainable, it is but just to exhibit, also, some of the defects as well as the advantages of such schools; and to suggest such further measures as appear calculated to obviate such defects.

The instruction afforded by common schools, such as are contemplated in the bill for a general system of education, being only *elementary,* must, of necessity, produce but a very limited development of the human faculties. It would indeed diminish, but could not destroy, the present injurious monopoly of talent. While the higher branches of literature and science remain accessible only to the children of the wealthy, there must still be a balance of knowledge, and with it a "balance of power," in the hands of the privileged few, the rich and the rulers.

Another radical defect in the best system of common schools yet established, will be found in its not being adapted to meet the wants and necessities of those who stand most in need of it. Very many of the poorest parents are totally unable to clothe and maintain their children while at school, and are compelled to employ their time, while yet very young, in aiding to procure a subsistence. In the city of New York, a much more efficient system of education exists than in this city, and common schools have been in successful operation for the last ten or twelve years; yet there are at the present time upwards of 24,000 children between the ages of 5 and 15 years, who attend no schools whatever, and this apparently criminal neglect of attending the schools is traced, chiefly, to the circumstance just mentioned. It is evidently therefore, of no avail, how free the schools may be, while those children who stand most in need of them, are, through the necessity of their parents, either retained from them altogether, or withdrawn at an improper age, to assist in procuring a subsistence.

The constitution of this state declares that "the legislature shall provide schools in which the poor may be taught gratis." If this signifies that the poor *shall have an opportunity* afforded for instruction, it must involve MEANS equal to the end. The poverty of the poor must be no obstruction, otherwise the constitution is a dead letter—nay, worse, an insult on their unfortunate codition [sic] and feelings.

The committees, therefore, believe, that one school, at least, should be established in each county, in which some principle should be adopted, calculated to obviate the defects that have been alluded to, and by which the children of all who desire it, may be enabled to procure, at their own expense, a liberal and scientific education. They are of opinion that a principle fully calculated to secure this object, will be found in a union of agricultural and mechanical with literary and scientific instruction; and they have therefore, in addition to a plan of common elementary schools, the substance of a bill providing for the establishment of high schools, or model schools, based upon this principle, which they also present for public deliberation.

Believing, as the committees do, that upon an equal education and proper training to industry, sobriety, and virtue, hangs the liberty and prosperity of the new world, and, perhaps, the ultimate emancipation of the old; and believing, as they do, that the union of industry with literature and science constitutes the only desideratum by which an equal education can be supplied and secured to all classes, they experience the most sincere pleasure in discovering that this good and great principle is gaining in popularity and dominion throughout the world. Not only are institutions of this kind established in France, Prussia, Germany, and Great Britain, in imitation of the original Hofwyl institutions in Switzerland, but in the United States, also, there are several. At Whitesborough, N.Y. there is one with from 30 to 40 pupils; at Princeton, Ky. another containing 80; a third exists at Andover, Mass. that accommodates 60 pupils; a fourth at Maysville, Tenn.; and a fifth has recently been established, at Germantown, in this county. At Monmouth, N.J. and at Cincinnati, Ohio, very extensive establishments, based upon this principle, have been or are about commencing.

The Germantown establishment had been commenced only seven months when its first report was made, in November last. The pupils are instructed in literature, the sciences, languages, morals, and manual labor. The latter consists of agriculture, gardening, and some mechanic arts. They are permitted to labor little or much, as their dispositions may incline them or their necessities dictate. The institution, at its commencement, on the 1st of May, 1829, had but four pupils — at the date of the report it had 25. By an estimate made by the board of managers, as early as July last, it appeared that the balances against several of them for board and tuition were but very small, and that some of them, by their labor, had almost cleared their expenses. They generally work from two to five hours per day.

The first institution in which manual labor appears to have been combined with literature and science, was established many years since by Fellenberg, at Hofwyl, in the Canton of Bern, Switzerland.

The pupils of this institution, in addition to a common or elementary education, were instructed in almost every branch of literature and science. They were taught agriculture, gardening, and the mechanic arts, and their choice of the latter was greatly facilitated by the numerous workshops on the premises. The elements of drawing, surveying and geometry, botany, mineralogy, music, and athletic exercises formed a part of their amusements.

Hofwyl was an independent, selfgoverning community, regulated by a constitution and bylaws formed by the pupils themselves.

It had its code of laws; its council of legislation; its representatives; its civil officers; its treasury. It had its annual elections, and each member had an equal vote; its labors and duties in which all took an equal share. It proposed, debated, and enacted its own laws independent even of Fellenberg himself, and never, writes one of the pupils after he had left it, "never perhaps were laws framed with a more single eye to the public good, nor more strictly obeyed by those who framed them."

The same writer considers this circumstance of forming the school into an independent juvenile republic, as the great lever that raised the moral and social character of the Hofwyl establishment to the height it ultimately attained. It gave birth, he says, to public spirit and to social virtues. It awakened in the young republic an interest in the public welfare, and a zeal for the public good, which might in vain be sought in older but not wiser communities.

Professor Griscom of New York, who, while in Europe in 1818–19, visited Hofwyl, observes, that "the principles on which it is conducted, appear calculated to afford the very best kind of education which it is possible to supply, whatever situation the pupil may be destined to fill in after life. But its greatest recommendation is in the moral charm which it diffuses throughout all its operations. Scholars thus educated, must become not only more intelligent men and better philosophers, but also more dignified members of society. I cannot," he further remarks, "but indulge a hope that this scheme of education, combining agricultural and mechanical with literary and scientific instruction, will be speedily and extensively adopted in the United States." This institution ranked among its pupils children from almost every country in Europe. It had dukes, and princes, some of them related to crowned heads, and children whose parents could not afford to pay for their education, yet all were on a perfect equality. There existed not the smallest distinction between princes and nobles on the one hand, and the objects of Fellenberg's charity on the other, save that in general the latter advanced more rapidly in their studies than the former, and became the best men and the greatest scholars.

The committees, however, are by no means disposed to urge the Fellenberg system as a model of educational perfection.

Doubtless, like all human institutions, it is susceptible of still higher improvements; and such indeed appears to be the opinion of individuals intimately acquainted with the detail of its operations. — But to the committees it does appear that the principle which forms the basis of this system — the union of agricultural and mechanical with literary and scientific instruction, is peculiarly adapted to the condition and necessities of the American people, and perfectly consistent with the nature and character of our free institutions.

Its principal features are essentially republican.

Its adoption and gradual extension in each county throughout the state, would, in time, remove every obstacle to education arising from poverty, and open the door of improvement equally wide to the children of all ranks and classes.

It would afford such an equal training and enlarged development of the physical, intellectual, and moral energies of the-rising generation, as would secure for ever their *real* liberties and equal prosperity and happiness.

To the children of those insolated yet numerous families, who reside in thinly populated sections of the state, it would afford an easy and certain acquisition of morals, intelligence, and *trades*, which they can never acquire by any other means.

There is one point in which the committees believe that the gradual extension and ultimate universal adoption of this system of education will produce a benefit, the value of which no human calculation can ascertain. It is but too well known that the growing effects of INTEMPERANCE — that assassinator of private peace and public virtue, are in this country terrific; and that this fearful pestilence, unless checked in its career by some more efficient remedy than has yet been resorted to, threatens to annihilate, not only the domestic peace and prosperity of individuals, but also the moral order and political liberties of the nation. No people can long enjoy liberty who resign themselves to the slavery of this tyrant vice. Yet does it appear to the committees, that all efforts to root this moral poison from the constitution of society will prove futile until the trial shall be made upon our youth. When we behold the hundreds, perhaps thousands of youth, who, between the ages of 14 and 21 are daily and nightly seduced around or into the innumerable dens of vice, licensed and unlicensed, that throng our suburbs, we are constrained to believe that in many if not in most cases, the unconquerable habit that destroys the morals, ruins the constitution, sacrifices the character, and at last murders both soul and body of its victim, is first acquired during the thoughtless period of juvenile existence. This plan of education, however, by its almost entire occupation of the time of the pupils, either in labor, study, or recreations; by the superior facilities it affords for engrossing their entire attention, and by its capability of embracing the whole juvenile population, furnishes, we believe, the only rational hope of ultimately averting, the ruin which is threatened by this extensive vice.

The committee are aware that any plan of common and more particularly of equal education that may be offered to the public, is likely to meet with more than an ordinary share of opposition. It is to be expected that political demagogueism, professional monopoly, and monied influence, will conspire as hitherto (with several exceptions more or less numerous) they ever have conspired against every thing that has promised to be an equal benefit to the whole population. Nevertheless, the appearance, that something will now be done for the intellectual as well as every thing for the physical improvement of the state are certainly very promising. The public mind is awake and favorably excited, while the press also is somewhat active on this subject. . . .

22. THE WORKING MAN'S MANUAL (1831)[1]

STEPHEN SIMPSON

❖ ❖ ❖

Nothing is so essentially connected with the wealth of nations, and the happiness of the people, as the proper cultivation, expansion, and discipline of the popular mind. Upon this depends not only the amount of public virtue and happiness—but the aggregate of industry, ingenuity, temperance, economy, and vigour.

When we look back to the small states of GREECE, so diminutive in extent, so trivial in *physical* resources, yet so colossal in all the moral grandeur of nations; so happy in peace, so blessed with abundance, so invincible in war, so inimitable in letters, so exquisite in taste, so unparalleled in the arts, so splendid in all things—we are compelled to refer all her transcendent excellences to her mind—her *education,* her literature, her science, and her philosophy. The example of ROME, not more extended in physical limits, and not less renowned in imperishable glory—extorts the judgment to the same acknowledgment of the supremacy of intellect over matter; and the all-powerful influence of public intelligence, in forming the national character, deciding its destiny, and moulding its people. In fine, the history of the world is but a repetition of the same truth illustrated by the same renown, tracking the career of intellect in the path of glory, and showing, that kingdoms, the most insignificant in magnitude, have, by the force of knowledge, eclipsed all their gigantic rivals in wealth, resources, and fame. We might contrast England with Russia—France with China—and Greece and Rome with all!

When history glares her blaze of truth in our eyes, let us not

---

[1]Stephen Simpson, *The Working Man's Manual: A New Theory of Political Economy on the Principle of Production the Source of Wealth* (Philadelphia, 1831), pp. 119–216. Author and editor, Simpson was the first candidate for Congress from the Workingmen's Party of Philadelphia. He wrote the Manual during his unsuccessful candidacy.

close them to its lessons. When the intellect of Rome was quenched by a barbarian deluge, what was the condition of the world?—To what era of all those blackened by crime, and debased by ignorance, do we look back, with the greatest horror? To the DARK AGES, to the midnight of mind that overspread the world, and permitted depravity to wage an unrestricted warfare upon virtue, knowledge, science, industry, and happiness. Sufficiently admonitory, then, is the lesson of the past, to urge us to the improvement of the present, and the perfection of the future. Cast upon the stage of existence in a *new era*, let us not disgrace our destiny by failing to make our advancement conform to our opportunities.

The spirit of the age, which now points to the universal education of the people, is an unavoidable effect of that law of our nature, which ordains that means must be adapted to ends, and that causes must conform to their consequences;—that as time rolls on, and reflection lights the torch of intellect, prejudice, bigotry, and superstition, must give place to reason, and humanity maintain her rights in defiance of prejudice or interest, riches or ambition. When, as a people, we inscribed the holy precepts of justice and of truth on our declaration of independence—proclaiming that all men were created free and equal—with the same rights to the pursuit and enjoyment of happiness; we commenced the foundation, because we created the necessity of universal education, by adopting a form of government, whose existence and purity depended on the exercise of reason, and the preservation of public virtue. Where every man is an *elector,* and bound to judge and to choose those who may make laws, and administer the government;—every one ought to receive an education, commensurate to his duties, as such; and where individual opulence does not furnish the means, the public are bound to impart the blessing in the fullest measure, and to the widest extent, at the common cost of society: not, however, as a *bounty,* or a *charity,* but as a *right;* that as *all* contribute their share of labour to the expense and support of government, so *all* are equally entitled to the great benefits of popular instruction. In the same manner, that the *constitution* protects our liberties, and that the law secures our rights of person and of property, without becoming a charity to the poor; so ought *education* to be dispensed to all who desire to receive its vivifying beams, and investigating spirit. Indeed, to conceive of a *popular government* devoid of a system of *popular education,* is as difficult as to conceive of a civilized society destitute of a *system of industry.* This truth has been generally received in this country, and never, I believe, directly denied; although its force has been attempted to be evaded by the *rich* and *opposed by the aristocracy,* who have heretofore, unfortunately, been our sole *law makers,* through the odious system of *charity schools* — the bare idea of which impresses a consciousness of degradation, and leads to results the very reverse of those that ought to be produced by popular instruction. I will not, however, enlarge upon this subject, which must be familiar to all; yet all may not have remarked, that the scanty pittance of education termed *charitable,* has never realized the *equal benefits of instruction,* to which the working people have been entitled as the producers of all the wealth of society. When it is solemnly inscribed upon our constitution, that education is an essential preliminary of government, its diffusive dispensation becomes a duty and a right of the first importance and magnitude: we are bound to consider it, not as an *accidental* but as an *integral* part of government, which, when we neglect or overlook, we violate the most sacred obligations, which, as good citizens, we have sworn to discharge.

A proper understanding as to the basis of American education, is essential to just legislative enactments to provide for its diffusion. The errors and misconceptions that have heretofore been formidable obstructions in the path of popular education, have had their origin in that fertile spring of most of our misfortunes, the FEUDAL HEREDITARY SYSTEM of the English government; which is based on principles radically opposite, and eternally repugnant to ours; but from which, unfortunately, we have drawn all our models for action, while we have resorted to truth and justice for principles in the *abstract.* Hence that collision between our form of government, whose soul is intelligence and knowledge, and our practice, and our institutions, which are subversive of both. In Europe, education being a *grace and bounty,* coming from an hereditary king and nobility, to their *feudal* vassals, or *inferior* subjects, may well be called a *charity,* and can hardly be termed a blessing; for it must lead them to the sight of truths, which revolt from all their systems of injustice and oppression; which reveals to their astonished eyes all the charms of liberty and equality, and yet denies them their enjoyment and protection. A new system of education must, therefore, in this country, be adopted, conformable to our constitution, and conducive to the happiness of the people. I mean *new*, not in relation to the *method of teaching*, although this is every way susceptible of improvement; — but in respect to the condition of its gift, and the universality of its influence and operation, by which I mean knowledge imparted to the people as a matter of right and duty, and received by all, whether they choose to refuse or to accept it, under the obligation of good citizenship.

Intimately connected as general education is with human happiness and virtue, the philanthropist, the statesman, and the patriot, perceive in its adoption, an increase of the moral energies of the nation, as well as an augmented power in the lever of government. I hold it to be an indisputable maxim, that knowledge not only prevents crime, but increases industry — that it adds to the excellence of the human character in all its bearings — that it snatches men from low and grovelling vices, and gives them a fresh impulse to the acquisition of perfection of every kind. How seldom do we behold a *tavern* frequented by men of good education, and cultivated intellect? How seldom do we find men of educated minds, slaves to the beastly vice of intemperance? — Give education to the people, and you give them the spur to every virtue; the rein to every vice. Look into the cells of your prisons! By whom are they tenanted? By the *ignorant*, or the recipients of *charity schools*, who, perhaps, had better have been left among the unsophisticated mass of intellectual darkness.

It is cheering to the heart of the philanthropist, at all times, to perceive the cause of human happiness in its diffusive sense, as affecting the great mass of mankind, engaging public attention; but more especially so at an era, when the lust of gain appears to be the grand absorbing passion of our race: I say the CAUSE OF HUMAN HAPPINESS, for such do I consider the cause of popular education, which shall bring into *action* that immensity of intellect which now lies dormant; and which, in respect to its influence on happiness, is precisely as if it did not exist.

It does not, however, appear so unquestionable, whether the entire mass of mind can by culture be brought *actively to the aid of* governments, and of nations. If, however, it be only maintained

185

that education can be brought to produce that effect by the diminution of crime and the augmentation of industry, I concur in the position; but some appear to give a different construction to the effects of a system of popular education, which reaches beyond the limits of *"mere reading and writing,"* and that they look to the participation of *nearly the whole race* in the moral government of nations, as a natural consequence of giving the multitude of men the command of their minds in ethics, science, and politics. There appears to me to be two ways only, in which this effect can be produced,—1st, by the adoption of the *representative system* of government, as a *preliminary* step; or, 2d, by superinducing it *through the influence* of popular education. Representative government may exist *nominally*, but not effectually, without the diffusion of the higher kind of popular instruction. To be complete, representation must exhibit a *moral fitness* between the representative and his station, and his constituents. A people incompetent from ignorance or vice, of choosing a *proper* representative, never can enjoy that kind of government, except in *form and name*. There must exist in a majority of the people an ability to discriminate character, and a disposition to appreciate talents, or the substance of representation is lost in the *form*. Electors ought, on all occasions, to be competent to a just conception of the fitness or unfitness of representatives. By this method only do I conceive it possible to bring the mass of the people to the efficient aid of government and nations, as far as *moral power* is concerned. Looking beyond the limits of mere *reading and writing*, the cause of diffusive education assumes a magnitude so great, and becomes enveloped in difficulties so embarrassing, as to claim the most intense investigation. How is it to be accomplished? Is it not indispensable, as a preliminary measure, to remove from the face of society that redundance of *taverns* and *liquor stores*, that poison and debauch eighty per cent of the mass of the people? For, on what principle can we expect education to take root in society, when a majority of that society are in the hourly habit of destroying the power of thought, and inhaling the steam of excitement? These are serious questions; but they receive, I am disposed to think, a conclusive answer in the adoption of a *general system of popular education*, reaching beyond the mere attainment of reading and writing. Knowledge is the grand remedy of

186

intemperance; for in proportion as we elevate men in the scale of existence, and give them reason to esteem and respect themselves, so do we reclaim them from all temptations of degrading vice, and ruinous crimes. A reading and intellectual people were never known to be sottish; — but those who are ignorant, or stupid, are forever wallowing in drunkenness and debauchery. Thus sobriety and political honesty, are the twin offspring of education. Make the people enlightened, and liberty will prove her own sentinel, virtue her own protector, truth her own champion! — Under our present system, the evil from which we most suffer is the *ignorance of teachers;* an evil that has been very generally felt and acknowledged; and which, in Europe, has given rise to the preliminary measure of a *school for teachers.* In most of our seminaries, this deficiency is palpably obvious, and forms a subject of general complaint. When every other business fails, people open schools, as if NO EDUCATION in themselves was sufficient to qualify them to teach others. The same remark will apply to most of our legislators. We are shrewd and cunning, and rest satisfied with the consciousness of being smart; but without knowledge, cunning can only produce knavery and deception. The richest soil must be cultivated, if we hope to make it produce aught but weeds.

It has been maintained by some, that *females* ought to be embraced in a comprehensive and judicious system of popular instruction; and that *common schools,* in which our daughters could be fully prepared to discharge their various duties in life, ought to be provided for all, at the public cost. As this idea is one of great delicacy and importance, it deserves to be considered with a single eye to the serious consequences that it appears to involve.

Nature has left nothing dubious or equivocal in the laws and properties that regulate the grandeur of her beautiful and sublime system; and reason and instinct alternately direct us in the true and appropriate path that conducts us to perfection of *principle* and imperfection of practice. Among the unerring indications of her wisdom, which made this complicated world to move in harmony, is that decisive instinct, that all-controlling and overpowering bias of nature, that impels *woman* to retire into the privacy of domestic life; to cherish the tender sympathies of the heart; to cultivate those arts that minister to the comfort of man, and which are positively necessary and indispensable to the pleasure, happiness and preservation of *her offspring*. And it is in this that we perceive the all-powerful *law of nature* that destines her to be the *passive*, not the active member of society; that causes her to seek *privacy*, not obtrude herself among the rulers of the world. As the MOTHER of the human race, quiet, seclusion, and domestic tranquility, together with much suffering, is her lot. Without the protecting shadow of quietude, and the soft arts of gentle love and persuasive peace, the end of her being, *as the mother of our kind*, would be utterly frustrated. Without these endearing qualities in the breast of woman, the word *home*, now so filled with magic sounds and replete with sweet associations of bliss, quiet and repose, would be empty, hollow, and unmeaning; — nay, without the *passive* character of woman, stamped so by the great God of nature, and confirmed as such by reason and by instinct, the harmonious structure of the world would be disrupted and overturned — and sad, sad indeed, would be the wretched condition of man.

Knowledge, always ready to improve mankind, genius, ever keen and active to suggest new discoveries, and curiosity, restless and unsatisfied with old possessions, are ever devising plans to lead man to perfection; plans in which *imagination* often has more agency than reason, and fiction a greater share than philosophy. An age of intelligence is, therefore an age of peril. *Invention* is like Mercury, too swiftly winged to wait for cold *discretion;* and zeal, when beckoned by virtue, obeys no signal of restraint. But a *just philosophy*, whose precepts are sanctioned by nature, may mitigate error, and arrest enthusiasm in her march to mischief. So let it be with the new fangled project of the celebrated reformers of the day, to *reduce the mother of our race* to a destructive equality with man. Let nature and a just philosophy step in to dispel the fatal delusion, and save us from the evils of a ruinous abation, in which the *loss is certain*, and the gain impossible! No — let us have no *common schools for woman!* Their duties are not public — their functions are not appropriate to the state — nature claims all their energies as the mother and the nurse of our kind — as the ornament and the *primum mobile* of the domestic circle. Their allegiance is not to the state but to their families: — their husbands — parents — children. We want no race of fabled *Amazons*, to drive man from the field of battle to the distaff; and supplant him at the forum by the intoxicated and intoxicating oratory of a *Corinna*!—God has drawn the line between the duties and functions of the two sexes. What! to behold a female warrior with a child at her nipple! or a female orator *mending her gown* in the interval of mental estuation!

There is but one circumstance that could justify the legislature in providing common schools for our females—and that never can exist—that females discharged *all* the duties of active citizens of the state. Why should they be qualified for tasks they are never to discharge? I anticipate the reply to this question. They are to be educated, and accomplished for *ladies*, at the public cost—not for *Amazons*! This answer settles the question—the legislature possess no *constitutional* power to educate *ladies*—their business is confined to the *citizens of the commonwealth*—to those who *bear arms, pay taxes,* serve as *jurors,* &c. Thus, we are very happily saved from a deluge of argument, by a sound barrier of our *organic law,* which justly forbids public education to the *ladies* of the commonwealth! However gothic and barbarous this prohibition may seem to some of the enthusiastic champions of the *march of mind,* the judicious must approve its wisdom, and the reflecting applaud its adherence to the philosophical fitness of things.

Zeal is always prone to overstep the boundaries of reason. Having discovered our error in this matter of popular education for females, let us retrace our steps; and thus establish our claim to the character of *rational reformers,* not wild enthusiasts, and bewitched zealots. Let the daughters of the land, then, remain under the sacred care of our household gods; to be privately educated according to the sphere they are destined to move in, and the circumstances that surround them—never forgetting that *usefulness* is the next quality to *virtue*—that to be modest, to be chaste, to be amiable, and to be industrious, are the chief ennobling traits in the beautiful character of *woman*.

This position does not imply a *denial* of education to the female, but simply declares, that her instruction shall conform to her destination by nature. To prove beneficial, every application of intellectual culture, must be regulated by the circumstances of the object. It would be the height of absurdity, to instruct our naval and military officers in *embroidery*, but it would be equally absurd, to initiate our females in *oratory, law,* government, and military tactics.

Prone to run into opposite extremes, no sooner do we consent to rescue the female from her degradation of complete ignorance, than we become infatuated with the thought of qualifying her for all the masculine duties of life. This visionary scheme is fraught with mischief; it unsettles the economy of life, it jars the harmony of nature, and tends to diminish the happiness of mankind, as well as prostrate the barriers of chastity and virtue.

In relation to the productive faculties of a nation, popular education assumes an importance, not suspected even by its best friends. By implanting the principles of science in the mass of intellect, *invention* is provided with materials for the production of improvements, that may change the whole face of society into one radiant smile of content and enjoyment. The invention of *machinery* is the fruit of an educated age, and the more we diffuse that education, the more we advance the arts and sciences, manufactures and agriculture, to perfection. Not one seed of knowledge dropped into the common mind is lost. On some occasion it will germinate to a profit, and recompense society ten fold for the gift; nor do I mean a merely intellectual reward, but a substantial one of labour, of an increase of the means of sustaining and enjoying life, at the least expenditure of time and toil.

Ignorance and inferiority of mind are the only causes of human degradation; except that of poverty, which is the general concomitant of ignorance—as ignorance is its invariable cause. In the progress of nations, civilized people are generally found to vanquish barbarians, either by the force of superior skill, or the charms of science, literature, and knowledge. Nations, like individuals, hold one another in contempt, or look up with respect and admiration, as they rise or fall in the scale of intelligence and wisdom, refinement and civilization. It is only, however, when we come to scrutinize more closely the elements of a single nation, that we can obtain an accurate and full perception of the debasing effects of ignorance. This becomes obvious, the moment we penetrate into the manners, and non-intercourse of different classes of society, which we may distinguish into the ignorant, or the enlightened. Between these two classes, one of whom labours, and the other remains in idleness, there exists so great a separation in all the social duties and associations, as almost to constitute them different species. The enlightened and educated look down upon the ignorant as a debased order of beings, and treat them as matter of course, with contempt; and the ignorant on their part, look up to the refined with a sensation approaching to hatred. It is found, that where vigorous intellect bursts the bonds of its ignorance, in this contemned class, that it is immediately merged into the higher and cultivated class; and, notwithstanding the stigma of labour, comes at length to excite respect. Thus the proof is afforded that it is the *ignorance,* not the *occupation* of the working people, that degrades them on the one hand, and empoverishes them on the other. Owing to this ignorance and degradation, it is, that the educated and enlightened, taking advantage of their contemned condition, have oppressed and bound them in the fetters of servile subjection. It is not ignorance that can make laws, organize governments, or administer justice. Education, therefore, is the key to government—it opens the path of power. In vain will you boast of equal rights, and a form of government that secures power to the most humble, when qualified for the task; the blessing will only be nominal whilst the *mass of people* remain ignorant, and incapable of performing those functions that belong to the great civil machine of society. The educated will still occupy the high posts of honour, and devise the system of law and justice; and law and justice thus devised will forever partake of the sentiments peculiar to wisdom and refinement. Hence the maxim that "those who think must govern those who toil;" a maxim, however, that is predicated on the *ignorance* of those who toil, as a necessary property of their condition. But educate those who toil—teach them to *think;* and they take the place of those who govern. This has been strenuously opposed by the great body of the enlightened, because they were fearful of losing their *exclusive privileges,* by imparting knowledge to the mass of the people.

A system of *general education,* one would hardly imagine, could meet with an opponent in an age so enlightened and so philanthropic—an age so distinguished for the *march of mind,* the diffusion of knowledge, and a severe scrutiny into all the principles that combine in the structure of society. And yet, wonderful to say, *public education for the people* has met with gothic adversaries, and illiberal, narrow-minded traducers. The extension of

191

the lights of knowledge, *by popular education,* to all the people of the republic, has ever been the avowed object of all of our most illustrious statesmen. It teems from the lips of the venerated Washington—it glows in the pen of the immortal Jefferson—it formed the daily toil and the midnight study of the lamented and great Clinton. The text of the friends of liberty was—*to enlighten the people is to promote and cement the public virtue!* The soundness of this text was never questioned *anterior* to the organization of a party, whose object it was to obtain it from the legislature, *as a right,* unjustly withheld. When public instruction was bestowed as the *boon of charity,* it found numerous advocates, and met with no opponents; but now, when we justly demand it as a *right*—and under our constitution it must be a *right* and not a charity—it is not only refused by some, but to our utter amazement, its consequences are painted as baneful to the people, and deprecated as having a fatal tendency upon the good order of government! We seem to have resuscitated from the tomb of time the very spirit of the *feudal ages,* in the breasts of certain bigots, intolerants, aristocrats, and narrow-minded *monopolists of knowledge,* who seem as averse to giving the people LIGHT, as they are to paying them for their labour in *hard money.* Actuated by this spirit of an era long past, it is pretended to have been suddenly discovered that *ignorance* is necessary to obedience, and that *public education* is incompatible with public virtue and public order! Sophistry like this is too flimsy to call for confutation; but it reveals a fact that may be useful to us: that although we live under a free constitution, much of the leaven of despotism still remains among us, and that our *theoretical* freedom demands eternal vigilance to preserve it in practice. It is said, that a tax to support common schools would be an *Agrarian Law,* an unjust taking away from the wealth of the rich, for the benefit of the common people. On this principle ALL laws are Agrarian laws; for the rich pay more than the poor individually, though not collectively, for the support of government.

Objections to popular education, however, at the present day, come too late to command attention, or require arguments to show their fallacy. The age has happily outrun those who would keep it stationary in ignorance, or arrest its progress towards general knowledge. The cloud of absolute power in governments has passed away from the firmament of the mind; and left it clear and unspecked by one of the fetters of passive submission, non-resistance, and blind credulity. In time long past, the sovereign power was in the king—now it is in the people; positions being thus reversed, it is incumbent on the people to conform their knowledge to their power.

The influence of education on the manners, is not less important than its operation on the mind; between which there exists so close an intimacy—so powerful a sympathy. Civility, politeness, deference, and all the amiable and softer virtues, are generally found to be residents of minds refined and educated; while ignorance assumes manners of corresponding rudeness, and imperious insolence. As it is the tendency of knowledge to inspire diffidence, the more the mind imbibes, the less it presumes to trespass upon the feelings or challenge the opinions of others. Besides that, in educated people there exists a natural assimilation, the general result of which is good breeding; hence one of the most salutary consequences of popular instruction—that those who labour, and have heretofore been rude and insolent, will gradually become polite and civil; and thus remove one of the most serious difficulties that prevents the working people emerging from that debasing condition in which they are now held by the customs of intellect and power. It is to *education,* therefore, that we must mainly look for a redress of that perverted system of society, which dooms the producer to ignorance, to toil, and to penury, to moral degradation, physical want, and social barbarism.

The power of the ballot boxes will do little, without the auxiliary help of our moral and intellectual energies. How can it be a marvel, that wealth practises oppression, when it holds as its allies, all the riches of knowledge, and the exterior semblances of virtue and truth? Moving in the high orbit of science, government and laws; ordaining justice and morality after their own images, how shall we ever counteract the principles of vassalage that now prevail, unless we procure EDUCATION for our offspring, and diffuse SCIENCE among our brethren? It is through this door that we must at last enter into the temple of justice, to consecrate on the altar of reason the true rights of man. Knowledge is *power,* in respect to the procurement of equity to the great mass of the sons of labour. It is the light of intelligence that abashes despotism—it is the fire of intellect that dissolves and melts the chains that enthral seven eighths of mankind to the caprice and luxury of the other few. *"In what way shall this evil be attacked and removed?"* I have answered, by giving our children equal or superior knowledge, virtue and intelligence, to the rich — by EDUCATION to direct and qualify us for government and laws; and by concentrating our SUFFRAGE to enable us to reach that point of influence, at which we shall be able to make the laws conform to the spirit of justice, and the government congenial to the equality of human rights.

CHAPTER 9

THE POLITICIAN AND EDUCATIONAL REFORM

*Ignorance . . . the cause as well as the effect
of bad government.*

DeWitt Clinton, 1809

23. FREE SCHOOLS (1809)[1]

DeWITT CLINTON

On an occasion so interesting to this Institution [Free School Society of New York City], when it is about to assume a more respectable shape, and to acquire a spacious and permanent habitation, it is no more than a becoming mark of attention to its patrons, benefactors and friends, assembled for the first time in this place, to delineate its origin, its progress, and its present situation. The station which I occupy in this Association, and the request of my much respected colleagues, have devolved this task upon me—a task which I should perform with unmingled pleasure if my avocations had afforded me time to execute it with fidelity. And I trust that the humble objects of your bounty, presented this day to your view, will not detract from the solemnity of the occasion — "That ambition will not mock our useful toil, nor grandeur hear with a disdainful smile the simple annals of the poor."

In casting a view over the civilized world, we find an universal accordance in opinion on the benefits of education; but the practical exposition of this opinion exhibits a deplorable contrast. While magnificent Colleges and Universities are erected, and endowed, and dedicated to literature, we behold few liberal appropriations for diffusing the blessings of knowledge among all descriptions of people. The fundamental error of Europe has been to confine the light of knowledge to the wealthy and the great, while the humble and the depressed have been as sedulously excluded from its participation as the wretched criminal, immured in a dungeon, is from the light of Heaven. This cardinal mistake is

---

[1] William W. Campbell, *The Life and Writings of DeWitt Clinton* (New York: Baker and Scribner, 1849), pp. 309–27. Clinton was Mayor of New York City when he delivered this address to the Free School Society in 1890 upon the occasion of the organization's move to new quarters.

not only to be found in the institutions of the old world and in the condition of its inhabitants, but it is to be seen in most of the books which have been written on the subject of education. The celebrated Locke, whose treatises on government and the human understanding have covered him with immortal glory, devoted the powers of his mighty intellect, to the elucidation of education — but in the very threshold of his book, we discover this radical error — his treatise is professedly intended for the children of gentlemen. "If those of that rank (says he), are by their education once set right, they will quickly bring all the rest in order;" and he appears to consider the education of other children as of little importance. The consequence of this monstrous heresy has been, that ignorance, the prolific parent of every crime and vice, has predominated over the great body of the people, and a corresponding moral debasement has prevailed. "Man differs more from man, than man from beast," says a writer, once celebrated. This remark, however generally false, will certainly apply with great force to a man in a state of high mental cultivation, and man in a state of extreme ignorance.

This view of human nature is indeed calculated to excite the most painful feelings; and it entirely originates from a consideration of the predominating error which I have exposed. To this source must the crimes and calamities of the old world be principally inputed. Ignorance is the cause as well as the effect of bad governments, and without the cultivation of our rational powers, we can entertain no just ideas of the obligations of morality or the excellencies of religion. Although England is justly renowned for its cultivation of the arts and sciences, and although the poor rates of that country exceed five millions sterling per annum, yet (I adopt the words of an eminent British writer), "there is no Protestant country where the education of the poor has been so grossly and infamously neglected as in England." If one-tenth part of that sum had been applied to the education of the poor, the blessings of order, knowledge, and innocence would have been diffused among them, the evil would have been attacked at the fountain head, and a total revolution would have taken place in the habits and lives of the people, favorable to the cause of industry, good morals, good order, and rational religion.

More just and rational views have been entertained on this

subject in the United States. Here, no privileged orders—no factitious distinctions in society—no hereditary nobility—no established religion—no royal prerogatives exist, to interpose barriers between the people, and to create distinct classifications in society. All men being considered as enjoying an equality of rights, the propriety and necessity of dispensing, without distinction, the blessings of education, followed of course. In New England the greatest attention has been invariably given to this important object. In Connecticut, particularly, the schools are supported at least three-fourths of the year by the interest of a very large fund created for that purpose, and a small tax on the people; the whole amounting to seventy-eight thousand dollars per annum. The result of this beneficial arrangement is obvious and striking. Our Eastern brethren are a well-informed and moral people. In those States it is as uncommon to find a poor man who cannot read and write, as it is rare to see one in Europe who can.

Pennsylvania has followed the noble example of New England. On the fourth of April last, a law was passed in that State entitled "An act to provide for the education of the poor, gratis." The expense of educating them is made a county charge, and the county commissioners are directed to carry the law into execution.

New York has proceeded in the same career, but on a different, and perhaps more eligible plan. For a few years back, a fund has been accumulating with great celerity, solemnly appropriated to the support of common schools. This fund consists at present of near four hundred thousand dollars in bank stock, mortgages, and bonds; and produces an annual interest of upwards of twenty-four thousand dollars. The capital will be augmented by the accumulating interest and the sale of three hundred and thirty-six thousand acres of land. When the interest on the whole amounts to fifty thousand dollars, it will be in a state of distribution. It is highly probable that the whole fund will, in a few years, amount to twelve hundred and fifty thousand dollars, yielding a yearly income of seventy-five thousand dollars. If population is taken as the ratio of distribution, the quota of this city will amount to seven thousand five hundred dollars, a sum amply sufficient on the plan of our establishment, if judiciously applied, to accommodate all our poor with a gratuitious education.

On a comparison of the plan of this State with that of Pennsylvania, it will probably be found that we are entitled to the palm of superior excellence. Our capital is already created, and nothing more is requisite than a judicious distribution—whereas the expense of school establishments in that State, is to be satisfied by annual burdens. The people of Pennsylvania are therefore interested against a faithful execution of the plan, because the less that is applied to education, the less they will have to pay in taxation. Abuses and perversions will of course arise and multiply in the administration of the public bounty. And the laws of that State being liable to alteration or repeal, her system has not that permanency and stability to which ours can lay claim. It is true that our Legislature may divert this fund, but it would justly be considered a violation of public faith, and a measure of a very violent character. As long as the public sentiment is correct in this respect, we have no reason to apprehend that any Legislature will be hardy enough to encounter the odium of their constituents, and the indignation of posterity. And we have every reason to believe, that this great fund, established for sinking vice and ignorance, will never be diverted or destroyed, but that it will remain unimpaired, and in full force and vigor to the latest posterity, as an illustrious establishment, erected by the benevolence of the State for the propagation of knowledge, and the diffusion of virtue among the people.

A number of benevolent persons had seen, with concern, the increasing vices of this city, arising in a great degree from the neglected education of the poor. Great cities are at all times the nurseries and hot-beds of crime. Bad men from all quarters repair to them, in order to obtain the benefit of concealment, and to enjoy in a superior degree the advantages of rapine and fraud. And the dreadful examples of vice, which are presented to youth, and the alluring forms in which it is arrayed, connected with a spirit of extravagance and luxury, the never-failing attendant of great wealth and extensive business, cannot fail of augmenting the mass of moral depravity. "In London," says a distinguished writer on its police, "above twenty thousand individuals rise every morning, without knowing how, or by what means they are to be supported through the passing day, and in many instances even where they are to lodge on the ensuing night." There can be no doubt that hundreds are in the same situation in this city, prowling about our streets for prey, the victims of intemperance, the slaves of idleness, and ready to fall into any vice, rather than to cultivate industry and good order. How can it be expected that persons so careless of themselves, will pay any attention to their children? The mendicant parent bequeaths his squalid poverty to his offspring, and the hardened thief transmits a legacy of infamy to his unfortunate and depraved descendants. Instances have occurred of little children, arraigned at the bar of our criminal courts, who have been derelict and abandoned, without a hand to protect, or a voice to guide them through life. When interrogated as to their connections, they have replied, that they were without home and without friends. In this state of turpitude and idleness, leading lives of roving mendicancy and petty depredation, they existed a burden and a disgrace to the community.

True it is, that Charity Schools, entitled to eminent praise, were established in this city, but they were attached to particular sects, and did not embrace children of different persuasions. Add to this that some denominations were not provided with those establishments, and that children, the most in want of instruction, were necessarily excluded, by the irreligion of their parents, from the benefit of education.

After a full view of the case, those persons of whom I have spoken, agreed that the evil must be corrected at its source, and that education was the sovereign prescription. Under this impression, they petitioned the Legislature, who, agreeably to their application, passed a law on the 9th of April, 1805, entitled, "An Act to incorporate the Society instituted in the city of New York for the Establishment of a Free School, for the education of poor children, who do not belong to, or are not provided for, by any religious society."—Thirteen Trustees were elected under this Act, on the first Monday of the ensuing May, with power to manage the affairs of the Corporation. On convening together, they found that they had undertaken a great task, and encountered an important responsibility; without funds, without teachers, without a house in which to instruct, and without a system of instruction; and that their only reliance must be on their own industry, on the liberality of the public, on the bounty of the constituted authorities, and on the smiles of the Almighty Dispenser of all good.

In the year 1798, an obscure man of the name of Joseph Lancaster, possessed of an original genius and a most sagacious mind, and animated by a sublime benevolence, devoted himself to the education of the poor of Great-Britain. Wherever he turned his eyes, he saw the deplorable state to which they were reduced by the prevalence of ignorance and vice. He first planted his standard of charity in the city of London, where it was calculated that forty thousand children were left as destitute of instruction as the savages of the desert. And he proceeded by degrees, to form and perfect a system, which is in education what the most finished machines for abridging labor and expense are in the mechanic arts.

It comprehends reading, writing, arithmetic, and the knowledge of the Holy Scriptures. It arrives at its object with the least possible trouble and at the least possible expense. Its distinguishing characters are economy, facility, and expedition, and its peculiar improvements are cheapness, activity, order, and emulation. It is impossible on this occasion to give a detailed view of the system. For this I refer you to a publication entitled, "Improvements in Education, &c., by Joseph Lancaster," and for its practical exposition, I beg you to look at the operations of this seminary. Reading in all its processes, from the alphabet upwards, is taught at the same time with writing, commencing with sand, proceeding to the slate, and from thence to the copy-book. And to borrow a most just and striking remark, "The beauty of the system is, that nothing is trusted to the boy himself—he does not only *repeat* the lesson before a superior, but he *learns* before a superior." Solitary study does not exist in the establishment. The children are taught in companies. Constant habits of attention and vigilance are formed, and an ardent spirit of emulation kept continually alive. Instruction is performed through the instrumentality of the scholars. The school is divided into classes of ten, and a chief, denominated a Monitor, is appointed over each class, who exercises a didactic and supervisional authority. The discipline of the school is enforced by shame, rather than by the infliction of pain. The punishments are varied with circumstances; and a judicious distribution of rewards, calculated to engage the infant mind in the discharge of its duty, forms the keystone which binds together the whole edifice.

Upon this system, Lancaster superintended in person a school of one thousand scholars, at an annual expense of three hundred pounds sterling. In 1806, he proposed, by establishing twenty or thirty schools in different parts of the kingdom, to educate ten thousand poor children, at four shillings per annum each. This proposition has been carried into effect, and he has succeeded in establishing twenty schools in different parts of the kingdom, all of which are under the care of teachers, educated by him, few of whom are more than eighteen years old. Several of the schools have each about three hundred scholars—that at Manchester has four hundred—his great school in Borough-Road, London, flourishes very much—it has sometimes eleven hundred children —seldom less than one thousand.

When I perceive that many boys in our school have been taught to read and write in two months, who did not before know the Alphabet, and that even one has accomplished it in three weeks—when I view all the bearings and tendencies of this system—when I contemplate the habits of order which it forms, the spirit of emulation which it excites—the rapid improvement which it produces—the purity of morals which it inculcates—when I behold the extraordinary union of celerity in instruction, and economy of expense—and when I perceive one great assembly of a thousand children, under the eye of a single teacher, marching with unexampled rapidity, and with perfect discipline, to the goal of knowledge, I confess that I recognize in Lancaster, the benefactor of the human race—I consider his system as creating a new era in education, as a blessing sent down from Heaven to redeem the poor and distressed of this world from the power and dominion of ignorance.

Although the merits of this apostle of benevolence have been generally acknowledged in his own country, and he has received the countenance and protection of the first men in Great Britain, yet calumny has lifted up her voice against him, and attempts have been made to rob him of his laurels. Danger to the Established Church and to Government, has been apprehended from his endeavors to pour light upon mankind. This insinuation has been abundantly repelled by the tenor of his life—his carefully steering clear in his instructions of any peculiar creed, and his confining himself to the general truths of Christianity. "I have," says Lancaster, "been eight years engaged in the benevolent work of superintending the education of the poor. I have had three thousand children, who owe their education to me, some of whom have left school, are apprenticed or in place, and are going on well. I have had great influence with both parents and children, among whom there is, nevertheless, no one instance of a convert to my religious profession." That knowledge is the parent of sedition and insurrection, and that in proportion as the public mind is illuminated, the principles of anarchy are disseminated, is a proposition that can never admit of debate, at least in this country.

But Lancaster has also been accused of arrogating to himself surreptitious honors, and attempts have been made to transfer the entire merit of his great discovery to Dr. Bell. Whatever he borrowed from that gentleman, he has candidly acknowledged. The use of sand in teaching, undoubtedly came to him through that channel, but it has been practised for ages by the Brahmins. He may also be indebted to Bell for some other improvements, but the vital leading principles of his system, are emphatically an original discovery.

The trustees of this institution, after due deliberation, did not hesitate to adopt the system of Lancaster, and in carrying it into effect, they derived essential aid from one of their body, who had seen it practised in England, and who had had personal communication with its author. A teacher was also selected who has fully answered every reasonable expectation. He has generally followed the prescribed plan. Wherever he has deviated, he has improved. A more numerous, a better governed school, affording equal facilities to improvement, is not to be found in the United States.

Provided thus with an excellent system and an able teacher, the school was opened on the 6th of May, 1806, in a small apartment in Bancker street. This was the first scion of the Lancaster stock engrafted in the United States; and from this humble beginning, in the course of little more than three years, you all observe the rapidity with which we have ascended.

One great desideratum still remained to be supplied. Without sufficient funds, nothing could be efficiently done. Animated appeals were made to the bounty of our citizens, and five thousand six hundred and forty-eight dollars were collected by subscription.

203

Application was also made to the Legislature of this State for assistance, and on the 27th of February, 1807, a law was passed, appropriating four thousand dollars, for the "purpose of erecting a suitable building, or buildings, for the instruction of poor children, and every year thereafter, the sum of one thousand dollars, for the purpose of promoting the benevolent objects of the Society." The preamble of this liberal act contains a legislative declaration of the excellence of the Lancaster system, in the following words: — "Whereas the trustees of the Society for establishing a Free School in the city of New York, for the education of such poor children as do not belong to, or are not provided for, by any religious society, have, by their memorial, solicited the aid of the Legislature; and whereas their plan of extending the benefits of education to poor children, and the excellent mode of instruction adopted by them, are highly deserving of the encouragement of Government."

Application was also made to the Corporation of the city for assistance, and the tenement in Bancker-street, being in all respects inadequate to the accommodation of the increasing establishment, that body appropriated a building adjacent to the Alms-house, for the temporary accommodation of the school, and the sum of five hundred dollars towards putting it in repair; the Society agreeing to receive and educate fifty children from the Alms-house. To this place the school was removed on the 1st of May, 1807, where it has continued until to-day.

The Corporation also presented the ground of this edifice, on which was an arsenal, to the Society, on condition of their educating the children of the Alms-house gratuitously; and also the sum of fifteen hundred dollars, to aid in the completion of this building. The value of this lot and the old building, may be fairly estimated at ten thousand dollars; and the Society have expended above thirteen thousand dollars in the erection and completion of this edifice and the adjacent buildings. The income of the school, during the last year, has been about sixteen hundred dollars, and its expense did not much differ from that sum. This room will contain near six hundred scholars, and below there are apartments for the family of the teacher, for the meeting of the trustees, and for a female school, which may contain one hundred scholars, and may be considered as an useful adjunct to this institution. This seminary was established about twelve years ago, by a number of young women belonging to, or professing with, the Society of Friends; who have, with meritorious zeal and exemplary industry, devoted much of their personal attention, and all their influence, to the education of poor girls in the elementary parts of education and needle-work. The signal success which attended this free-school animated the trustees with a desire to extend its usefulness, and to render it coextensive with the wants of the community, and commensurate with the objects of public bounty. A statute was accordingly passed, on their application, on the 1st of April, 1808, altering the style of this corporation, denominating it "The Free School Society of New York," and extending its powers to all children who are the proper objects of gratuitous education.

From this elevation of prosperity and this fruition of philanthropy, the Society had the satisfaction of seeing that the wise and the good of this and the neighboring States, had turned their attention to their establishment. A number of ladies of this city, distinguished for their consideration in society, and honored and respected for their undeviating cultivation of the charities of life, established a society for the very humane, charitable, and laudable purposes of protecting, relieving, and instructing orphan children. This institution was incorporated on the 7th of April, 1807, under the style of "The Orphan Asylum Society in the City of New York," and at a subsequent period the Legislature, under a full conviction of its great merits and claims to public patronage, made a disposition in its favor, which will, in process of time, produce five thousand dollars.

A large building, fifty feet square and three stories high, has been erected for its accommodation, in the suburbs of the city, and it now contains seventy children, who are supported by the zeal and benevolence of its worthy members, and educated on the plan of this institution, at an annual expense of two thousand dollars.

An economical school, whose principal object is the instruction of the children of the Refugees from the West Indies, was opened some time since in this city, where, in addition to the elementary parts of education, Grammar, History, Geography, and the French language, are taught. It is conducted on the plan of Lancaster, with modifications and extensions, and is patronized and cherished by French and American gentlemen, of great worth and respectability, who are entitled to every praise for their benevolence. Children of either sex are admitted, without distinction of nation, religion, or fortune. This Seminary is in a flourishing condition, and contains two hundred scholars. There are two masters in this Seminary, and two women who teach needle-work, and there is a printing-press; where such as have any talents in that way are taught that important art.

We have also the satisfaction of seeing the benefits of this system extended, either in whole or in part, to the Charity Schools of the Dutch, Episcopal, and Methodist Churches, and of the Presbyterian Church in Rutger's-street; and also to the school founded by the Manumission Society, for the education of the people of color; which has, in consequence of this amelioration, been augmented from seventy to one hundred and thirty children.

In Philadelphia, the same laudable spirit has been manifested. Two deputations from that city have visited us, for the express purpose of examining our school. One of these made so favorable a report on their return, that a number of the more enterprising and benevolent citizens, composed of members belonging to the Society of Friends, immediately associated under the name of the "Adelphi Society," and raised, by private subscription, a sum sufficient to purchase a suitable lot of ground, to erect a handsome two story brick building, seventy-five feet in length, and thirty-five in breadth, in which they formed two spacious rooms. The Adelphi School now contains two hundred children, under the care of one teacher, and is eminently prosperous. The other deputation made also a favorable report, and "the Philadelphia Free School Society," an old and respectable institution, adopted, in consequence, our system, where it flourishes beyond expectation.

Two female schools, one called the "Aimwell School," in Philadelphia, and another in Burlington, New Jersey, have also embraced our plan with equal success.

I trust that I shall be pardoned for this detail. The origin and progress of beneficial discoveries cannot be too minutely specified; and when their diffusion can only be exceeded by their excellence, we have peculiar reason to congratulate the friends of humanity. This prompt and general encouragement is honorable to our national character, and shows conclusively that the habits, manners, and opinions of the American people, are favorable to the reception of truth and the propagation of knowledge. — And no earthly consideration could induce the benevolent man, to whom we are indebted for what we see this day, to exchange his feelings, if from the obscure mansions of indigence, in which, in all human probability he now is, instilling comfort into the hearts, and infusing knowledge into the minds of the poor, he could hear the voice of a great and enlightened people pronouncing his eulogium, and see this parent seminary, and the establishments which have sprung from its bosom, diffusing light, imparting joy, and dispensing virtue. His tree of knowledge is indeed transplanted to a more fertile soil, and a more congenial clime. It has flourished with uncommon vigor and beauty—its luxuriant and wide-spreading branches afford shelter to all who require it—its ambrosial fragrance fills the land—and its head reaches the heavens!

Far be it from my intention to prevent future exertion. For although much has been done, yet much remains to do, to carry into full effect the system. It would be improper to conceal from you, that in order to finish this edifice we have incurred a considerable debt, which our ordinary income cannot extinguish; and that, therefore, we must repose ourselves on the public beneficence. It has been usual to supply the more indigent children with necessaries to protect them against the inclemencies of winter —for without this provision, their attendance would be utterly impracticable. This has hitherto been accomplished by the bounty of individuals, and to no other source can we at present appeal for success.

The law from which we derive our corporate existence does not confine us to one seminary, but contemplates the establishment of schools. A restriction to a single institution would greatly impair our usefulness, and would effectually discourage those exertions which are necessary in order to spread knowledge among all the indigent.

Col. Henry Rutgers, with his characteristic benevolence, has made a donation of two lots in Henry-street, worth at least twenty-five hundred dollars, to this Corporation. By a condition contained in one of the deeds, it is necessary that we should erect a school-house by June, 1811; and it is highly proper, without any reference to the condition, that this should be accomplished as soon as possible, in order to meet the wants of the indigent in that populous part of the city. If some charitable and public-spirited

207

citizen would follow up this beneficence, and make a similar conveyance on the opposite side of the city, and if the liberality of the public shall dispense the means of erecting the necessary buildings, then the exigencies of all our poor, with respect to education, would be amply supplied for a number of years.

After our youth are instructed in the elements of useful knowledge, it is indispensable to their future usefulness that some calling should be marked out for them. As most of them will undoubtedly be brought up in useful trades, pecuniary means to facilitate their progress to this object would, if properly applied, greatly redound to the benefit of the individual as well as to the good of the community.

In such an extensive and comprehensive establishment, we are to expect, according to the course of human events, that children of extraordinary genius and merit will rise up, entitled to extraordinary patronage. To select such from the common mass—to watch over their future destiny—to advance them through all the stages of education and through all the grades of knowledge, and to settle them in useful and honorable professions, are duties of primary importance and indispensable obligation. This, however, will require considerable funds: but of what estimation are pecuniary sacrifices when put in the scale against the important benefits that may result; and if we could draw aside the veil of futurity, perhaps we might see in the offspring of this establishment, so patronized and so encouraged, characters that will do honor to human nature. . . .

24. THE IMPORTANCE OF EDUCATION IN A REPUBLIC (1838)[1]

EDWARD EVERETT

MR PRESIDENT:

I rise, at the particular request of the secretary of the board, and in compliance with the wishes of other respected friends of education, to express to you the thoughts which occur to me on the great subject now under our consideration, and, more especially, on the resolution which has just been read. I do not come prepared to discuss the proposition which it contains in a maturely-digested discourse. My object only is to offer to you, and this large and respected audience, the thoughts, somewhat desultory, which present themselves to my mind on the principle advanced in the resolution; and, if I can do more, I shall be well contented with having offered to the convention this public testimony of the interest I take in the cause.

I will observe, in the first place, that, without designing any thing like adulation of our native state, we may claim for it the credit of having made provision for education from the earliest period of its settlement. The small New England republics, and especially Massachusetts, have been, in point of time, far in advance of the older governments of the world, in systematic provision for the education of the people at the public expense. In setting this example, we have certainly paid back to Europe no small part of the debt of civilization. I regard this hereditary care for education as a precious portion of our moral birthright; and I trust we shall transmit it, unimpaired, to after ages.

I would gladly believe, nay, I do firmly believe, that this attention—which, in this country, has never been withheld from educa-

[1]Edward Everett, *Orations and Speeches on Various Occasions* (10th ed., Boston, 1883), II, 313–21, 323–24. The address was given in 1838, when Everett was Governor of Massachusetts, to a Common School Convention.

tion, and which, of late, I am rejoiced to say, has greatly increased — does not manifest itself in an accidental, far less uncongenial association, with that general interest in political affairs which also characterizes our communities, and springs from popular systems of government. On the contrary, in the view I take of the subject, a country possessed of such institutions is precisely that where education is most important; where alone it is absolutely necessary for carrying on the system of government, and keeping up its natural healthy action. It is, of course, in such a country that we should most expect from the people an enlightened and vigilant care of education.

There are two simple plans of government, on which, either pure, and without qualification, or with such admixture of the two principles, all constitutions are constructed. One of them asserts that the people are the rightful source of power, both ultimate and direct; the other denies this proposition. When Charles I. stood upon the scaffold, and a moment before he laid his head upon the block, so firm was his faith in the last-named principle, that he declared, with his dying breath, that "the people's right was only to have their life and their goods their own, a share in the government being nothing pertaining to them." The other plan is announced, in clear terms, in the constitution of Massachusetts: "The people of this commonwealth have the sole and exclusive right of governing themselves, as a free, sovereign, and independent state."

Now, it might be thought, that, even on the theory of government which Charles sealed with his blood, education would be deemed a great popular interest, as teaching the methods, and furnishing some of the means, of preserving life and acquiring property, which he admitted to be within the right of the people. It does not appear, however, that, at that time, nor till long after, this right was understood as imposing any correlative duty on the prince; consequently, such a thing as a scheme of popular education, promoted by the state, was, at that time, unthought of. It is not, certainly, my intention to intimate that there was no education in England, before the revolution of 1688, but such as was compatible with the spirit and policy of a purely arbitrary government. There was always a temperament of popular institutions in the British monarchy, inviting and forcing the minds of men, in various ways, to improvement and progress. The administration of affairs had never, in practice, for any long period of time, been brought down to the platform of Oriental despotism, to which the theory of Charles I. reduced it.

There were always parliaments, courts of justice, and juries, in the worst of times. The universities were seats of scholastic learning, and the practice of dispensing religious instruction from the pulpit forced upon the church a certain kind of popular education; but I suppose it was obtained at schools and colleges founded by pious and charitable individuals. Nothing resulted from the theory of the government, but that the prince, and those associated with him, needed the advantages of education, to fit them for the administration of affairs. Accordingly, we find that, with the popular reforms which have been made in the government of England, in modern times, and especially in our own day, attention has been given, for the first time, to national education. The best efforts of the Broughams and Wyses, and other liberal statesmen, have been strenuously made in this cause; and I learn, with satisfaction, from a distinguished gentleman from that country, who is now present with us, (Mr George Combe, of Edinburgh,) that a greatly-increased interest in the subject has marked the progress of the political reforms of a recent date, in the land of our fathers. In like manner, in France, every thing that has been done for popular education, by the enlightened zeal and labors of M. Cousin, and its other distinguished friends in that country, dates from the period of the political reforms of the government of the country. It reflects lasting credit on the Prussian monarchy, that, without admitting the people to an efficient share in the government, it has had the wisdom and the courage to bestow upon them an admirable system of public education.

But on the system established in the United States, where the people are not only in theory the source of power, but in practice are actually called upon, constantly, to take an efficient part in constituting and administering the government, it is plain that education is universally and indispensably necessary, to enable them to exercise their rights and perform their duties. This will be put beyond question by considering a few particulars.

I. The first duty, in a popular government, is that which is attached to the elective franchise; though I fear it is too little regarded in this light. It is not merely the right, but it is the duty, of the citizen, by the exercise of the right of suffrage, to take a part, at periods recurring after short intervals, in organizing the government. This duty cannot be discharged with rectitude, unless it be discharged with intelligence; and it becomes the duty of the citizen to make up his own mind on all the great questions which arise in administering the government. How numerous and important these questions are, I need not say. Since you and I, Mr President, have been of years to observe the march of affairs, the people of the United States have been called to make up a practical judgment on the following, among other great questions,—the *protective policy,* that is, on the legislation necessary to introduce and establish an infant branch of manufactures; a question, however easily disposed of by theorists, on both sides, of infinite practical difficulty; on *internal improvement,* that is, the construction of public works of communication between the various parts of the country, at the expense of the general government; on the *circulating medium,* and how far the currency, which is the representative of value, must have intrinsic value itself; on the *different families of the human race* existing in the country, and the rights and duties which result from their relation to each other; on the *relations* of the country with *foreign* powers, in reference to colonial trade, disputed boundaries, and indemnification for wrongs and spoliations; on the disposal of the *public domain,* and its bearings on the progress of population and of republican government in the mighty west; on the nature of our political system, as consisting in the harmonious *adjustment of the federal and state governments.* I have named only a part of the questions which, within the last twenty years, have been, some of them constantly, before the community—the turning-points of municipal, state, and national elections. The good citizen, who is not willing to be the slave of a party because he is a member of it, must make up his mind for himself on all those great questions, or he cannot exercise the right of suffrage with intelligence and independence. As the majority of the people are well or ill informed on these subjects, the public policy of the country will be guided by wisdom and truth, or the reverse.

I do not mean that it is necessary that every citizen should receive an education which would enable him to argue all these questions, at length, in a deliberative or popular assembly; but, while it is his right and his duty to give effect to his judgment at the polls, and while the constitution necessarily gives as much weight to the vote of the uninformed and ignorant as to that of the well-instructed and intelligent citizen, it is plain that the avenues to information should be as wide and numerous as possible; and that the utmost practicable extension should be given to a system of education which will confer on every citizen the capacity of deriving knowledge, with readiness and accuracy, from books and documents. The whole energy of the state should be directed to multiply the numbers of those capable of forming an independent and rational judgment of their own, and to diminish as much as possible the numbers of the opposite class, who, being blinded by ignorance, are at the mercy of any one who has an interest and the skill to delude them.

II. But the exercise of the elective franchise is only the beginning of the duties of the citizen. The constitution makes it the right, the laws make it the duty, of all citizens, within certain ages, to bear arms. It may sound strangely to connect this duty with the subject of education. I hope no practical demonstration of the connection of the topics will ever arise among us. But this right and this duty, lightly esteemed in quiet times, may become of fearful import. Arms are placed in the hands of the citizen for the most important purposes; not for parade and holiday display, but to defend his country against violence from abroad; to maintain the supremacy of the laws; to preserve the peace of the community. Heaven grant that the day may be far distant when our citizens shall be called to wield them for either purpose. But if the experience of the past warrant an anticipation of the future, the time may come when this duty, also, is to be performed. It will not then be a matter of indifference whether the honor and peace of the community are committed to an ignorant and benighted multitude, like those which swell the ranks of the mercenary standing armies of Europe, or to an educated and intelligent population, whose powers of reflection have been strengthened by exercise, and who are able to discriminate between constitutional liberty and arbitrary power on the one hand, and anarchy on the other.

III. There are other civil duties to be performed, for which education furnishes a still more direct and appropriate prepara-

213

tion. The law of tne land calls the citizen to take a part in the administration of justice. Twelve men are placed in the jury-box, to decide on the numberless questions which arise in the community—questions of character, of property, and of life. The jury passes on your fortune and your reputation; pronounces whether you live or die. Go into the courts: are they light matters which those twelve men are to decide? Look in the anxious faces of those whose estates, whose good name, whose all, is at stake, hanging on the intelligence of those twelve men, or any one of them. What assurance is there, but that which comes from our schools, that these men will understand and do their duty? Those little boys, now sporting in the streets, or conning their tasks in our town schools, in a few short years will be summoned, in their turns, to discharge this important trust. Can we deem it a matter of indifference whether or not their minds have been early accustomed to follow a train of thoughts or a statement of facts? Did not the secretary give us, this morning, from his own experience, the instance of a witness who, in a case of slander, where every thing turned on his testimony, first swore that what he saw, he saw through one window, and then through another, and then through a door? Woe to the community, where the degree of stolidity and ignorance, necessary to constitute such a witness, abounds; and where it must appear, not only on the stand, but in the jury-box. It appears to me a most imperative duty, on the part of a state which calls its citizens to discharge this momentous office, to do all in its power to qualify them for it by a general system of education. Is it said, there is learned counsel to argue and explain the cause to a jury, however ignorant? But there is counsel on both sides; the jury must decide after hearing them both. But the court will instruct the jury. No doubt, as far as the law is concerned; but the court's instructions are addressed to minds supposed to be capable of following out an argument, estimating evidence, and making up an independent opinion. I do not say, that there are not some minds to whom the best opportunities of education would not impart the requisite qualifications of an intelligent juror. But I may appeal to every professional character and magistrate in this convention, that, in an important case, if he were to be called on to select a jury on which he could place full reliance, he would select men of good common sense, who had received a good common education.

214

IV. But I have not yet named all the civil duties for which education is needed, as the preparatory discipline. The various official trusts in society are to be filled, from a commission of the peace to the place of chief justice; from a constable up to the president of the United States. The sphere of duty of some of these functionaries is narrow; of others, large and inexpressibly responsible; of none, insignificant. Taken together, they make up the administration of free government—the greatest merely temporal interest of civilized man. There are three courses, between which we must choose. We must have officers unqualified for their duties; or we must educate a privileged class, to monopolize the honors and emoluments of place; or we must establish such a system of general education, as will furnish a supply of well-informed, intelligent, and respectable citizens, in every part of the country and in every walk of life, capable of discharging the trusts which the people may devolve upon them. The topic is of great compass, but I cannot dwell upon it. It is superfluous to say which of the three courses is most congenial with the spirit of republicanism.

V. I have thus far spoken of those reasons for promoting common school education, which spring from the nature of our government. There are others, derived from the condition of our country. Individual enterprise is every where stimulated; the paths of adventure are opened; the boundless west prevents the older settlements from being overstocked, and gives scope for an unexampled development of energy. Education is wanted, to enlighten and direct those active, moving powers. Without it, much wild vigor will be exerted in vain. Energy alone is not enough; it must be turned to feasible objects, and work by sound principles.

Again, this spirit of enterprise runs naturally towards the acquisiton of wealth. In this I find no matter of reproach; only let it not be a merely Carthaginian prosperity. Let a taste for reading and reflection be cultivated, as well as property acquired. Let us give our children the keys of knowledge, as well as an establishment in business. Let them, in youth, form habits and tastes which will remain with them in after-life, in old age, and furnish rational entertainment at all times. When we collect the little circle, at the family board and at the fireside, in our long winter evenings, let us be able to talk of subjects of interest and importance,—the pro-

215

ductions and institutions of our own and foreign countries; the history of our venerated fathers; the wonders of the material universe; the experience of our race; great moral interests and duties; — subjects surely as important as dollars and cents. Let us, from early years, teach our children to rise above the dust beneath their feet, to the consideration of the great spiritual concerns of immortal natures. A mere bookworm is a worthless character; but a mere money-getter is no better.

It is a great mistake, to suppose that it is necessary to be a professional man, in order to have leisure to indulge a taste for reading. Far otherwise. I believe the mechanic, the engineer, the husbandman, the trader, have quite as much leisure as the average of men in the learned professions. I know some men, busily engaged in these different callings of active life, whose minds are well stored with various useful knowledge acquired from books. There would be more such men, if education in our common schools were, as it well might be, of a higher order; and if common school libraries, well furnished, were introduced into every district, as I trust, in due time, they will be. It is surprising, sir, how much may be effected, even under the most unfavorable circumstances, for the improvement of the mind, by a person resolutely bent on the acquisition of knowledge. . . .

✿ ✿ ✿

No leisure, Mr President, for reading? Is there a man in the community, of an intelligent mind, and with any, the least, tincture of improvement, derived from education, who, when coming, at nightfall, from his labor, (I care not how hard or humble,) if told that, beneath his roof, he would find Shakspeare, or Milton, or Scott, or Irving, or Channing, seated in actual presence by his fireside, and waiting to converse with him, would talk of wanting leisure, or of fatigue? Would he not bound forward to meet them, as the panting hart bounds to the water-brooks? Would not the stars grow pale in the sky before he would think of weariness? Well, sir, there is not an individual in the community who cannot, for a few dollars, surround his fireside with these and kindred spirits, the lights and guides of humanity; not in bodily, but in intellectual presence. They will speak to his understanding, not through the ear, but through the eye. They will discourse to him, not in their every-day language, in which the most gifted do not

216

always greatly excel their fellows, but in the choicest and purest strains to which, by study and meditation, and I had almost said, by inspiration, they have elevated their thoughts; and this they will do, not for a hasty moment, in a brief visit, but again and again, for days and for years; yea, until, by long-continued intercourse with the noblest intellects of our race, his own becomes exalted and purified.

VI. There is one other topic to which I ought to allude, more important than all others; but I have only time for a single remark. Man is a religious being, and, as far as human means and influences go, education is the natural basis of a rational belief. It is the peculiarity of Christianity, as distinguished from other religions, that it addresses the understanding as well as the heart. It commands us to search the Scriptures; to be ready to give a reason for the hope that is in us; and invites us, on the Sabbath, to listen to a *discourse*, that is, a connected, well-reasoned address, on its evidence, duties, hopes, and sanctions. Can this be done, to a good purpose, (humanly speaking,) without education? The heathen might offer incense on the altar of Jupiter with a vacant mind; he might scrutinize the palpitating viscera of animals with a grovelling spirit; he might consult the oracle at Delphi, and shape his conduct by the response, with a benighted understanding. It is but little to say that there was nothing in his religion that invited the exercise of his reasoning powers. We are blessed with a faith which calls into action the whole intellectual man; which prescribes a reasonable service; challenges the investigation of its evidences; and which, in the doctrine of immortality, invests the mind of man with a portion of the dignity of Divine Intelligence. In whatever other respects the advantages of education may be dispensed with, when we consider man as a religious and immortal being, it is a shocking spectacle to see him growing up dark and benighted, ignorant of himself, of his duties, and of his destination.

But this subject is too vast for the occasion. I forbear to enlarge. I trust, sir, the resolution will be adopted, and that the people of Massachusetts, of this generation, will show by their conduct as a powerful commonwealth, not less than as a community of individuals, that they perceive the intimate connection between education and the existence and prosperity of free institutions of government.

217

CHAPTER 10

THE REFORMER

Education. . . the great equalizer
of the condition of men.

Horace Mann, 1848

25. A Concise View of the General State of Education in the United States (1832)[1]

WALTER ROGERS JOHNSON

Among the various topics of interest connected with the history, progress and actual condition of the United States, none deserves a more attentive consideration than that of the means by which the public *mind* is developed and matured.

Whatever *peculiar* interest may be attached to the United States as a nation, must obviously be attributable to other causes than mere local and physical advantages. Whatever hopes may be entertained in regard to the amelioration of man's social condition and political relations, as developed in the western hemisphere, must be founded on the presence and action of causes not operative in the despotic nations of Europe. The acknowledgement, both theoretical and practical, of a few important maxims in politics, and the wide and general diffusion of *intelligence* by all the appropriate means, constitute the main differences between the population of this country and that of several nations in the eastern hemisphere. The original individual dispositions of men here are probably much the same as in Europe; and it would be vain to expect, from the mere advantage of local situation, an exemption from the evils which beset the race, whether in their individual or their social capacity, so long as the intelligent principle of the mass of society lies dormant, and those moral energies which prove conservative in all times of difficulty and danger, are permitted to receive but a partial development, or a meager aliment, when brought into action.

[1]*Hazard's Register of Pennsylvania*, X (Oct. 27, 1832), 257–65. Johnson, Massachusetts-born and Harvard-educated, was a well-known scientist, a dedicated educator, and a supporter of the universal education movement. He was, successively, a teacher, a principal, a professor of Mechanics and Natural Philosophy at the Franklin Institute in Philadelphia, and a member of the Smithsonian Institution.

It is proposed in the following sketch, after a brief account of the early efforts which were made to promote the cause of intelligence among the first colonists, and a concise statement of the results of those attempts previous to the revolution, to consider the means and the authority by which public provision for general education has been made.

Referring next to the different classes of seminaries and institutions by which education is promoted, we may consider in particular the number and character of each class, with its influence on the state of general intelligence.

We shall then present some statements respecting institutions peculiarly appropriated to certain classes or professions of the community; and finally, note the influence of voluntary associations, having for their avowed object the advancement of learning or the promotion of education.

Education, regarded as a great public interest, is necessarily considered in close connexion with the means provided, and the institutions established for the purposes of public *instruction.* Though some affect to draw a broad distinction between these two things, they are in fact so intimately connected, that any reference to a system of public *education,* of which instruction is not the predominant and most important feature, becomes almost ridiculous. It may be added that much of what is called *teaching* is neither instruction nor education, as it neither conveys knowledge nor developes the understanding. Such is all that species of dogmatising which consists in forcing upon the mind general truths without the concomitant, or rather the antecedent examination of the facts on which they are established.

The amount of *public patronage* to seminaries of learning, must not be assumed as the absolute measure of education in any part of the country, and least of all in those states where public schools, academies, and colleges have been longest established. The amount of money paid and the quantity of instruction given in private schools and families, is, in all the states, very considerable; and, though it does not effect all the objects of education, and though it confines the views of youth, and limits the number of those parents who take a deep interest in public instruction, yet it serves to bound, in some degree, the inroads of ignorance and error, vice and superstition.

The early colonists of the eastern portion of the Union brought from the parent country some just and admirable ideas of the true basis of liberty, which they endeavoured to establish on the foundation of universal intelligence. One of the first acts of legislation of the colony of Massachusetts Bay, which received its royal charter in 1628, was a law for the education of every child in the colony. This law merely made it obligatory on parents to educate their own children and apprentices; but in 1647 the same colony enacted a law to establish schools for instruction in the common branches of an English education in every *town* containing fifty families; and a school for the higher branches in each town containing one hundred families. The germ of all the common school systems of the United States, may thus be regarded as coeval with the settlement of the country; and the spirit which dictated this admirable provision for universal intelligence (though blended in the minds of the early colonists with much of that puritanical austerity which is equally opposed to nature, reason, and rational religion) is to be commended as the essential principle of free government and of equal rights. A penalty of twenty pounds was affixed to the neglect of this law on the part of any town.

There is some difficulty, if not an utter impossibility, in obtaining authentic information respecting the exact state of the schools erected in early times, in accordance with these laws. They were managed and controlled solely by the little corporations called in the eastern states *towns;* elsewhere known by the designation of *townships.* No regular general report of their condition and operation was rendered, and the government of the colony was not authorised to interfere in their management farther than to grant the remedy for neglect to provide schools, where the law authorised and required such provision. But public opinion appears to have been ever in advance of the requirements of the law; as few, if any penalties were incurred by the towns for remissness in this particular. The colony of Connecticut was early engaged in the cause of universal education; and her system of public common schools has at all times constituted the chief object of care and anxiety. The same provision and the same limitations as to number of families required to oblige a town to support schools, were found as in the older colony of Massachusetts.

But notwithstanding the obvious policy and usefulness of the system of general education, it will require but little reflection to convince us that the greater part of the efforts of a public nature made for the diffusion of education, have been applied to those classes whose moral and intellectual culture least requires the fostering care of government. With the exception of some of the New England states, particularly Massachusetts and Connecticut, little had been done for common schools before the commencement of the present century. In the two states just named, provisions for universal education were, as already stated, among the *first* objects of their pilgrim founders. Their reason for wishing the blessings of knowledge to be widely diffused, are certainly as cogent under the independent as they could have been under the colonial government.

In the first law of Massachusetts, it was provided "that none of them (the colonists) shall suffer so much barbarism in any of their families, as not to endeavour to teach, by themselves or others, their children and apprentices so much learning as may enable them to read the English tongue, *and knowledge of the capital laws.*"

. . . Up to the time of the revolution in 1776, only eight [colleges] had been formed for a population of three millions. This number it will also be seen is now increased eight fold, for about a quadruple population; and other schools of a higher class have doubtless been multiplied in a proportionate degree.

Harvard college, the oldest in the United States, had, during the ten years immediately preceding the American revolution, about one hundred and seventy students. The other seven colleges did not probably, at that time, average more than half that number each, but the wealthier and more loyal part of the colonists were in the practice of sending their sons to England for education—a practice which, while it fostered a colonial dependence, withdrew a portion of encouragement from the institutions founded in America.

The constitution of the United States has not confided to congress the superintendence of public instruction, rightly judging, perhaps, that such a power could be best exercised by those who were most immediately concerned in the faithful execution of laws respecting this matter. The bestowment of a portion of the public lands to be held by the several states for purposes of education, is, in fact, an acknowledgement that congress does not possess the power to regulate the details of instruction, at the same time that it indicates a just estimate of the important cause, for the promotion of which the appropriations in question have been made.

The local legislatures of the twenty-four states are therefore the only acknowledged organs for declaring and executing the public will in this particular.

But though the minute arrangements for promoting education, are not under the control of the general government, there is one mode in which it may conduce directly to the advancement of the cause of instruction; and that is, by furnishing, at the time of taking each census, a full account of the number of persons receiving education in every precinct of the country: such statistics are a great desideratum, and could in no manner essentially impede the progress of those employed to make the enumeration.

The different kinds of institutions for education established by public authority, may be reduced to the following classes:

1. Primary or "common" schools.
2. Academies, high schools, or gymnasia.
3. Schools and institutes for practical popular instruction.
4. Colleges and universities.
5. Professional schools.

To which may be added several establishments for the instruction of particular classes, who from certain peculiar circumstances are precluded from a participation in the benefits of the general provisions for instruction. Such are the *deaf* and *dumb*, for whom several flourishing institutions have been erected, and the *blind*, who are likely soon to enjoy such a measure of the blessing of instruction as their unfortunate deprivation will admit.

It will be evident that the cause of education is one on which the American people set a high and a just estimate, when we recollect that the establishment of public seminaries, of all the above descriptions, has never been made to prejudice the right of any individual or company to establish similar institutions on their private account and responsibility; and that no authority and no inquisitorial power whatever can be exercised to limit or abolish that right, but, on the contrary, numerous establishments of the first respectability have from the earliest times been maintained on that footing. The seminaries of a private kind have, indeed, sometimes far surpassed those which claim public patronage, both in the liberality of their provisions, the ability of their teachers, and the numbers of their pupils. They are useful in giving that free scope to the choice of methods and range of studies which is seldom allowed in those public institutions, especially of a higher class, which rest on the basis of chartered privileges. . . .

In two of the New England states, Massachusetts and Connecticut, laws for the establishment of common schools, where all classes of society might together receive the elements of an English education, were enacted at a period far anterior to the revolution. The system of general education in Massachusetts was commenced prior to the establishment of any college in the country. So far, therefore, as precedent and prescription have authority, the common school system ought to be regarded as the *national system*, and cherished accordingly. This appears to be, at present, the general feeling throughout the community, and it is probable that no considerable legislative action in favour of education will hereafter take place, which does not involve the acknowledgement of this as the basis, and admit the *right to be educated* as a preliminary to the obligation to submit to the authority of law or to bear a part in the national defence.

In several of the southern and in some of the middle states, the public provision for instruction in common schools has reference solely to *the poor*. This peculiarity has tended little to render the plan either acceptable or useful. The feeling of degradation connected with the acceptance of a boon, is, in many instances, strong enough to deter the people altogether from receiving the proffered instruction. And though panegyric has been exhausted and efforts multiplied to force this system into popularity, yet they have been so far from succeeding, that the people often prefer total ignorance to knowledge *on such terms;* and the poorer classes of population in the states where it exists, are accordingly among the worst instructed poor in the Union—perhaps in the world.

It may be inferred from recent movements among the people themselves, as well as among their representatives, that the estimate in which eleemosynary instruction is held, cannot be very high. The former claim as a *right*, and as an indispensable incident to their condition as freemen, the equal enjoyment of at least elementary instruction, since this is the only means of enabling them to comply with the duties and obligations imposed by the constitutions and laws under which they live.

Plain sense and some experience have concurred to justify the remark of an able advocate of public education, which we take the liberty to transcribe.

"Only allow the rich (no matter under what pretext, whether of philanthropy, or patriotism, or interest) to prescribe the education of the poor, and they prescribe their condition and relative importance. If any thing be anti-republican, it certainly is so, directly or indirectly, to maintain that although a hundred dollars a year is not too much to expend for the mental improvement of the son of the wealthy merchant, lawyer, and physician, a two dollar education is quite sufficient for the children of the poor; or in other words, the mass of our fellow citizens."

The system of common schools has in some instances been so modified as to include a department exclusively appropriated to children under seven years of age. They are sometimes called *primary* in contradistinction to the remaining portion of the common schools; and sometimes *infant schools* — the latter designation, as well as the general features of the system itself, being derived from the establishment of Mr. Owen, at New Lanark, where the first infant school is said to have been put in operation.

Wherever the system of common schools has been established on a solid basis, and managed *by the people* on just and liberal principles, it has not failed to display the most gratifying results on the character and habits of the people. It has diminished crime, promoted temperance, quickened industry, abated pauperism, substituted mental for animal pleasures, implanted a general desire for useful information, and rendered the spirit of liberty and of patriotism a living and energetic *principle* of action. It has made the enormity of slavery more apparent to the general mind, and has followed close in the rear of that odious system, wherever the force of public sentiment has caused its abolition. Female character is observed to possess more universal esteem wherever the system of universal education has been adopted. Both sexes are alike the subjects of its salutary and sustaining influences, and mutually aid each other to maintain the virtue and intelligence of the social system.

2. *Academies, high schools, gymnasia.* — The term *academy*, as

225

applied to a species of schools intermediate between the colleges and the common or English schools, has long been known as a denomination of a valuable class of seminaries which abound in all the United States, and which have probably been instrumental in sustaining the general intelligence of the population in a degree quite equal to that of the colleges, and inferior only to that of common schools.

The advantage possessed by these institutions is, that not being fettered by any exclusive course of studies and operations, they are enabled to extend the range of studies and adopt such improvements in instruction as the spirit of the age shall from time to time render expedient or useful; they can provide practical instruction precisely adapted to the situation and circumstances of the community in which they are established; they can dispense with the waste of time incident to the study of branches that can never be rendered available, and can substitute those which are directly connected with the duties and occupations of life; they can afford to youth in moderate circumstances the means of becoming adequately qualified for any of the stations and relations of general society, and they are often made to furnish a portion of classical and other instruction entirely sufficient for entering on any of the learned professions. Many highly distinguished members of all those professions have received no other education than that furnished by an academy, high school, or gymnasium.

The mode of sustaining the academies is generally that of uniting a small fund sufficient to provide buildings and furniture, and to pay some portion of the wages of the teachers, with a moderate quarterly charge upon the students. The funds of some academies amount to fifty or sixty, and of a few to nearly one hundred thousand dollars. Their concerns are chiefly managed by trustees, the mode of whose appointment is various according to the directions of their respective charters. The *gymnasia* which have been erected in the United States have been mostly the results of individual enterprize, and constructed on the plan of similar establishments in Germany. The high schools derive their name from an establishment long known under the title of the High School of Edinburgh. They generally embrace a course of classical, mathematical and English education, with the study of modern languages and several departments of natural science. Like their prototype, they have in many instances availed themselves of the effectual aid of monitorial instruction and with the best results, employing it not as a *substitute* but as an *auxiliary* for the regular teacher. Prejudice and jealousy have sometime been found combined to counteract the diffusive usefulness of these establishments, but it is believed their number has not been thereby essentially diminished. The education of females on this plan has been particularly successful.

3. *Popular Education.* — It would be unjust to omit a notice of the very meritorious exertions which in many parts of the United States have assumed the form of systematic efforts for the purposes of *popular instruction.* In the principal cities and in many of the larger towns and villages the business of giving instruction of this kind is carried on in regularly organized societies. The method of teaching, which is chiefly by lectures, resembles essentially that employed by the mechanics' institutions and other popular societies of Europe. Among us these establishments are known by the names of "Lyceums," — "Societies for the promotion of useful knowledge," — "Mechanics' Institutions," — "Franklin Institutions," &c., and their influence wherever situated has been highly useful in exciting a spirit of inquiry, in rousing an attention to the great topics which engaged the minds of men and render them sensible of the dignity and value of a cultivated intellect, and in substituting a fountain of innocent and rational gratification for the idle gossip or the low dissipation into which the mass of an ignorant community is ever liable to fall.

There are, it is believed not less than one thousand of these institutions scattered throughout the whole extent of the United States. But few of them have received any direct aid from legislation. They are mostly voluntary associations for mutual aid and encouragement in the prosecution of a common interest. Besides lectures on the more popular departments of science, they generally embrace discussions, oral or written, on topics interesting for their practical bearing, but they very judiciously avoid the profitless questions of theology, and party politics. It is not the least of the recommendations of these useful societies, that they offer to teachers and others concerned in the business of education, an

opportunity to enlarge the sphere of their usefulness and to benefit the cause of instruction by the discussion of methods and the
development of principles, pertaining to youthful education.

The establishment of several periodical works of a highly
useful character is due to the exertions of these popular institutions.

It is worthy of remark in this connexion, that the first Journal
of Education in the English language, was commenced in the
United States and was for several years conducted with a spirit
and liberality of tone which deserve high commendation. In the
mean time the British press has begun to labour in the cause, and
a quarterly periodical of most respectable promise has recently
been sent forth. Other efforts to the same purpose have likewise
been made in America, but their influence has been less direct and
beneficial, owing in some instances to the want of due qualifications in their conductors and in others to the partial and sectarian
tone which they have assumed.

Among the objects of practical instruction which the friends of
education have desired to embrace in their plans of improvement,
is that of agriculture. And they have anxiously sought for some
modification of the foreign establishments which might be adapted to the genius and feelings of America. The establishment of
Hofwyl in Switzerland has features wholly repugnant to the republican character, and which must therefore be abandoned
before any considerable success will attend these efforts. The
manual labour schools, of which several have been erected in the
United States, have too frequently partaken of the theological and
sectarian character to admit of general public patronage. . . .

26. EDUCATION AND PROSPERITY (1848)[1]

HORACE MANN

[A] cardinal object which the government of Massachusetts, and all the influential men in the State, should propose to themselves, is the physical well-being of all the people, — the sufficiency, comfort, competence, of every individual in regard to food, raiment, and shelter. And these necessaries and conveniences of life should be obtained by each individual for himself, or by each family for themselves, rather than accepted from the hand of charity or extorted by poor-laws. It is not averred that this most desirable result can, in all instances, be obtained; but it is, nevertheless, the end to be aimed at. True statemanship and true political economy, not less than true philanthropy, present this perfect theory as the goal, to be more and more closely approximated by our imperfect practice. The desire to achieve such a result cannot be regarded as an unreasonable ambition; for, though all mankind were well fed, well clothed, and well housed, they might still be but half civilized.

Poverty is a public as well as a private evil. There is no physical law necessitating its existence. The earth contains abundant resources for ten times — doubtless for twenty times — its present inhabitants. Cold, hunger, and nakedness are not, like death, an inevitable lot. There are many single States in this Union which could supply an abundance of edible products for the inhabitants of the thirty States that compose it. There are single States capable of raising a sufficient quantity of cotton to clothe the whole nation; and there are other States having sufficient factories and machinery to manufacture it. The coal-fields of Pennsylvania are sufficiently

---

[1]*Old South Leaflets*, VI (Boston, n.d.) No. 144. The excerpt is from Mann's Twelfth Annual Report as Secretary of the Massachusetts State Board of Education (1848).

abundant to keep every house in the land at the temperature of sixty-five degrees for centuries to come. Were there to be a competition, on the one hand, to supply wool for every conceivable fabric, and, on the other, to wear out these fabrics as fast as possible, the single State of New York would beat the whole country. There is, indeed, no assignable limit to the capacities of the earth for producing whatever is necessary for the sustenance, comfort, and improvement of the race. Indigence, therefore, and the miseries and degradations incident to indigence, seem to be no part of the eternal ordinances of Heaven. The bounty of God is not brought into question or suspicion by its existence; for man who suffers it might have avoided it. Even the wealth which the world now has on hand is more than sufficient to supply all the rational wants of every individual in it. Privations and sufferings exist, not from the smallness of its sum, but from the inequality of its distribution. Poverty is set over against profusion. In some all healthy appetite is cloyed and sickened by repletion; while in others the stomach seems to be a supernumerary organ in the system, or, like the human eye or human lungs before birth, is waiting to be transferred to some other region, where its functions may come into use. One gorgeous palace absorbs all the labor and expense that might have made a thousand hovels comfortable. That one man may ride in carriages of Oriental luxury, hundreds of other men are turned into beasts of burden. To supply a superfluous wardrobe for the gratification of one man's pride, a thousand women and children shiver with cold; and for every flash of the diamonds that royalty wears there is a tear of distress in the poor man's dwelling. Not one Lazarus, but a hundred, sit at the gate of Dives. Tantalus is no fiction. The ancient one might have been fabulous; but the modern ones are terrible realities. Millions are perishing in the midst of superfluities.

According to the European theory, men are divided into classes, — some to toil and earn, others to seize and enjoy. According to the Massachusetts theory, all are to have an equal chance for earning, and equal security in the enjoyment of what they earn. The latter tends to equality of condition; the former, to the grossest inequalities. Tried by any Christian standard of morals, or even by any of the better sort of heathen standards, can any one hesitate, for a moment, in declaring which of the two will produce the greater amount of human welfare, and which, therefore, is the more conformable to the divine will? The European theory is blind to what constitutes the highest glory as well as the highest duty of a State. Its advocates and admirers are forgetful of that which should be their highest ambition, and proud of that which constitutes their shame. How can any one possessed of the attributes of humanity look with satisfaction upon the splendid treasures, the golden regalia, deposited in the Tower of London or in Windsor Palace, each "an India in itself," while thousands around are dying of starvation, or have been made criminals by the combined forces of temptation and neglect? The present condition of Ireland cancels all the glories of the British crown. The brilliant conception which symbolizes the nationality of Great Britain as a superb temple, whose massive and grand proportions are upheld and adorned by the four hundred and thirty Corinthian columns of the aristocracy, is turned into a loathing and a scorn when we behold the five millions of paupers that cower and shiver at its base. The galleries and fountains of Versailles, the Louvre of Paris, her Notre Dame, and her Madeleine, though multiplied by thousands in number and in brilliancy, would be no atonement for the hundred thousand Parisian *ouvriers* without bread and without work. The galleries of painting and of sculpture at Rome, at Munich, or at Dresden, which body forth the divinest ideals ever executed or ever conceived, are but an abomination in the sight of Heaven and of all good men, while actual living beings — beings that have hearts to palpitate, and nerves to agonize, and affections to be crushed or corrupted — are experimenting all around them upon the capacities of human nature for suffering and for sin. Where standards like these exist, and are upheld by council and by court, by fashion and by law, *Christianity is yet to be discovered;* at least, it is yet to be applied in practice to the social condition of men.

Our ambition as a State should trace itself to a different origin, and propose to itself a different object. Its flame should be lighted at the skies. Its radiance and its warmth should reach the darkest and the coldest abodes of men. It should seek the solution of such problems as these: To what extent can competence displace pauperism? How nearly can we free ourselves from the low-minded and the vicious, not by their expatriation, but by their elevation?

231

To what extent can the resources and powers of Nature be converted into human welfare, the peaceful arts of life be advanced, and the vast treasures of human talent and genius be developed? How much of suffering, in all its form, can be relieved? or, what is better than relief, how much can be prevented? Cannot the classes of crimes be lessened, and the number of criminals in each class be diminished? Our exemplars, both for public and for private imitation, should be the parables of the lost sheep and of the lost piece of silver. When we have spread competence through all the abodes of poverty, when we have substituted knowledge for ignorance in the minds of the whole people, when we have reformed the vicious and reclaimed the criminal, then may we invite all neighboring nations to behold the spectacle, and say to them in the conscious elation of virtue, "Rejoice with me, for I have found that which was lost." Until that day shall arrive, our duties will not be wholly fulfilled, and our ambition will have new honors to win.

But is it not true that Massachusetts, in some respects, instead of adhering more and more closely to her own theory, is becoming emulous of the baneful examples of Europe? The distance between the two extremes of society is lengthening instead of being abridged. With every generation, fortunes increase on the one hand, and some new privation is added to poverty on the other. We are verging towards those extremes of opulence and of penury, each of which unhumanizes the human mind. A perpetual struggle for the bare necessaries of life, without the ability to obtain them, makes men wolfish. Avarice, on the other hand, sees, in all the victims of misery around it, not objects for pity and succor, but only crude materials to be worked up into more money.

I suppose it to be the universal sentiment of all those who mingle any ingredient of benevolence with their notions on political economy that vast and overshadowing private fortunes are among the greatest dangers to which the happiness of the people in a republic can be subjected. Such fortunes would create a feudalism of a new kind, but one more oppressive and unrelenting than that of the middle ages. The feudal lords in England and on the Continent never held their retainers in a more abject condition of servitude than the great majority of foreign manufacturers and capitalists hold their operatives and laborers at the present day. The means employed are different; but the similarity in results is striking. What force did then, money does now. The villein of the middle ages had no spot of earth on which he could live, unless one were granted to him by his lord. The operative or laborer of the present day has no employment, and therefore no bread, unless the capitalist will accept his services. The vassal had no shelter but such as his master provided for him. Not one in five thousand of English operatives or farm-laborers is able to build or own even a hovel; and therefore they must accept such shelter as capital offers them. The baron prescribed his own terms to his retainers: those terms were peremptory, and the serf must submit or perish. The British manufacturer or farmer prescribes the rate of wages he will give to his work-people: he reduces these wages under whatever pretext he pleases; and they, too, have no alternative but submission or starvation. In some respects, indeed, the condition of the modern dependent is more forlorn than that of the corresponding serf class in former times. Some attributes of the patriarchal relation did spring up between the lord and his lieges to soften the harsh relations subsisting between them. Hence came some oversight of the condition of children, some relief in sickness, some protection and support in the decrepitude of age. But only in instances comparatively few have kindly offices smoothed the rugged relation between British capital and British labor. The children of the work-people are abandoned to their fate; and notwithstanding the privations they suffer, and the dangers they threaten, no power in the realm has yet been able to secure them an education; and when the adult laborer is prostrated by sickness, or eventually worn out by toil and age, the poor-house, which has all along been his destination, becomes his destiny.

Now two or three things will doubtless be admitted to be true, beyond all controversy, in regard to Massachusetts. By its industrial condition, and its business operations, it is exposed, far beyond any other State in the Union, to the fatal extremes of overgrown wealth and desperate poverty. Its population is far more dense than that of any other State. It is four or five times more dense than the average of all the other States taken together; and density of population has always been one of the proximate causes of social inequality. According to population and territorial extent there is far more capital in Massachusetts — capital which is movable, and instantaneously available — than in any other State in the Union;

and probably both these qualifications respecting population and territory could be omitted without endangering the truth of the assertion. It has been recently stated in a very respectable public journal, on the authority of a writer conversant with the subject, that from the last of June, 1846, to the first of August, 1848, the amount of money invested by the citizens of Massachusetts "in manufacturing cities, railroads, and other improvements," is "fifty-seven millions of dollars, of which more than fifty has been paid in and expended." The dividends to be received by citizens of Massachusetts from June, 1848, to April, 1849, are estimated by the same writer at ten millions, and the annual increase of capital at "little short of twenty-two millions." If this be so, are we not in danger of naturalizing and domesticating among ourselves those hideous evils which are always engendered between capital and labor, when all the capital is in the hands of one class and all the labor is thrown upon another?

Now surely nothing but universal education can counterwork this tendency to the domination of capital and the servility of labor. If one class possesses all the wealth and the education, while the residue of society is ignorant and poor, it matters not by what name the relation between them may be called: the latter, in fact and in truth, will be the servile dependants and subjects of the former. But, if education be equably diffused, it will draw property after it by the strongest of all attractions; for such a thing never did happen, and never can happen, as that an intelligent and practical body of men should be permanently poor. Property and labor in different classes are essentially antagonistic; but property and labor in the same class are essentially fraternal. The people of Massachusetts have, in some degree, appreciated the truth that the unexampled prosperity of the State — its comfort, its competence, its general intelligence and virtue — is attributable to the education, more or less perfect, which all its people have received; but are they sensible of a fact equally important, — namely, that it is to this same education that two-thirds of the people are indebted for not being to-day the vassals of as severe a tyranny, in the form of capital, as the lower classes of Europe are bound to in the form of brute force?

Education, then, beyond all other devices of human origin, is the great equalizer of the conditions of men, — the balance-wheel of the social machinery. I do not here mean that it so elevates the moral nature as to make men disdain and abhor the oppression of their fellow-men. This idea pertains to another of its attributes. But I mean that it gives each man the independence and the means by which he can resist the selfishness of other men. It does better than to disarm the poor of their hostility towards the rich: it prevents being poor. Agrarianism is the revenge of poverty against wealth. The wanton destruction of the property of others—the burning of hay-ricks and corn-ricks, the demolition of machinery because it supersedes hand-labor, the sprinkling of vitriol on rich dresses—is only agrarianism run mad. Education prevents both the revenge and the madness. On the other hand, a fellow-feeling for one's class or caste is the common instinct of hearts not wholly sunk in selfish regards for person or for family. The spread of education, by enlarging the cultivated class or caste, will open a wider area over which the social feelings will expand; and, if this education should be universal and complete, it would do more than all things else to obliterate factitious distinctions in society.

The main idea set forth in the creeds of some political reformers, or revolutionizers, is that some people are poor *because* others are rich. This idea supposes a fixed amount of property in the community, which by fraud or force, or arbitrary law, is unequally divided among men; and the problem presented for solution is how to transfer a portion of this property from those who are supposed to have too much to those who feel and know that they have too little. At this point, both their theory and their expectation of reform stop. But the beneficent power of education would not be exhausted, even though it should peaceably abolish all the miseries that spring from the co-existence, side by side, of enormous wealth and squalid want. It has a higher function. Beyond the power of diffusing old wealth it has the prerogative of creating new. It is a thousand times more lucrative than fraud, and adds a thousand-fold more to a nation's resources than the most successful conquests. Knaves and robbers can obtain only what was before possessed by others. But education creates or develops new treasures,—treasures not before possessed or dreamed of by any one. . . .

For the creation of wealth, then,—for the existence of a wealthy people and a wealthy nation,—intelligence is the grand condition.

The number of improvers will increase as the intellectual constituency, if I may so call it, increases. In former times, and in most parts of the world even at the present day, not one man in a million has ever had such a development of mind as made it possible for him to become a contributor to art or science. Let this development precede, and contributions, numberless, and of inestimable value, will be sure to follow. That political economy, therefore, which busies itself about capital and labor, supply and demand, interest and rents, favorable and unfavorable balances of trade, but leaves out of account the element of a widespread mental development, is naught but stupendous folly. The greatest of all the arts in political economy is to change a consumer into a producer; and the next greatest is to increase the producer's producing power, — an end to be directly attained by increasing his intelligence. For mere delving, an ignorant man is but little better than a swine, whom he so much resembles in his appetites, and surpasses in his powers of mischief. . . .

27. Lecture on Existing Evils and Their Remedy (1819)[1]

FRANCES WRIGHT

Having now traced with you what knowledge is in matter and
in mind; what virtue is in human conduct, where its rules are to be
sought, and how they may be found; tested, by the standard thus
supplied, the ruling topic of discussion and instruction throughout
this country; shown that, while this topic subtracts from the wealth
of the country twenty millions per annum, and from the hearts and
minds of the people social fellowship and common sense, it has in
nature no real existence—is not knowledge, but only imagination—is not fact, but only theory; and, having shown, moreover,
that theory can supply no subject matter of instruction; that the
teaching of opinions is as erroneous in principle as it is dangerous
in practice; that the duty of the instructor is simply to enrich the
mind with knowledge, to awaken the eye, and the ear, and the
touch, to the perception of things, the judgment to their comparison and arrangement, and to leave the free, unbiased mind to draw
its own conclusions from the evidence thus collected,—I shall
now present a few observations on the necessity of commencing,
and gradually perfecting a radical reform in your existing outlays
of time and money—on and in churches, theological colleges,
privileged and exclusive seminaries of all descriptions, religious
Sabbath schools, and all their aids and adjuncts of Bibles, tracts,
missionaries, priests and preachers, multiplied and multiplying
throughout the land, until they promise to absorb more capital
than did the temple of Solomon, and to devour more of the first
fruits of industry than did the tribe of Levi in the plenitude of its
power;—on the necessity I say, of substituting for your present

[1]*The Free Enquirer* (New York), II, no. 7, Dec. 12, 1829, pp. 49–53. The speech
was delivered in Philadelphia on June 2, 1819.

cumbrous, expensive, useless, or rather pernicious, system of partial, opinionative, and dogmatical instruction, one at once national, rational, and republican; one which shall take for its study our own world and our own nature; for its object the improvement of man; and for its means, the practical developement of truth, the removal of temptations to evil, and the gradual equalization of human condition, human duties, and human enjoyments, by the equal diffusion of knowledge without distinction of class or sect—both of which distinctions are inconsistent with republican institutions as they are with reason and with common sense, with virtue and with happiness.

Time is it in this land to commence this reform. Time is it to check the ambition of an organized clergy, the demoralizing effects of a false system of law; to heal the strife fomented by sectarian religion and legal disputes; to bring down the pride of ideal wealth, and to raise honest industry to honor. Time is it to search out the misery in the land, and to heal it at the source. Time is it to remember the poor and the afflicted, ay! and the vicious and the depraved. Time is it to perceive that every sorrow which corrodes the human heart, every vice which diseases the body and the mind, every crime which startles the ear and sends back the blood affrighted to the heart—is the product of one evil, the foul growth from one root, the distorted progeny of one corrupt parent—IGNORANCE.

Time is it to perceive this truth; to proclaim it on the housetop, in the market place, in city and forest, throughout the land; to acknowledge it in the depths of our hearts, and to apply all our energies to the adoption of those salutary measures which this salutary truth spontaneously suggests. Time is it, I say, to turn our churches into halls of science, our schools of faith into schools of knowledge, our privileged colleges into state institutions for all the youth of the land. Time is it to arrest our speculations respecting unseen worlds and inconceivable mysteries, and to address our enquiries to the improvement of our human condition, and our efforts to the practical illustration of those beautiful principles of liberty and equality enshrined in the political institutions, and, first and chief, in the national declaration of independence.

And by whom and how, are these changes to be effected? By

whom! And do a free people ask the question? By themselves. By themselves — *the people.* . . .

Hitherto, my friends, in government as in every branch of morals, we have but too much mistaken words for truths and forms for principles. To render men free, it sufficeth not to proclaim their liberty; to make them equal, it sufficeth not to call them so. True, the 4th of July '76 commenced a new era for our race. True, the sun of promise then rose upon the world. But let us not mistake for the fulness of light what was but its harbinger. Let us not conceive that man in signing the declaration of his rights secured their possession; that having framed the theory he had not, and hath not still, the practice to seek.

Your fathers, indeed, on the day from which dates your existence as a nation, opened the gates of the temple of human liberty. But think not they entered, nor that you have entered, the sanctuary. They passed not, nor have you passed, even the threshold.

Who speaks of liberty while the human mind is in chains? Who of equality while the thousands are in squalid wretchedness, the millions harrassed with health-destroying labor, the few afflicted with health-destroying idleness, and all tormented by health destroying solicitude? Look abroad on the misery which is gaining on the land! Mark the strife, and the discord, and the jealousies, the shock of interests and opinions, the hatreds of sect, the estrangements of class, the pride of wealth, the debasement of poverty, the helplessness of youth unprotected, of age uncomforted, of industry unrewarded, of ignorance unenlightened, of vice unreclaimed, of misery unpitied, of sickness, hunger, and nakedness unsatisfied, unalleviated, and unheeded. Go! mark all the wrongs and the wretchedness with which the eye and the ear and the heart are familiar, and then echo in triumph and celebrate in jubilee the insulting declaration — *all men are free and equal!* . . .

The noble example of New England has been imitated by other states, until all not possessed of common schools blush for the popular remissness. But, after all, how can *common schools,* under their best form, and in fullest supply, effect even the purpose which they have in view?

The object proposed by common schools (if I rightly understand it) is to impart to the whole population those means for the acquirement of knowledge which are in common use: reading and writing. To these are added arithmetic, and, occasionally perhaps, some imperfect lessons in the simpler sciences. But, I would ask, supposing these institutions should even be made to embrace all the branches of intellectual knowledge, and, thus, science offered gratis to all the children of the land, how are the children of the very class, for whom we suppose the schools instituted, to be supplied with food and raiment, or instructed in the trade necessary to their future subsistence, while they are following these studies? How are they, I ask, to be fed and clothed, when, as all facts show, the labor of the parents is often insufficient for their own sustenance, and, almost universally, inadequate to the provision of the family without the united efforts of all its members? In your manufacturing districts you have children worked for twelve hours a day; and, in the rapid and certain progress of the existing system, you will soon have them, as in England, *worked to death,* and yet unable, through the period of their miserable existence, to earn a pittance sufficient to satisfy the cravings of hunger. At this present time, what leisure or what spirit, think you, have the children of the miserable widows of Philadelphia, realizing, according to the most favorable estimate of your city and county committee, sixteen dollars per annum, for food and clothing—what leisure or what spirit may their children find for visiting a school, although the same should be open to them from sunrise to sunset? Or what leisure have usually the children of your most thriving mechanics, after their strength is sufficiently developed to spin, sew, weave, or wield a tool? It seems to me, my friends, that to build school houses nowadays is something like building churches. When you have them, you need some measure to ensure their being occupied.

But, as our time is short, and myself somewhat fatigued by continued exertions, I must hasten to the rapid development of the system of instruction and protection which has occurred to me as capable, and alone capable, of opening the door to universal reform.

In lieu of all common schools, high schools, colleges, seminaries, houses of refuge, or any other juvenile institution, instructional or protective, I would suggest that the state legislatures be directed (after laying off the whole in townships or hundreds) to organize, at suitable distances, and in convenient and healthy situations, establishments for the general reception of all the children resident within the said school district. These establishments to be devoted, severally, to children between a certain age. Say, the first to infants between two and four, or two and six, according to the density of the population, and such other local circumstances as might render a greater or less number of establishments necessary or practicable. The next to receive children from four to eight, or six to twelve years. The next from twelve to sixteen, or to an older age if found desirable. Each establishment to be furnished with instructors in every branch of knowledge, intellectual and operative, with all the apparatus, land, and conveniences necessary for the best developement of all knowledge; the same, whether operative or intellectual, being always calculated to the age and strength of the pupils.

To obviate, in the commencement, every evil result possible from the first mixture of a young population, so variously raised in error or neglect, a due separation should be made in each establishment; by which means those entering with bad habits would be kept apart from the others until corrected. How rapidly reform may be effected on the plastic disposition of childhood, has been sufficiently proved in your houses of refuge, more especially when such establishments have been under *liberal* superintendence, as was formerly the case in New York. Under their orthodox directors, those asylums of youth have been converted into jails.

It will be understood that, in the proposed establishments, the children would pass from one to the other in regular succession, and that the parents, who would necessarily be resident in their close neighborhood, could visit the children at suitable hours, but, in no case, interfere with or interrupt the rules of the institution.

In the older establishments, the well directed and well protected labor of the pupil would, in time, suffice for, and, then, exceed, their own support; when the surplus might be devoted to the maintenance of the infant establishments.

In the beginning, and until all debt was cleared off, and so long as the same should be found favorable to the promotion of these best palladiums of a nation's happiness, a double tax might be at once expedient and politic.

First, a moderate tax per head for every child, to be laid upon its parents conjointly or divided between them, due attention being always paid to the varying strength of the two sexes, and to the undue depreciation which now rests on female labor. The more effectually to correct the latter injustice, as well as to consult the convenience of the industrious classes generally, this parental tax might be rendered payable either in money, or in labor, produce, or domestic manufactures, and should be continued for each child until the age when juvenile labor should be found, on the average, equivalent to the educational expenses, which, I have reason to believe, would be at twelve years.

This first tax on parents to embrace equally the whole population; as, however moderate, it would inculcate a certain forethought in all the human family; more especially where it is most wanted—in young persons, who, before they assumed the responsibility of parents, would estimate their fitness to meet it.

The second tax to be on property, increasing in percentage with the wealth of the individual. In this manner I conceive the rich would contribute, according to their riches, to the relief of the poor, and to the support of the state, by raising up its best bulwark—an enlightened and united generation.

Preparatory to, or connected with, such measures, a registry should be opened by the state, with offices through all the townships, where, on the birth of every child, or within a certain time appointed, the same should be entered, together with the names of its parents. When two years old, the parental tax should be payable, and the juvenile institution open for the child's reception; from which time forward it would be under the protective care and guardianship of the state, while it need never be removed from the daily, weekly, or frequent inspection of the parents.

Orphans, of course, would find here an open asylum. If possessed of property, a contribution would be paid from its revenue to the common educational fund; if unprovided, they would be sustained out of the same.

In these nurseries of a free nation, no inequality must be allowed to enter. Fed at a common board; clothed in a common garb, uniting neatness with simplicity and convenience; raised in the exercise of common duties, in the acquirement of the same knowledge and practice of the same industry, varied only according to individual taste and capabilities; in the exercise of the same virtues; in the enjoyment of the same pleasures; in the study of the same nature; in pursuit of the same object—their own and each other's happiness—say! would not such a race, when arrived at manhood, and womanhood work out the reform of society—perfect the free institutions of America? . . .

CHAPTER 11

THE OPPOSITION

No confidence in any compulsory equalizations.

The National Gazette, 1830

28. The National Gazette (1830)[1]

We can readily pardon the editor of the United States Gazette for not perceiving that the scheme of Universal Equal Education at the expense of the State is virtually "Agrarianism." It would be a compulsory application of the means of the richer, for the direct use of the poorer classes; and so far *an arbitrary division of property among them.* The declared object is to procure the opportunity of instruction for the child or children of every citizen; to elevate the standard of the education of the working classes; or *equalize the standard for all classes;* which would, doubtless, be to lower or narrow that which the rich may now compass. But the most sensible and reflecting possessors of property sufficient to enable them to educate their children in the most liberal and efficacious way, and upon the broadest scale, would prefer to share their means for any other purpose, or in any other mode than such as would injuriously affect or circumscribe the proficiency of their offspring. A public meeting of 'the Mechanics and other Working Men of the City and County of New York,' was held in the city, on the 17th inst., and among the principles for which they have 'resolved' to contend, we find the following:

'*In Education*—the adoption of a general system of instruction at the expense of the State, which shall afford to children, however rich or poor, equal means to obtain useful learning. To effect this, it is believed that a system of direct taxation will not be necessary, as the surplus revenue of the State and United States Governments will, in a very few years, afford ample means—but even if it were necessary to resort to direct taxation to accomplish this all-important object, and the amount paid by the wealthy should be far greater than that paid by our less eligibly situated fellow-citizens, an equivalent to them would be found in the increased ability and usefulness of the educated citizens to serve and to

---

[1]*The National Gazette* (Philadelphia), Editorial, August 19, 1830.

promote the best interests of the State; in the increased permanency of our institutions — and in the superior protection of liberty,
person and property.'

Thus, a direct tax for 'the equal means of obtaining useful
learning' is not deemed improbable, and it is admitted that the
amount which would be paid by the wealthy would be 'far greater'
than that paid by their 'less eligibly situated fellow citizens.' Here,
we contend, would be the action, if not the name, of the Agrarian
system. Authority — that is, the State — is to force the more eligibly
situated citizens to contribute a part (which might be very considerable) of their means, for the accomodation of the rest; and this is
equivalent to the idea of an actual compulsory partition of their
substance. The more thriving members of the 'mechanical and
working classes' would themselves feel the evil of the direct
taxation; — they would find that they had toiled for the benefit of
other families than their own. One of the chief excitements to
industry, among those classes, is the hope of earning the means of
educating their children respectably or liberally; that incentive
would be removed, and the scheme of State and equal education
be thus a premium for comparative idleness, to be taken out of the
pockets of the laborious and conscientious. — What is said in the
New York resolution, of the advantages of the ultimate equality, is
of no particular weight in the question as we now consider its
character. Similar advantages might be pleaded for a more direct
comprehensive Agrarian project; indeed, we have seen the general distribution of the means of the rich, — the total destruction of
what is called the aristocracy, — argued, in some of the New York
publications, upon the same grounds of beneficial consequence
— additional strength to our republican institutions, and so forth.

We have no confidence in any compulsory equalizations; it has
been well observed that they pull down what is above, but never
much raise what is below, and often 'depress high and low together beneath the level at what was originally the lowest.' By no
possibility could a perfect equality be procured. A scheme of
universal equal education, attempted in reality, would be an
unexampled *bed of Procrustes* for the understandings of our youth;
and in fact, could not be used with any degree of equality or profit,
unless the dispositions and circumstances of parents and children
were nearly the same to accomplish which phenomenon, in a

nation of many millions, engaged in a great variety of pursuits, would be beyond human power. For the original, prodigious, and splendid conceptions of his modern philosophers, Swift chose an island,—the far-famed Laputa—of only ten thousand acres of surface. No one of his professors in the school of political projectors, in the Grand Academy of Lagado, even imagined any thing more difficult than what is now seriously proposed to the working classes of the United States.

We have thrown out the foregoing remarks cursorily, and as it were accidentally,—without meaning to develope now a question which may be made,—advantageously for the public mind,—to embrace a consideration of the nature of our political institutions, the order and constitution of American society, and the condition of the working classes particularly, compared with those of Europe. It is a fundamental part of the Republican system to yield no power to *government* or to state except what is necessary—to leave as much as possible to individual enterprise and individual discretion;—to interfere only from imperative motives and for public ends of the highest and clearest utility, with the direction of private industry and the disposal of private fortune. Upon all this, the idea of committing to the State the regulation and care of the education of all citizens, with a uniform plan, is a broad encroachment,—a bold and momentous innovation. A number of the soundest and most patriotic thinkers, among us, might chose [*sic*] rather to assign to the State a general control over private property for any other object; or a multitude of parents would be glad to escape to any other land,—whatever might be the designation of its government,—where they could enjoy at least freedom of choice as to the tuition of their children. The New York Meeting have coupled with the project above mentioned, another hopeful one —'the gradual extinguishment of all chartered monoplies,' that is, the destruction of all banks and all paper-money—the Bank of the United States being specially denounced.

CHAPTER 12

THE SOUTH

Not yet prepared to educate all.

George Fitzhugh, 1854

29. On Public Education
in South Carolina (1853)[1]

JAMES H. THORNWELL

HIS EXCELLENCY GOVERNOR MANNING:

I ask the favor of presenting to your excellency a few reflections upon the subject of public instruction in South Carolina. As I feel that I am addressing one whose interest and zeal in the prosperity of letters will induce him to weigh with candor, to estimate with charity, and even to invest with disproportionate value the crudest hints which spring from the desire to increase the educational facilities of the State, I shall dismiss all apprehensions of being suspected of an officious obtrusion upon your notice. You are the man above all others to whom the head of this institution should look with confidence to give fresh impulse to the general cause of education; and you will excuse me for saying that if all the suggestions which shall fall from me or the maturer recommendations which shall come from yourself shall terminate auspiciously to the wishes of us both, there will be furnished a beautiful instance of providential retribution in connecting the name of the first conspicuous benefactor of the South Carolina College with the establishment of an adequate system of common schools. A proud distinction in itself to be the friend and patron of learning, the honor is increased in your case in that it has been preeminently your care in its higher and lower culture to dispense its blessings to the poor. Apart from fellowship with God, there can not be a sweeter satisfaction than that which arises from the con-

---

[1]Thornwell was President of South Carolina College in 1853 when he submitted his educational report to Governor Manning. A printed copy of this letter is in the Library of Congress. The City Council of Charleston, considering the ideas so pertinent to the public school movement in 1885, ordered the letter published by *The News and Courier*.

sciousness of being a father to the fatherless; and if the ends which I know are dear to your heart can only be achieved, every indigent child in the State, looking upon you as its real father, may address you in the modest and glowing terms. . . .

DIFFICULTIES OF THE SUBJECT

I am not insensible to the dangers and difficulties which attend the discussion of this subject. It is so seductive to the fancy that the temptation is almost irresistible to indulge in schemes and visionary projects. In the effort to realize the conception of a perfect education we are apt to forget that there is no such thing as absolute perfection in the matter, that all excellence is relative, and that the highest recommendation of any plan is that it is at once practicable and adjusted to the wants and condition of those for whom it is provided. A system of public instruction, like the form of government, must spring from the manners, maxims, habits, and associations of the people. It must penetrate their character, constitute an element of their national existence, be a portion of themselves, if it would not be suspected as an alien or distrusted as a spy. The success of the Prussian scheme is ascribed . . . to the circumstance that it existed in the manners and customs of the country before it was enacted into law. It was not a foreign graft, but the natural offshoot of popular opinion and practice. It is an easy thing to construct a theory when nothing is to be done but to trace the coherencies and dependencies of thought; but it is not so easy to make thought correspond to reality, or to devise a plan which shall overlook none of the difficulties and obstructions in the way of successful application. In the suggestions which I have to offer I shall endeavor to keep steadily in view the real wants of the citizens of this Commonwealth, and, avoiding all crotchets and metaphysical abstractions, shall aim exclusively at what experience or the nature of case demonstrates to be practicable. I have no new principle to ventilate, but I shall think myself happy if I can succeed in setting in a clearer light, or vindicating from prejudice and misconstruction, the principles which have already been embodied in our laws. It is, perhaps, not generally known that the legislature of South Carolina contemplates a scheme of public instruction as perfect in its conception of the end as it is defective in its provision of the means. The order, too, in which the Legislature's attention has been turned to the various branches of the subject, though not the most popular or the most obvious, is percisely the order of their relative importance. It began where it ought to have begun, but, unfortunately, stopped where it ought not to have stopped. To defend what it has already done and stimulate it to repentance for what it has not done is the principal motive of this communication. . . .

ELEVATION OF THE MASSES

In the next place, it should not be admitted that general education is the true source of the elevation of the masses and of the demand for popular instruction. Every educated man is a center of light, and his example and influence create the consciousness of ignorance and the sense of need from which elementary schools have sprung. Defective culture is never conscious of itself until it is brought into contact with superior power. There may be a conviction of ignorance in reference to special things and a desire of knowledge as a means of accomplishing particular ends, but the need of intellectual improvement on its own account never is awakened spontaneously. We never lament our inferiority to angels. The reason is we are not brought into contact with them, and are, consequently, not sensible of the disparity that exists. If we had examples before us of angelic amplitude of mind, the contrast would force upon us a lively impression of the lowness of our intellectual level. If we had never been accustomed to any other light but that of the stars, we should never have dreamed of the sun nor felt the absence of his rays as any real evil. . . . We must know the good in order to understand the evil; we must be familiar with the day to comprehend night and darkness. Hence it is that civilization never has been and never can be of spontaneous growth among a people. It has always been an inheritance or an importation. If men had been originally created savages, they would all have been savages to-day.

Those ingenious theories which undertake, from principles of human nature, to explain the history of man's progress from barbarism to refinement are nothing better than speculative romances. They are contradicted by experience as well as by the laws of the human mind. Philosophy coincides with the Bible —man was created in the image of God, and the rudeness and coarseness of uncivilized communities are states of degradation into which he has apostatized and sunk, and not his primitive and original condition. Civilization has migrated from one center to another, has found its way among barbarians and savages, and restored them to something of their forfeited inheritance, but in every such instance it has been introduced from without, it has never developed itself from within. Where all is darkness, whence is the light to spring? What planet is the source of the rays that shine on it? Hence it is knowledge which creates the demand for knowledge, which causes ignorance to be felt as an evil; and hence it is the education, in the first instance, of the few which has awakened the strong desire for the illumination of the many. Let knowledge, however, become stagnant, let no provision be made for the constant activity of the highest order of minds in the highest sphere of speculation, and the torpor would be communicated downward until the whole community was benumbed.

THE PROGRESS OF SOCIETY

The thinkers in the most abstract departments of speculation keep the whole of society in motion, and upon its motion depends its progress. Scholars, therefore, are the real benefactors of the people, and he does more for popular education who founds a university than he who institutes a complete and adequate machinery of common schools. The reason is obvious—the most potent element of public opinion is wanting where only a low form of culture obtains. The common schools, having no example of anything higher before them, would soon degenerate and impart only a mechanical culture, if they did not—which I am inclined to think would be the case, from their want of life—permit the people to relapse into barbarism. Colleges, on the other hand, will create the demand for lower culture, and private enterprise, under the stimulus imparted, would not be backward in providing for it. The college will diffuse the education of principles, of maxims, a tone of thinking and feeling which are of the last importance without the schools. The schools could never do without the college. If we must dispense with one or the other, I have no hesitation in saying that on the score of public good alone it were wise to dispense with the schools. One sun is better than a thousand stars.

There never was, therefore, a more grievous error than that the college is an antagonism to the interests of the people. Precisely the opposite is the truth; and because it is preeminently a public good, operating directly or indirectly to the benefit of every citizen in the State, the legislature was originally justified in founding, and in still sustaining this noble institution. It has made South Carolina what she is; it has made her people what they are; and from her mountains to her seaboard there is not a nook or corner of the State that has not shared in its healthful influence. The very cries which are coming up from all quarters for the direct instruction of the people, cries which none should think of resisting, are only echoes from the college walls. We should never have heard of them if the state of things had continued among us which existed when the college was founded. The low-country would still have sent its sons to Europe or the North, and the up-country would have been content with its fertile lands and invigorating hills. . . .

THE FREE SCHOOLS

The next part of our system in the order of legislation is the free schools. And here I am sorry to say that the law is not only inadequate, but there is a very extraordinary discrepancy between the law and the practice which increases the difficulty and has added to the inefficiency of the standing appropriation. It is clear from the face of it that the Act of 1811 was designed as the first step towards the establishment of a system of common schools that should bring the means of elementary education within the reach of every child in the State. It was not intended to be a provision for *paupers*. Throughout our statutes free schools mean public schools, or schools which are open to every citizen. The first Act in which I find the expression is that of the 8th of April, 1710, entitled "An Act for the founding and erecting of a free school for the use of the inhabitants of South Carolina." This act created and incorporated a Board of Trustees for the purpose of taking charge of such funds as had already been contributed, or might afterwards be contributed, for public instruction in the Province. In it the epithet *free* is synonymous, not with *pauper*, but *public*, or *common*. The same is the case in the Act of the 7th of June, 1712, entitled "An Act for the encouragement of learning." Although the school was a *free* school, every pupil was required to *pay* for his tuition. But the meaning of the phrase is made still clearer by the extended Act of the 12th December of the same year. There the school was manifestly open to all. Special inducements were held out to patronize and encourage it, and provisions made for educating a certain number free of expense. The Act of 1811, which is the basis of our present system, is so clear and explicit as to the kind of schools to be founded, that I am utterly unable to account for the partial and exclusive interpretation which has been put upon its words. The Third Section provided "that every citizen of this State shall be entitled to send his or her child or children, ward or wards, to any free school in the district where he or she may reside, free from any expense whatever on account of tuition; and where more children shall apply for admission at any one school than can be conveniently educated therein, a preference shall always be given to poor orphans and children of indigent and necessitous parents."

I have no doubt that, if this Act had been executed according to its true intent and meaning, and public schools had been established in every district of the State corresponding to the number of members in the House of Representatives, the advantages would have been so conspicuous that the Legislature could not have stopped until the means of instruction had been afforded to every neighborhood, to every family, and to every child. The law was wise; it was strictly tentative and provisional, but its benevolent intention has been defeated by a singular misconception of its meaning. As a provisional law, it was defective in unity of plan. The Commissioners in each district were absolutely independent and irresponsible. There was no central power which could correct mistakes, and which could infuse a common spirit and a common life into the whole scheme. The consequence is that, after all our legislation and all our expenditures, we have not even the elements in practical operation of a system of public schools. We have the whole work to begin anew.

You will permit me to suggest a few reasons why we should begin it heartily and at once, and then to imitate the nature and extent of our incipient efforts.

In the first place, it is the duty of the State to provide for the education of its citizens. Even Adam Smith, who . . . was opposed to the direct interference of the Government in higher, or liberal education, is constrained to admit that the education of the common people forms an exception to his principle. He makes it the care of the Government, upon the same general ground with the cultivation of a martial spirit. We should be as solicitous that our citizens should not be ignorant as that they should not be cowards. The whole passage is so striking that you will excuse me for quoting it in full:

THE DUTY OF THE STATE

"But a coward, or a man incapable either of defending or revenging himself, evidently wants one of the most essential parts of the character of a man. He is as much mutilated and deformed in his mind as another is in his body, who is either deprived of some of his most essential members, or has lost the use of them. He is evidently the more wretched and miserable of the two, because happiness and misery, which reside altogether in the mind, must necessarily depend more upon the healthful or unhealthful, the mutilated or entire state of the mind, than upon that of the body. Even though the martial spirit of the people were of no use towards the defence of the society, yet to prevent that sort of mental mutilation, deformity and wretchedness, which cowardice necessarily involves in it, from spreading themselves through the great body of the people, would still deserve the most serious attention of Government — in the same manner as it would deserve its most serious attention to prevent a leprosy, or any other loathsome and offensive disease, from spreading itself among them; though, perhaps, no other public good might result from such attention besides the prevention of so great a public evil.

255

"The same thing may be said of the gross ignorance and stupidity which, in a civilized society, seems so frequently to benumb the understanding of all the inferior ranks of people. A man without the proper use of the intellectual faculties of a man is, if possible, more contemptible than even a coward, and seems to be mutilated and deformed in a still more essential part of the character of human nature. Though the State was to derive no advantage from the instruction of the inferior ranks of the people, it would still deserve its attention that they should not be altogether uninstructed. The State, however, derives no considerable advantages from their instruction. The more they are instructed the less liable they are to the delusions of enthusiasm and superstition, which, among ignorant nations, frequently occasion the most dreadful disorders. An instructed and intelligent people, besides, are always more decent and orderly than an ignorant and stupid one. They feel themselves, each individually, more respectable, and more likely to obtain the respect of their lawful superiors, and they are, therefore, more disposed to respect those superiors. They are more disposed to examine, and more capable of seeing through, the interested complaints of faction and sedition; and they are, upon that account, less apt to be misled into any wanton or unnecessary opposition to the measures of Government. In free countries, where the safety of Government depends very much upon the favorable judgment which the people may form of its conduct, it must surely be of the highest importance that they should not be disposed to judge rashly or capriciously concerning it."

"If the community wish to have the benefit of more knowledge and intelligence in the laboring classes," says Say, "it must dispense it at the public charge. This object may be obtained by the establishment of primary schools, of reading, writing and arithmetic. These are the groundwork of all knowledge, and are quite sufficient for the civilization of the lower classes. In fact, one cannot call a native civilized, nor consequently possessed of the benefits of civilization, until the people at large be instructed in these three particulars; till then it will be but partially reclaimed from barbarism."

I might multiply authorities to an indefinite extent, showing that it is the general opinion of political philosophers that popular instruction is one of the most sacred duties of the Commonwealth. The opinion obviously rests upon two grounds — the importance of education in itself and in its relation to the State, and the impossibility of adequately providing for it without the assistance of the Legislature. The alternative is either that the education of the people must be abandoned as hopeless, or the Government must embark in the work. Surely, if this be really the state of the case, South Carolina cannot hesitate a moment as to which brance of the proposition she will choose.

THE FOLLY OF INDIVIDUAL EFFORT

When it is remembered that education makes the citizen as well as the man — that it is precisely what fits a human being to be a living member of a Commonwealth — we cannot hesitate as to whether our people shall be ciphers or men. And that this is the alternative is clear, both from the nature of the case and from fact. Whoever considers what it is to provide an adequate system of instruction for all the children of a country, the amount of funds necessary to erect school-houses, to found libraries, to procure the needful apparatus, to pay teachers, and to keep the machinery, once set in motion, in steady and successful operation, will perceive the folly of entrusting such a task to the disjointed efforts of individuals, or the conflicting efforts of religious denominations. In either case there will be no unity of plan, no competency of means: what is done must be done partially, and, because partially, must be done amiss.

"All experience," says Sir Wm. Hamilton, "demonstrates the necessity of State interference. No countries present a more remarkable contrast in this respect (in regard to popular education) than England and Germany. In the former the State has done nothing for the education of the people, and private benevolence more than has been attempted elsewhere; in the latter, the Government has done everything, and left to private benevolence almost nothing to effect. The English people are, however, the lowest, the German people the highest, in the scale of knowledge. All that Scotland enjoys of popular education above the other kingdoms of the British Empire she owes to the State, and among the

257

principalities of Germany, from Russia down to Hesse Cassel, education is uniformly found to prosper exactly in proportion to the extent of interference and to the unremitting watchfulness of the Government. The experience of the last half century in Germany has, indeed, completely set at rest the question. For thirty years no German has been found to maintain the doctrine of Smith. In their generous rivalry the Governments of that country have practically shown what a benevolent and prudent policy could effect for the University as well as for the school, and, knowing what they have done, who is there now to maintain that for education, as for trade, the State can prevent evil, but cannot originate good?"

There are those among us who admit that no complete system of popular education can be instituted without the intervention of the State, and yet maintain that the true method of intervention is simply to supplement individual exertions; that is, they would have those who are able to do so educate their children in schools sustained by themselves, and solicit the aid of the Legislature only for paupers. It is obvious, in the first place, that in this there is no system at all; the schools are detached and independent, they have no common life, and the State knows nothing of the influences which may be exerted within them. Education is too complicated an interest, and touches the prosperity of the Commonwealth in too many points, to be left, in reference to the most important class of its subjects, absolutely without responsibility to the Government. The homogeneousness of the population can only be sustained by a general system of public schools.

In the next place, the scheme is invidious — it makes a reproachful distinction betwixt the children of the Commonwealth, and in the last place it must, from this very circumstance, be inefficient. Parents will scorn a favor rather than permit their children to be stigmatized as the condition of receiving it. The true policy of the State is to recognize no distinction betwixt the rich and the poor; to put them all upon the same footing; to treat them all upon the same footing; to treat them simply as so many minds whose capacities are to be unfolded and whose energies are to be directed. The rich and the poor in the school-house, as in the house of God, should meet together upon the ground of their common relations, and the consequences of this promiscuous elementary

258

training would soon be felt in harmonizing and smoothing all the unevenness, harshness and inequalities of social life.

In the second place, the State should make some speedy provision for popular education in consequence of the unusual demand which, in some form or other, is indicated as existing in every section of the country.

THE DEMAND FOR SCHOOLS

There never was a greater cry for schools; the people are beginning to appreciate their importance, and at no period within my recollection have such strenuous efforts been made to establish and support them. The extraordinary exertions of the various sects — exertions, too, which deserve all praise when considered as attempts to satisfy an acknowledged public want, and the success which has attended them — are proofs that public opinion is ripe in South Carolina for the interference of the Legislature; and if it should not speedily interfere this great and mighty interest will pass completely out of its hands and be beyond its regulation or control. It is a critical period with us in the history of education. The people are calling for schools and teachers, and if the State will not listen to their cries they will be justified in adopting the best expedients they can, and in acceding to the provisions which religious zeal proposes to their acceptance. Our people are not, as a body, in favor of sectarian education. They prefer a general and inexclusive system, and if they adopt the narrower one it will be because their own Government has been inattentive to their interests. I sincerely hope that the Legislature may be duly sensible of the delicate posture of this subject. To my mind it is clear as the noonday sun that, if anything is to be done, it must be done at once. Now or never is the real state of the problem.

In the third place, the State should take the subject in hand, because this is the only way by which consistency and coherence can be secured in the different departments of instruction. Education is a connected work, and its various subdivisions should be so arranged that, while each is a whole in itself, it should be at the same time a part of a still greater whole. The lower elementary education should, for example, be complete for those who aspire

259

to nothing more; it should likewise be naturally introductory to a higher culture. It should be a perfect whole for the one class, and a properly adjusted part for the other. So, also, the higher elementary education, that of the grammar school, should be complete for those who are not looking to liberal education, and yet, in relation to others, subsidiary to the College or the scientific schools. This unity in the midst of variety cannot be secured without a common centre of impulse and of action. There must be one presiding spirit, one head, one heart. Education will become a disjointed and fragmentary process if it is left to individuals, to private corporations and religious sects. Each will have his tongue and his psalm, and we shall have as many crotchets and experiments as there are controlling bodies. The competition excited will be a competition not for efficiency in instruction, but for numbers; each will estimate success by the hosts that can be paraded at its annual festivals, or the pomp and pretension of a theatrical pageant, played off under the name of an examination. This is not the language of reproach; it is a result which, from the principles of human nature, will be inevitably necessitated by the condition in which they shall find themselves placed. . . .

Let me add, in this place, that public education is recommended by considerations of economy. Absolutely it is the cheapest of all systems. It saves the enormous expense of boarding schools, or the still heavier expense of domestic tutors, one of which must be encountered when it is left to private enterprise to supply the means of education. If the amount which is annually expended in South Carolina upon the instruction of that portion of her children who are looking to a liberal education could be collected into one sum, we would be amazed at the prodigality of means in comparison with the poverty of the result. The same sum judiciously distributed would go very far towards supplying every neighborhood with a competent teacher. From the want of system there is no security that, with all this lavish expenditure, efficient instructors shall be procured. Those who employ the teachers are not always competent to judge of their qualifications, and the consequence is that time and money are both not infrequently squandered in learning what has afterwards to be unlearned. The danger, too, of sending children from home at an early age, the evil of exemption from parental influence and discipline, are not to be lightly hazarded. The State should see to it that the family is preserved in its integrity, and enabled to exert all its mighty power in shaping the character of the future citizens of the Commonwealth. Comparatively, public education is cheap, as general intelligence contributes to general virtue, and general virtue diminishes expenditures for crimes; it is cheap, as it develops the resources of the country and increases the mass of its wealth. It is not labor, but intelligence that creates new values; and public education is an outlay of capital that returns to the coffers of the State with an enormous interest. Not a dollar, therefore, that is judiciously appropriated to the instruction of the people will ever be lost. The five talents will gain other five, and the two talents other two; while to neglect this great department of duty is to wrap the talent in a napkin and bury it in the bowels of the earth.

THE REAL DIFFICULTY

But, after all, the practical question is one of real difficulty. What shall the State do? This is a point of great delicacy, and demands consummate wisdom. Nothing should be done abruptly and violently, no measures should be adopted that are not likely to recommend themselves, no attempt made to force an acquiescence into any provisions, however salutary they may have proved elsewhere, which are not founded in the habits and predilections of the people, or obviously indispensable to elevate and improve them. The public mind should be prepared for every great movement before it is begun. Popular enthusiasm should, if possible, be awakened by addresses and disputations, which, like pioneers, prepare the way for the law by making rough places plain and the crooked straight. Above all, we should guard against attempting to make our system too perfect at the outset. The words of Cousin are as applicable to us now as they were to France at the time he wrote them: "God grant that we may be wise enough to see that any law on primary instruction passed now must be a provisional and not a definite law; that is must of necessity be reconstructed at the end of ten years, and that the only thing now is to supply the most urgent

wants, and to give legal sanction to some incontestable points."
Festina lente contains a caution which it becomes States as well as
individuals to respect.

What we first need is a collection of the facts from which the
data of a proper system may be drawn. We must know the number
of children in the State of the ages at which children are usually
sent to school, the kind and degree of education demanded, the
relative distances of the residence of parents, the points at which
school-houses may be most conveniently erected, the number of
buildings required, the number of teachers, and the salaries which
different localities make necessary to a competent support. Facts
of this sort must constitute the ground-work. In possession of these
we may then proceed to compare different systems, adopting from
among them that which seems to be best adapted to our own circumstances, or originate a new one if all should prove unsatisfac-
tory.

All, therefore, that in my judgment the Legislature should
undertake at present is to acquire this preliminary information,
including the accumulation of facts, the comparison of different
common-school systems, and the digest of a plan suited to the
wants of our own people. This can be done by the appointment of
a minister of public instruction, who shall be regarded as an officer
of the Government, compensated by a large salary, and who shall
give himself unreservedly to this great interest. Let him be required to traverse the State, to inspect the condition of every
neighborhood, and from personal observation and authentic testimony let him become acquainted with the number, the extent and
the circumstances of the children. Let him be prepared to say
where school-houses can be most conveniently erected, the distance at which they should be removed from each other, the kind
of teacher needed in each neighborhood, and let him indicate
what sections of the State are unprepared for schools in consequence of the dispersion of their inhabitants. Let him be able to
give some probable estimate of the expenses incident to the successful operation of an adequate scheme. In the next place, it
should be his duty to master the existing systems, whether in this
country or Europe, and to lay before the Legislature a succinct
account of their fundamental provisions. Let him propose the
scheme which he thinks ought to be adopted here, and let his

report be referred to an able and learned commissioner, charged with the final preparation of such a scheme as we may be ready to enact into law.

I shall not disguise from your Excellency that upon many points connected with details of any and every scheme my own opinion has long ago been definitely settled. The extent or degree of elementary education, the best mode of securing competent teachers, the principle which should regulate their salaries, the introduction of religion into the schools — these and many other similar topics I have investigated to my own satisfaction. But, in the present condition of the whole subject, it would be obviously premature to express the opinions of any individual. The minister of public instruction should have the whole subject before him, and whatever discussions may take place upon details should be consequent upon and not prior to this report. All, therefore, that I would now press upon your Excellency is to have public instruction erected into a department of the Government. That is the first and indispensable step, and until that is done there never can be a plan adequate, consistent, successful. I have only to add here that this is substantially the recommendation which I had the honor to make in concert with the Bishop of Georgia some fourteen or fifteen years ago [1838], and time and observation have only strengthened my convictions of the wisdom and necessity of the measure.

MILITARY SCHOOLS

The third and last part of our system is the military schools. What I have to suggest in regard to them is that they be made to supply a want which is constantly increasing as the country advances in trade and in the arts. It is a great evil that there should be nothing intermediate between the grammar school and the college, and that all who wish to acquire nothing more than the principles of physical science, on account of their application to various branches of industry, should be compelled to purchase this privilege by bearing what to them is the heavy burden of liberal education. They do not want Latin, Greek, and philosophy, and it is hard that they can not be permitted to get a little chemistry, a little engineering, or a little natural philosophy, without going through Homer and Virgil, Aristotle and Locke. "Two great evils" (I use the words of Cousin, who is deploring a similar state of things in France)—"two great evils are the consequence. In general these boys, who know they are not destined to any very distinguished career, go through their studies in a negligent manner; they never get beyond mediocrity; when at about 18 they go back to the habits and the business of their fathers. As there is nothing in their ordinary life to recall or to keep up their studies, a few years obliterate every trace of the little classical learning they acquired. On the other hand, these young men often contract tastes and acquaintances at college which render it difficult, nay, almost impossible, for them to return to the humble way of life to which they are born; hence a race of men restless, discontented with their position, with others, and with themselves; enemies of a state of society in which they feel themselves out of place, and with some acquirements, some real or imagined talent, and unbridled ambition, are ready to rush into any career of servility or revolt." Our colleges ought, without doubt, to remain open to all who can pay the expences of them, but we ought by no means to force the lower classes into them; yet this is the inevitable effect of having no intermediate establishment between the primary schools and colleges.

The remedy, as I have already shown, is not to change the construction of the college, but to employ the elements which we confessedly have, and which are essentially suited to the purpose.

I shall trespass upon the patience of Your Excellency no longer. In all that I have said, I have had an eye to the prosperity and glory of my native State. Small in territory and feeble in number, the only means by which she can maintain her dignity and importance is by the patronage of letters. A mere speck compared with several other States in the Union, her reliance for the protection of her rights and her full and equal influence in Federal legislation must be the genius of her statesmen and the character of her people. Let her give herself to the rearing of a noble race of men, and she will make up in moral power what she wants in votes. Public education is the cheap expedient for uniting us among ourselves and rendering us terrible abroad. Mind, after all, must be felt, and I am anxious to see my beloved Carolina preeminently distinguished for the learning, eloquence, and patriotism of her sons. Let us endeavor to make her in general intelligence what she is in dignity and independence of character—the brightest star in the American constellation. God grant that the time may soon come when not an individual born within our borders shall be permitted to reach maturity without having mastered the elements of knowledge

I am, with consideration of the highest respect,

J. H. Thornwell.

30. Sociology for the South (1854)[1]

GEORGE FITZHUGH

The abolitionists taunt us with the ignorance of our poor white citizens. This is a stigma on the South that should be wiped out. Half of the people of the South, or nearly so, are blacks. We have only to educate the other half. At the North, they educate all. Our Southern free-trade philosophy, our favorite maxim, "every man for himself," has been the cause of the neglect of popular education. The civilized world differ from us and censure us. They say it is the first duty of government to provide for the education of all its citizens. Despotic Prussia compels parents to send their children to schools supported at public expense. All are educated and well educated. As our's is a government of the people, no where is education so necessary. The poor, too, ask no charity, when they demand universal education. They constitute our militia and our police. They protect men in possession of property, as in other countries; and do much more, they secure men in possession of a kind of property which they could not hold a day but for the supervision and protection of the poor. This very property has rendered the South merely agricultural, made population too sparse for neighborhood schools, prevented variety of pursuits, and thus cut the poor off as well from the means of living, as from the means of education.

Universal suffrage will soon attempt to remedy these evils. But rashness and precipitancy may occasion failure and bring about despondency. We are not yet prepared to educate all. Free schools should at once be established in all neighborhoods where a sufficient number of scholars can be collected in one school. Parents should be compelled to send their children to school. The obliga-

---

[1]George Fitzhugh, *Sociology for the South or the Failure of Free Society* (Richmond, 1854), pp. 144–48. Fitzhugh, a Virginia lawyer and sociologist, was a fervent defender of the institution of slavery.

tion on the part of government, to educate the people, carries with it the indubitable right to employ all the means necessary to attain that end. But the duty of government does not end with educating the people. As far as is practicable, it should open to them avenues of employment in which they may use what they have learned. The system of internal improvements now carried on in the South, will directly and indirectly, quite suffice to attain this end, so far as government can aid properly in such an object. Government may do too much for the people, or it may do too little. We have committed the latter error.

The mail and the newspaper-press might be employed, as cheap and efficient agents, in teaching the masses. No family in the Union is so dull, stupid and indifferent, as not to be curious about the news of the day. Contemporaneous history is the most interesting and important part of history. That is to be had alone from newspapers. But newspapers contain on all subjects the most recent discoveries, and the most valuable information.

A large weekly newspaper might be furnished to every poor family in the State, at less than a dollar a family. If there were not a teacher within fifty miles, some member of each family would learn to read, first to get at the neighborhood news and scandals, the deaths, and marriages, and murders. Gradually they would understand and become interested in the proceedings of our government, and the news from foreign countries. The meanest newspaper in the country is worth all the libraries in Christendom. It is desirable to know what the ancients did, but it is necessary to know what our neighbors and fellow country-men are doing.

Our system of improvements, manufactures, the mechanic arts, the building up of our cities, commerce, and education should go hand in hand. We ought not to attempt too much at once. 'Tis time we were attempting something. We ought, like the Athenians, to be the best educated people in the world. When we employ all our whites in the mechanic arts, in commerce, in professions, &c., and confine the negroes to farm-work, and coarse mechanical operations, we shall be in a fair way to attain this result. The abolition movement is a harmless humbug, confined to a handful of fanatics, but the feeling of antipathy to negroes, the hatred of race, and the disposition to expel them from the country is daily increasing, North and South. Two causes are in active operation to fan and increase this hostility to the negro race. The one, the neglect to educate and provide means of employment for the poor whites in the South, who are thereby led to believe that the existence of negroes amongst us is ruin to them. The other, the theory of the Types of Mankind, which cuts off the negro from human brotherhood, and justifies the brutal and the miserly in treating him as a vicious brute. Educate all Southern whites, employ them, not as cooks, lacqueys, ploughmen, and menials, but as independent freemen should be employed, and let negroes be strictly tied down to such callings as are unbecoming white men, and peace would be established between blacks and whites. The whites would find themselves elevated by the existence of negroes amongst us. Like the Roman citizens, the Southern white man would become a noble and a privileged character, and he would then like negroes and slavery, because his high position would be due to them. Poor people can see things as well as rich people. We can't hide the facts from them. It is always better openly, honestly, and fearlessly to meet danger, than to fly from or avoid it. The last words we will utter on this subject are,— The path of safety is the path of duty! Educate the people, no matter what it may cost!

31. NEGRO EDUCATION IN THE SOUTH (1740–1854)[1]

SOUTH CAROLINA PROHIBITS
THE TEACHING OF SLAVES TO WRITE, 1740

And *whereas,* the having of slaves taught to write, or suffering them to be employed in writing, may be attended with great inconveniences; *Be it therefore enacted* by the authority aforesaid, That all and every person or persons whatsoever, who shall hereafter teach, or cause any slave or slaves to be taught, to write, or shall use or employ any slave as a scribe in any manner of writing whatsoever, hereafter taught to write, every such person and persons, shall, for every such offence, forfeit the sum of one hundred pounds current money. (*The Statutes at Large of South Carolina,* VII, 413)

A NEGRO TEACHER AND PREACHER ANNOUNCES THE OPENING
OF HIS SCHOOL IN RALEIGH, NORTH CAROLINA,
IN WHICH HE TAUGHT
BOTH WHITE AND NEGRO STUDENTS, 1808

John Chaves takes this method of informing his Employers, and the Citizens of Raleigh in general, that the present Quarter of his School will end the 15th of September, and the next will commence on the 19th. He will, at the same time, open an Evening School for the purpose of instructing Children of Colour, as he intends, for the accommodation of some of his employers, to exclude all Children of Colour from his Day School.

The Evening School will commence at an hour by Sun. When the white children leave the House, those of colour will take their places, and continue until ten o'clock.

The terms of teaching the white children will be as usual, two and a half dollars per quarter; these of colour, one dollar and three

---

[1]Knight, *Documentary History of Education in the South before 1860,* (1953) V, 461, 467, 470, 475–77, 485–86, 488–89, 490–93.

quarters. In both cases, the whole of the money to be paid in advance to Mr. Benjamin S. King. Those who produce Certificates from him of their having paid the money, will be admitted.

Those who think proper to put their Children under his care, may rely upon the strictest attention being paid, not only to their Education but to their Morals, which he deems an *important* part of Education.

He hopes to have a better School House by the commencement of next quarter. (*The Raleigh Register*, August 20, 1808)

A NORTH CAROLINA EDITOR PRAISES THE SCHOOL OF JOHN CHAVIS, NEGRO TEACHER AND PREACHER, 1830

On Friday last, we attended an examination of the free children of color, attached to the School conducted by John Chavis, also colored, but a regularly educated Presbyterian minister, and we have seldom received more gratification from any exhibition of a similar character. To witness a well regulated school, composed of this class of persons—to see them setting an example both in behavior and scholarship, which their white superiors might take pride in imitating, was a cheering spectacle to a philanthropist. The exercises throughout, evinced a degree of attention and assiduous care on the part of the instructor, highly creditable, and of attainment on the part of his scholars almost incredible. We were also much pleased with the sensible address which closed the examination. The object of the respectable teacher, was to impress on the scholars, the fact, that they occupied an inferior and subordinate station in society, and were possessed but of limited privileges; but that even they might become useful in their peculiar sphere, by making a proper improvement of the advantages afforded them. (*The Raleigh Register*, April 22, 1830)

VIRGINIA PROHIBITS THE TEACHING OF SLAVES TO READ OR WRITE, 1831

Be it further enacted, That if any white person or persons assemble with free negroes or mulattoes, at any school-house, church, meeting-house, or other place for the purpose of instructing such free negroes or mulattoes to read or write, such person or persons shall, on conviction thereof, be fined in a sum not exceeding fifty dollars, and moreover may be imprisoned at the discretion of the jury, not exceeding two months.

Be it further enacted, That if any white person, for pay or compensation, shall assemble with any slaves for the purpose of teaching and shall teach any slave to read or write, such person, or any white person or persons contracting with such teacher, so to act, who shall offend as aforesaid, shall for such offence, be fined at the discretion of a jury, in a sum not less than ten, nor exceeding one hundred dollars, to be recovered on any information or indictment. (Acts Passed at the General Assembly of the Commonwealth of Virginia, 1830–31)

ALABAMA PROHIBITS THE TEACHING
OF SLAVES TO READ OR WRITE, 1832

And be it further enacted, That any person or persons who shall endeavor or attempt to teach any free person of color, or slave to spell, read, or write, shall upon conviction thereof by indictment, be fined in a sum not less than two hundred and fifty dollars nor more than five hundred dollars. (Acts Passed at the Thirteenth Annual Session of the General Assembly of the State of Alabama, 1831–32)

SOUTH CAROLINA FORBIDS THE TEACHING OF SLAVES
TO READ AND WRITE, 1834

Be it enacted, by the honorable Senate and House of Representatives, now met and sitting in General Assembly, and by the authority of the same, If any person shall hereafter teach any slave to read or write, or shall aid or assist in teaching any slave to read or write, or cause or procure any slave to be taught to read or write, such person, if a free white person, upon conviction thereof, shall, for each and every offence against this Act, be fined not exceeding one hundred dollars, and imprisoned not more than six months; or if a free person of color, shall be whipped, not exceeding fifty lashes, and fined not exceeding fifty dollars, at the

271

discretion of the court of magistrates and freeholders before which such free person of color is tried; and if a slave, to be whipped at the discretion of the court, not exceeding fifty lashes; the informer to be entitled to one half of the fine, and to be a competent witness. And if any free person of color or slave shall keep any school, or other place of instruction for teaching any slave or free person of color to read or write, such free person of color or slave shall be liable to the same fine, imprisonment and corporal punishment, as are by this act imposed and inflicted on free persons of color and slaves for teaching slaves to read or write. (*The Statutes at Large of South Carolina,* 1840, VII)

A SPECIAL LEGISLATIVE ACT PERMITS A VIRGINIA SLAVE TO BE TAUGHT TO READ AND WRITE, 1842

Whereas, it appearing to the general assembly that Henry Juett Gray, of the county of Rockingham, a blind youth of reputable character and exemplary deportment, who has made considerable progress in scientific attainments, is desirous of qualifying himself to become a teacher of the blind; and that in order to his comfort and extensive usefulness, it is necessary that he should have the services of a servant capable of reading and writing, which object cannot be permanently secured otherwise than by the education of a young slave named Randolph, the property of said Henry Juett: and it further appearing that Robert Gray, the father of said Henry Juett, is willing to indemnify the public against any possible injury which might be apprehended from the misconduct of said slave:

Be it therefore enacted, That it shall be lawful for the said Henry Juett Gray, or any friend for him, to employ from time to time any competent white person or persons to teach the said slave Randolph reading and writing, and for such white person or persons so to teach said slave without incurring any of the penalties prescribed by law in such cases: Provided, however, that this act shall be of no force or effect until the said Robert Gray, or some other responsible person, shall execute before the county court of Rockingham county bond with two or more sufficient sureties, payable to the sitting justices thereof, and their successors, in a penalty to be fixed by said court, but not less than double the value of said slave at mature age, and conditioned for indemnifying the commonwealth and the citizens thereof against any improper use of said slave of the art of reading and writing, and for the sale and removal of said slave by said Henry Juett Gray, or any future proprietor thereof, beyond the limits of this commonwealth, in the event of his conviction of any crime, unless the judgement of conviction shall have the effect of preventing such sale or removal; which bond may be sued on and prosecuted from time to time, in the names of said justices, for the use of the commonwealth, or any citizen thereof aggrieved, for the recovery of any damages which may be sustained by reason of any breach of the condition thereof: *And provided also,* That to give effect to this act, the county court of Rockingham county shall be satisfied and cause to be certified of record, that the said slave is a boy of good moral character and correct deportment: *And provided moreover,* That the general assembly reserves to itself full power to alter, modify or repeal this act at any time hereafter, and to require the sale and removal of said slave beyond the limits of this commonwealth. (Acts of Virginia, 1841–42)

CHANCELLOR WILLIAM HARPER OF SOUTH CAROLINA COMMENTS
ON THE EDUCATION OF SLAVES, 1852

Odium has been cast upon our legislation, on account of its forbidding the elements of education to be communicated to slaves. But, in truth, what injury is done to them by this? He who works during the day with his hands, does not read in intervals of leisure for his amusement, or the improvement of his mind—or the exceptions are so very rare, as scarcely to need the being provided for. Of the many slaves whom I have known capable of reading, I have never known one to read anything but the Bible, and this task they impose on themselves as a matter of duty. Of all methods of religious instruction, however, this, of reading for themselves, would be the most inefficient—their comprehension is defective, and the employment is to them an unusual and laborious one. There are but very few who do not enjoy other means more effectual for religious instruction. There is no place of worship opened for the white population, from which they are excluded. I believe it a mistake, to say that the instructions there given are not adapted to their comprehension, or calculated to improve them. If they are given as they ought to be—practically, and without pretension, and are such as are generally intelligible to the free part of the audience, comprehending all grades of intellectual capacity, —they will not be unintelligible to slaves. I doubt whether this be not better than instruction, addressed specially to themselves —which they might look upon as a device of the master's, to make them more obedient and profitable to himself. Their minds, generally, show a strong religious tendency, and they are fond of assuming the office of religious instructors to each other; and perhaps their religious notions are not much more extravagant than those of a large portion of the free population of our country. I am not sure that there is a much smaller proportion of them than of the free population, who make some sort of religious profession. It is certainly the master's *interest* that they should have proper religious sentiments, and if he fails in his duty towards them, we may be sure that the consequences will be visited not upon them, but upon him.

If there were any chance of their elevating their rank and condition in society, it might be matter of hardship, that they should be debarred those rudiments of knowledge which open the way to further attainments. But this they know cannot be, and that further attainments would be useless to them. Of the evil of this, I shall speak hereafter. A knowledge of reading, writing, and the elements of arithmetic, is convenient and important to the free laborer, who is the transactor of his own affairs, and the guardian of his own interests—but of what use would they be to the slave? These alone do not elevate the mind of character, if such elevation were desirable.

A CAROLINIAN DEFENDS LAWS AGAINST
TEACHING SLAVES TO READ, 1852

As far as the facilities of education go, the slave is secured at least from physical want, the greater temptation to crime, from idleness, and from excessive labor. And the growing spirit of religious teaching secures him from that dependence upon immoral influences, which the mind unaided can so rarely resist. This growing spirit of religious teaching is a far safer reliance than the uncertain influences surrounding the poor laborers of other countries. It is fostered by a sense of responsibility in the master, by his Christian feeling, by the dependent condition of the slave, and by all the kindness that grows out of the relation. At the North, it has been thought a fanciful notion that the white man should regard himself as the natural protector of the black. At least it will be granted that such an opinion will have its influence upon the moral education of the slave. An answer to much of this is ready for us in the taunt that we should not boast of the education of the slave as long as the reading of the Bible is shut out from him by our laws. We shall be content to say on this point, that this furnishes us with another instance of the insufficiencies of legislation being corrected by what we have called the *vis medicatrix* of nature. The slave's inability to read has given rise to a more kindly feeling, and to a closer connection between the races, than if each slave could read his own Bible. It has induced oral teaching; and the effect of this upon both races no man at the North can conceive. As a proof that the slave who cannot read the Bible is not beyond the reach of religious instruction, we may recall the policy of Lycurgus, who refused to write his laws, that they might be the better preserved in memory. We are sure that we need not repeat what has been so often said of this subject, — that the laws against reading were the only barrier we could devise against the flood of incendiary publications that threatened our safety. The responsibility must rest upon other shoulders than ours. ([Edward J. Pringle:] *Slavery in the Southern States*, 1852)

THE CASE OF MRS. MARGARET DOUGLASS

[Editor's note: Mrs. Margaret Douglass was a slave-owner and the daughter of one, but she was deeply concerned about the religious and moral welfare of Negro children. She moved to Norfolk, Virginia, from Charleston, South Carolina, in 1845 and in the following decade converted part of her house into a school for free Negro children. She and her daughter taught them principles of religion and reading and writing. In time she was presented to the mayor for teaching contrary to the law, but she pleaded innocence on the grounds that she instructed only free Negroes and that she was unaware of any prohibition regarding training of all blacks. The mayor dismissed the case, since she had acted in good faith. The Grand Jury, however, indicted her. She was tried for violating the Virginia code which prohibited the assemblage of Negroes for the purpose of religious worship, where it was conducted by one of their race, and every assemblage of such people for the purpose of instruction in reading and writing or for any other reason. And the white person assembled with the Negroes to teach them was liable to fine and imprisonment. Mrs. Douglass defended herself and pointed out that Sunday schools in the city had been engaged in such activities for years. Nonetheless, the jury convicted her but fined her only one dollar. The judge overruled such leniency and sentenced her to imprisonment for one month. Mrs. Douglass wrote of her experiences in *The Personal Narrative of Mrs. Margaret Douglass, a Southern Woman, Who was Imprisoned for One Month in the Common Jail, Under the Laws of Virginia, for the Crime of Teaching Free Colored Children to Read*. This was published in Boston in 1854.]

AN EDITORIAL CONCERNING THE CASE
OF MRS. MARGARET DOUGLASS
FROM THE *DAILY SOUTHERN ARGUS* (NORFOLK, VIRGINIA),
FEBRUARY 9, 1854

We publish today the judgment of Hon. Judge Baker in the case of Mrs. Douglass, which has much excited our citizens. The first time within the passage of the act forbidding the teaching of slaves or free colored persons to read or write, has a case of this description come under the jurisdiction of our Court, and it was singular that this case should be a woman. The jury found a verdict of guilty, and the law had to be sustained. Sympathy was aroused for Mrs. Douglass. It was revolting to the citizens to have a woman imprisoned in our jail, and every inducement was offered Mrs. Douglass to escape the punishment. The Court was obliged to adjourn its judgment over, and although a copias was awarded, yet it was the hope and wish of every one that she would leave the city. But no; "a martyr" she "would be to the cause of benevolence"; and to cap the climax, she brought her daughter, a maiden of some seventeen summers, who had obeyed the injunctions of her mother as a child should, to try the stern realities of the laws, and to use her own language in defending her cause, "to glory in works of benevolence and charity to a race downtrodden." Then sympathy departed, and in the breast of every one rose a right-eous indignation towards a person who would throw contempt in the face of our laws, and brave the imprisonment for "the cause of humanity."

The decision of Judge Baker is cogent and pungent, and will be read with interest. The laws must be upheld. It is not for the Judge to set upon the constitutionality or justice of the law; it is for him a sacred duty to impose the punishment meted out in the code. Virginia must keep in restraint the wire-workings of abolition sentiments. We have in this town suffered much from the agression of Northern foes, and a strong cordon must encircle our domestic institutions.

We must preserve from discord and angry passions our firesides and homesteads. We must preserve inviolate the majority of laws necessary for the protection of our rights; and there is no one of intelligence and foresight who will pronounce the judgment unrighteous.

Mrs. Douglass' time will run out this week, and we have heard it stated from good authority that her imprisonment will be a pecuniary reward to her. We hope that our citizens will prevent by all possible means any attempt to aid this woman, but let her depart hence with only one wish, that her presence will never be intruded upon us again. Let her seek her associates at the North, and with them commingle, but let us put a check to such mischievous views as fell from her lips last November, sentiments unworthy a resident of the state, and in direct rebellion against our Constitution.

Index

279

Females, education of
  in colonial period, 20, 31–32, 42–43, 80–81, 83
  in early national era, 111, 128, 144
  and free school movement, 153, 158, 187–89
Fithian, Philip Vickers, 14, 80–96
Fitzhugh, George, 161, 266–68
Franklin, Benjamin, 9, 14, 65–78
Free schools, 118–19
  See also Public schools; Popular education
Free school movement, 151–63
  Opposition to, 160–61, 192, 245
  Press and, 156–57
  Political leadership of, 159, 195–217
  and Reformers, 153, 218–243
  and Workingmen's organizations, 156–58, 164–94
  See also Massachusetts; New York; Pennsylvania

High Schools
  See Academies and high schools

Indentures, 9, 41
Indians, education of, 6, 9–12, 32, 54–63

See also Missionaries

Jefferson, Thomas, 102, 109–16
Johnson, Walter, 159, 219–28

Knox, Samuel, 102–03, 130–37

Lancaster, Joseph, 200–03
Latin grammar education and schools, 3, 5, 8, 13, 22, 23, 69, 82–83, 88, 112

Mann, Horace, 155, 159, 229–36
Massachusetts
  in colonial period, 3
  common schools in, 209, 221, 229–30
  and free school movement, 154
  laws of 1642 and 1647, 4, 6, 221
  See also Everett, Edward; Mann, Horace; Puritans
Mather, Cotton, 7, 17–23
  See also Puritans
Mechanics
  See Workingmen and education
Middle-class, education for, 14, 64–78

Printed in U.S.A.